Postfeminism and Contemporary Vampire Romance

Library of Gender and Popular Culture

From *Mad Men* to gaming culture, performance art to steampunk fashion, the presentation and representation of gender continues to saturate popular media. This series seeks to explore the intersection of gender and popular culture, engaging with a variety of texts – drawn primarily from Art, Fashion, TV, Cinema, Cultural Studies and Media Studies – as a way of considering various models for understanding the complementary relationship between 'gender identities' and 'popular culture'. By considering race, ethnicity, class and sexual identities across a range of cultural forms, each book in the series adopts a critical stance towards issues surrounding the development of gender identities and popular and mass cultural 'products'.

For further information or enquiries, please contact the library series editors:

Claire Nally: claire.nally@northumbria.ac.uk
Angela Smith: angela.smith@sunderland.ac.uk

Advisory Board:

Dr Kate Ames, Central Queensland University, Australia
Dr Michael Higgins, University of Strathclyde, UK
Prof Åsa Kroon, Örebro University, Sweden
Dr Andrea McDonnell, Emmanuel College, USA
Dr Niall Richardson, University of Sussex, UK
Dr Jacki Willson, University of Leeds, UK

Published and forthcoming titles:

The Aesthetics of Camp: Post-Queer Gender and Popular Culture
By Anna Malinowska

Ageing Femininity on Screen: The Older Woman in Contemporary Cinema
By Niall Richardson

All-American TV Crime Drama: Feminism and Identity Politics in Law and Order: Special Victims Unit
By Sujata Moorti and Lisa Cuklanz

Are You Not Entertained?: Mapping the Gladiator Across Visual Media
By Lindsay Steenberg

Bad Girls, Dirty Bodies: Sex, Performance and Safe Femininity
By Gemma Commane

Beyoncé: Celebrity Feminism in the Age of Social Media
By Kirsty Fairclough-Isaacs

Conflicting Masculinities: Men in Television Period Drama
By Katherine Byrne, Julie Anne Taddeo and James Leggott (Eds)

Fat on Film: Gender, Race and Body Size in Contemporary Hollywood Cinema
By Barbara Plotz

Fathers on Film: Paternity and Masculinity in 1990s Hollywood
By Katie Barnett

Film Bodies: Queer Feminist Encounters with Gender and Sexuality in Cinema
By Katharina Lindner

From the Margins to the Mainstream: Women On and Off Screen in Television and Film
By Marianne Kac-Vergne and Julie Assouly (Eds)

Gay Pornography: Representations of Sexuality and Masculinity
By John Mercer

Gender and Austerity in Popular Culture: Femininity, Masculinity and Recession in Film and Television
By Helen Davies and Claire O'Callaghan (Eds)

Gender and Early television: Mapping Women's Role in Emerging US and British Media, 1850–1950
By Sarah Arnold

The Gendered Motorcycle: Representations in Society, Media and Popular Culture
By Esperanza Miyake

Gendering History on Screen: Women Filmmakers and Historical Films
By Julia Erhart

Girls Like This, Boys Like That: The Reproduction of Gender in Contemporary Youth Cultures
By Victoria Cann

"Guilty Pleasures": European Audiences and Contemporary Hollywood Romantic Comedy
By Alice Guilluy

The Gypsy Woman: Representations in Literature and Visual Culture
By Jodie Matthews

Love Wars: Television Romantic Comedy
By Mary Irwin

Male and Female Violence in Popular Media
By Elisa Giomi and Sveva Magaraggia

Masculinity in Contemporary Science Fiction Cinema: Cyborgs, Troopers and Other Men of the Future
By Marianne Kac-Vergne

Paradoxical Pleasures: Female Submission in Popular and Erotic Fiction
By Anna Watz

Positive Images: Gay Men and HIV/AIDS in the Culture of 'Post-Crisis'
By Dion Kagan

Queer Horror Film and Television: Sexuality and Masculinity at the Margins
By Darren Elliott-Smith

Queer Sexualities in Early Film: Cinema and Male-Male Intimacy
By Shane Brown

Screening Queer Memory: LGBTQ Pasts in Contemporary Film and Television
By Anamarija Horvat

Steampunk: Gender and the Neo-Victorian
By Claire Nally

Television Comedy and Femininity: Queering Gender
By Rosie White

Tweenhood: Femininity and Celebrity in Tween Popular Culture
By Melanie Kennedy

Women Who Kill: Gender and Sexuality in Film and Series of the post-Feminist Era
By David Roche and Cristelle Maury (Eds)

Wonder Woman: Feminism, Culture and the Body
By Joan Ormrod

Young Women, Girls and Postfeminism in Contemporary British Film
By Sarah Hill

Postfeminism and Contemporary Vampire Romance

Representations of Gender and Sexuality in Film and Television

Lea Gerhards

BLOOMSBURY ACADEMIC
LONDON • NEW YORK • OXFORD • NEW DELHI • SYDNEY

BLOOMSBURY ACADEMIC
Bloomsbury Publishing Plc
50 Bedford Square, London, WC1B 3DP, UK
1385 Broadway, New York, NY 10018, USA
29 Earlsfort Terrace, Dublin 2, Ireland

BLOOMSBURY, BLOOMSBURY ACADEMIC and the Diana logo are trademarks of Bloomsbury Publishing Plc

First published in Great Britain 2022

Copyright © Lea Gerhards

Lea Gerhards has asserted her right under the Copyright, Designs and Patents Act, 1988, to be identified as Author of this work.

For legal purposes the Acknowledgements on p. xiii–xiv constitute an extension of this copyright page.

Cover design: Ben Anslow
Cover image: Vampire stock photo (© jentakespictures / iStock)

All rights reserved. No part of this publication may be reproduced or transmitted in any form or by any means, electronic or mechanical, including photocopying, recording, or any information storage or retrieval system, without prior permission in writing from the publishers.

Bloomsbury Publishing Plc does not have any control over, or responsibility for, any third-party websites referred to or in this book. All internet addresses given in this book were correct at the time of going to press. The author and publisher regret any inconvenience caused if addresses have changed or sites have ceased to exist, but can accept no responsibility for any such changes.

A catalogue record for this book is available from the British Library.

A catalog record for this book is available from the Library of Congress.

ISBN: HB: 978-1-3502-1568-9
ePDF: 978-1-3502-1565-8
eBook: 978-1-3502-1566-5

Series: Library of Gender and Popular Culture

Typeset by Deanta Global Publishing Services, Chennai, India
Printed and bound in Great Britain

To find out more about our authors and books visit www.bloomsbury.com and sign up for our newsletters.

Contents

List of illustrations	x
Series editors' introduction	xi
Acknowledgements	xiii
Introduction: The cultural politics of contemporary vampire romance	1
1 More than a backlash: The contradictions of postfeminist culture	23
2 Paranormal romance: A quintessentially postfeminist genre?	37
3 The politics of looking: Female protagonists between subject and object	69
4 Vampire transformation as makeover: The making of ideal postfeminist subjects	119
5 Fantasy solutions to postfeminist culture: Vampire heroes and postfeminist masculinity	157
Conclusion: Paradoxical pleasures	201
Notes	217
References	229
Index	265

Illustrations

3.1	Bella and her friends becoming objects of the male gaze. *Twilight*	76
3.2	POV shot from Bella's perspective. *Twilight*	77
3.3	James staring at Bella/the viewer. *Twilight*	77
3.4	Extreme close-up of Edward's eyes. *Twilight*	86
3.5	Close-up of Bella gazing at Edward. *Twilight*	88
3.6	Close-up of Edward's sparkling torso. *Twilight*	88
3.7	Sookie posing in sexy lingerie (4.9). *True Blood*	95
3.8	Elena secretly gazing at Stefan (1.3). *The Vampire Diaries*	99
3.9	Elena zooming in on Stefan (1.5). *The Vampire Diaries*	100
3.10	Damon performing for the female gaze (3.1). *The Vampire Diaries*	107
3.11	Eric relaxing in the bath (1.8). *True Blood*	108
4.1	Bella's 'mirror moment'. *Breaking Dawn – Part 2*	132
4.2	Caroline standing up to Damon (2.2). *The Vampire Diaries*	139
4.3	Jessica, startled by her vampire body's impulses (3.6). *True Blood*	145
5.1	Stefan as James Dean (5.5). *The Vampire Diaries*	183

Series editors' introduction

Postfeminism and Contemporary Vampire Romance addresses the cultural icon of the vampire, following the emergence of the *Twilight* franchise (2008–12), the Sookie Stackhouse novels and their TV adaptation, *True Blood* (2008–14), and *The Vampire Diaries* (2009–17). In these texts, the undead became synonymous with paranormal romance in a specifically twenty-first-century guise. Of course, the vampire is a cornerstone of Gothic literature and culture more widely. While Bram Stoker's *Dracula* (1897) is the obvious touchstone for many readers and viewers, somewhat lesser-known vampire texts such as Le Fanu's *Carmilla*, about a lesbian vampire, as well as a plethora of films in the Hammer Horror tradition, identify how far the vampire can prompt a reflection on sexuality and identity. Indeed, Gerhards notes that more recent adaptations and appropriations clearly situate the vampire as a symbol for discussions about gender, sexuality and romance. We might only think of Anne Rice's works in the *Vampire Chronicles* novel series (1976–2018), or Francis Ford Coppola's 1992 film, *Dracula*.

Other books in the Library of Gender and Popular Culture explore related themes. Darren Elliott-Smith's *Queer Horror* (2016) uses psychoanalytic theories to read queer masculinity and monstrosity as represented in the wider horror genre (including figures such as zombies, or productions like Gothic soap operas). By comparison, Leah Gerhards specifically explores the twenty-first-century phenomenon of the vampire as featured in literature, film and television. Specifically, Gerhards identifies her texts as being instrumental to a contemporary American Gothic, using an intersectional approach which accounts for ethnicity and social class in order to evaluate specific characters and texts.

Gerhards uses a postfeminist lens in order to interrogate some of the key issues surrounding women's scopic pleasure in the romance genre, particularly the way in which postfeminism envisages empowerment for women through choice and agency. She maintains her choice of modern Gothic material reflects a broader move in film and television to construct and represent the heterosexual female gaze, and female desire. By centralizing this female gaze, she also adds a note of caution: many of the texts under discussion are also white and resolutely straight, but they nonetheless provide a point of identification for teen viewers. Therefore, in common with other books in the series, such as Sarah Hill's *Young Women, Girls and Postfeminism in Contemporary British Film* (2020) and Melanie Kennedy's *Tweenhood: Femininity and Celebrity in Tween Popular Culture* (2018), each identifies the value of girls' culture for academic study. Similarly, Gerhards's book ultimately demonstrates the importance of providing narratives and foregrounding the experiences of young women and girls in contemporary culture.

Acknowledgements

The research for this book originated as my PhD thesis completed at Saarland University, Germany, in 2018. I am hugely thankful to Astrid M. Fellner for her generous support throughout the supervision process and for encouraging me to find my own voice. My work is better thanks to her insightful and constructive feedback. In her research colloquium, she managed to bring together a group of like-minded scholars and to create a welcoming space in which I could regularly discuss my work in a friendly atmosphere.

My gratitude also goes to Stacey Abbott, whose work on horror TV and film has been fundamental for my research, and who kindly agreed to be my second examiner. She has been nothing but supportive of me and my work on this project, even beyond the PhD process. 'TV Fandom' and 'Daughter of Fangdom', two conferences on television vampires she co-organized together with Lorna Jowett and Mike Starr at the University of Northampton in 2013 and 2015, were events that spurred me on and gave me the opportunity to discuss some of my ideas with a wider audience.

My work benefited greatly from the insight and critical feedback provided by my fellow PhD students and everyone who participated in our research colloquium at Saarland University. My thanks to you all. I also gratefully acknowledge the intellectual input and motivational boosts I received from countless audience members and fellow conference-goers over the years, whose questions and comments contributed to my thinking on this project.

I extend my thanks to Angela Smith and Claire Nally, the series editors of the Library of Gender and Popular Culture, for their interest in and support of my work. Special thanks are due to Camilla Erskine, Anna Coatman, Veidehi Hans and all the staff at Bloomsbury Academic who were involved in the editorial and production process of this book. I would also like to thank the anonymous peer reviewers for giving valuable advice and helping me sharpen my argument. Thank you, Lisa, for providing feedback on my manuscript from a native speaker's perspective.

Last but not least, I am extremely grateful for the unflagging support provided by my family and friends, with some of whom I share a passion for all things vampire. A special thank you goes to my partner Gerrit, with whom I have discussed my ideas innumerable times, and whose support I can always count on.

Parts of Chapter 4 were originally published in 2016 under the title 'Vampires "on a Special Diet": Identity and the Body in Contemporary Media Texts' in I. Ermida (ed.), *Dracula and the Gothic in Literature, Pop Culture and the Arts*, 235–56, and in 2017 under the title 'The Legacy of Lucy Westenra: Female Postfeminist Subjects in *The Vampire Diaries*, *True Blood* and *The Twilight Saga*' in A. M. Fellner, M. Fernández Morales and M. Martausová (eds), *Rethinking Gender in Popular Culture in the 21st Century: Marlboro Men and California Gurls*, 89–109. This material is published here with the permission of Brill Rodopi and Cambridge Scholars Publishing.

The author and publisher gratefully acknowledge the permission granted to reproduce the copyright material in this book. The third party copyrighted material displayed in the pages of this book are done so on the basis of 'fair dealing for the purposes of criticism and review' or 'fair use for the purposes of teaching, criticism, scholarship or research' only in accordance with international copyright laws, and is not intended to infringe upon the ownership rights of the original owners. Every effort has been made to trace copyright holders and to obtain their permission for the use of copyright material. The publisher apologizes for any errors or omissions in the earlier list and would be grateful if notified of any corrections that should be incorporated in future reprints or editions of this book.

Introduction

The cultural politics of contemporary vampire romance

Contextualizing vampire romance

At the beginning of the new millennium, American popular culture fell under the spell of the vampire, and the reign of the bloodsucker has not faltered. By 2011, a vast array of shelves in bookstores was expressly reserved for 'books with bite', and in the same year, the Teen Choice Awards created the special category of 'Choice Vampire' to account for the wide range of vampire characters in film and television. Although the undead have been a constant presence in US media texts at least since the 1970s, the popular cultural fascination with the vampire reached new heights in the first fifteen years of the twenty-first century, with 'vampiric infiltration [being] evident everywhere' (Ní Fhlainn 2019: 14) and vampires attaining 'blockbuster status' (Abbott 2016b: 3) on a global scale. Particularly prominent was the development of 'a massive vampire romance industry, now generally considered to be the most popular subgenre of paranormal romance' (Byron 2008: 172). Having started out as a largely literary genre, paranormal romance has subsequently made a huge impact on film and television through the adaptation of some of the genre's most popular novels, most notably the *Twilight* series by American author Stephenie Meyer (Crawford 2014: 4). Thus, after *Twilight*'s tremendous success, the book market was flooded with vampire romance narratives taking place in a contemporary setting and often spotlighting the romantic adventures of female teenage protagonists.[1] These paranormal romance narratives swiftly spilled over into television and film. A pivotal text that influenced narratives in a range of different media, Meyer's book series thus propelled the figure of the vampire to a level of popularity and mainstream appeal that was unprecedented (ibid.: 159; George and Hughes 2013a: 1; Bucciferro 2014a: 5; Abbott 2016b: 3). Underlining 'the widespread popularity and profitability of vampires' in the contemporary era, Maria Mellins has pointed out that 'the vampire assumes a prized and privileged position in twenty-first-century popular culture' (2013: 7).

Conceiving this cultural obsession with the vampire as a phenomenon that needs to be reckoned with from an academic perspective, I draw on three popular romance texts featuring the vampire motif to examine and interrogate them as critical objects. In this book, I examine the film adaptations of the *Twilight* series[2] (2008–12) as well as the television series *The Vampire Diaries* (The CW, 2009–17) and *True Blood* (HBO, 2008–14) with regard to their construction of concepts such as femininity, masculinity, subjectivity and sexuality. Adopting a Cultural Studies framework, which I will elaborate on later, this book presents an analysis of these popular cultural products in relation to the larger cultural phenomenon of postfeminism. The *Twilight* Saga's recent ten-year anniversary celebrations (which were accompanied by the publication of a gender-swapped retelling of the first book in the series, *Life and Death: Twilight Reimagined*), the 2020 publication of Meyer's *Twilight* companion novel *Midnight Sun*, and the sustained popularity of *The Vampire Diaries* spin-off TV series *Legacies* (2018–) suggest that these mid-aughts vampire romances continue to have a distinct presence in contemporary popular culture and fandoms. At the same time, the temporal distance to the series' original running time facilitates a new critical look at both the parallels and differences between these three related texts. Putting the *Twilight* Saga, *The Vampire Diaries* and *True Blood* under the microscope, this book provides in-depth studies of these popular vampire series. Having shaped the contemporary landscape of American Gothic in profound ways, the chosen texts constitute particularly compelling cases via which to explore the early twenty-first-century (popular) cultural discourses of postfeminism.

As demonstrated through the targeted analyses undertaken within the frame of this book, these paranormal romances function as extraordinarily suitable vessels for postfeminism's contradictory politics due to their generic structure, their central use of the vampire figure and their conception as texts narrativizing and foregrounding the experiences of young women and girls in contemporary culture.

The *Twilight* novel tetralogy, which was published between 2005 and 2008, already had a strong fan base before the release of the first movie. During the release of her novel series, Meyer was the bestselling author in the United States, selling just under 26.5 million books in 2009 (Roback 2010). However, the *Twilight* movie adaptations, which include *Twilight* (2008), *New Moon* (2009), *Eclipse* (2010), *Breaking Dawn – Part 1* (2011) and *Breaking Dawn – Part 2* (2012), 'have greatly contributed to the saga's prominence' (Bucciferro 2014a: 5). In fact, it was after the release of the first film – a 'blockbuster that surpassed all initial expectations' (ibid.) – that the franchise became the cultural phenomenon as which it is known today. Grossing over $1.36 billion in the United States alone and reaching a massive audience worldwide ('Twilight'), the *Twilight* Saga has had a lasting effect on filmmaking investments and schedules of major studios (Clayton and Harman 2014a: 1). Due to their considerable cultural influence, it therefore makes sense to draw upon the film versions of the *Twilight* series for the analysis in this book. Because the *Twilight* Saga, *The Vampire Diaries* and *True Blood* emerged in close temporal proximity to each other, it will be interesting to investigate both their collective relationship with the discourses of postfeminism and the ways in which they are in dialogue with each other. Importantly, a focus on the cinematic/television versions of the texts will open up my examination of postfeminism to an analysis of the visual representation of the female gaze, which emerges as a central postfeminist feature of all three key texts.

The *Twilight* Saga, *The Vampire Diaries* and *True Blood* apparently captured the zeitgeist of the early 2000s; their success was not necessarily something production companies had reckoned with, at least in the case of the *Twilight* Saga (Crawford 2014: 240). However, being rooted in a decade-long history of vampire literature, film and television, their emergence did not entirely come out of thin air. Over the course of the twentieth century, the vampire in film, TV and literature had become increasingly motivated not by its thirst for power but by romantic feelings for a human woman (ibid.: 54). This shift was even palpable in retellings and adaptations of Bram Stoker's *Dracula* (1897) and culminated in Francis Ford Coppola's 1992 film adaptation of Stoker's novel, which ultimately transformed its literary source into a story of timeless love (ibid.: 238). As Fred Botting points out, 'Coppola's version has gone further than any other Dracula adaptation in romanticising and liberalising the vampire story' (2008: 3). Another important precursor of twenty-first-century vampire romance was Anne Rice's *Vampire Chronicles* novel series (1976–2018), whose 'impact . . . on subsequent vampire fiction can scarcely be overstated' (Crawford 2014: 55). Although Rice's stories are not romances, her vampire characters were often driven by their love for, 'or at least erotic fixation with, those whom they transformed; and while their undead bodies were incapable of normal sex, their murderous acts of vampirism were frequently described in overtly sexual terms' (ibid.: 57). Some of Rice's most significant contributions to the evolving vampire genre were thus the humanization as well as eroticization of the vampire figure. Alongside Laurell K. Hamilton's *Anita Blake: Vampire Hunter* novel series (1993–), another cornerstone in the recent development of the paranormal romance was the *Buffy the Vampire Slayer* TV series (The WB/UPN, 1997–2003). Both of these series featured strong female protagonists who functioned as action heroines, vampire huntresses and investigators of supernatural mysteries, which can be linked to discourses surrounding 'girl power' emerging in the 1990s (McLennon 2014). As Joseph Crawford argues, *Buffy* can be credited with establishing the sympathetic, romantic vampire as a mainstream character (2014: 135). The series' influence on the vampire productions analysed in this book can be clearly felt; the texts follow in *Buffy*'s footsteps in many ways. For instance, both *The Vampire Diaries* and *True Blood* feature vampire characters that follow the tradition of a kind of binary construction of vampire figures introduced in *Buffy*: whereas Stefan and Bill mirror *Buffy*'s guilt-ridden Angel, Damon and Eric have many characteristics in common with the morally ambiguous fan favourite Spike (Busse 2010).

As a TV series concerned with a group of teenage protagonists making their way through the ambiguous period of adolescence, *Buffy* was representative of a noteworthy shift in audience make-up in the 1980s and 1990s: teen viewers/readers were increasingly recognized as consumers, with a range of teen-centric content being developed for different media (Crawford 2014: 89). This trend towards catering to young adult audiences continued throughout the early noughties. Immensely popular TV shows like *Dawson's Creek* (The WB, 1998–2003), *Roswell* (The WB/UPN, 1999–2002), *Degrassi: The Next Generation* (CTV/MuchMusic/MTV Canada, 2001–15), *The O.C.* (Fox, 2003–7) and *Veronica Mars* (UPN/The CW/Hulu, 2004–19), as well as films like *Ghost World* (2001), *Crossroads* (2002), *Mean Girls* (2004) and *The Sisterhood of the Traveling Pants* (2005) essentially paved the way for the teen-focused vampire romance genre emerging towards the end of the 2000s. Young people then starting to consume the *Twilight* books and films (as well as slightly later *The Vampire Diaries* and, depending on their age, *True Blood*) had been growing up with another franchise whose cultural impact cannot be discounted: J. K. Rowling's *Harry Potter* series (1997–2007). The publication of *The Deathly Hallows*, the final book in the series, had 'left a void, a need for another shared narrative' (Clarke 2010: 3) among a generation of fans. As Sorcha Ní Fhlainn argues, the *Twilight* phenomenon 'tapped into' (2019: 227) a young audience accustomed to Rowling's series. According to Ní Fhlainn, 'the timing of the [first *Twilight*] novel's publication was important as it swept up young adolescent readers into a seemingly gentle form of vampire fiction that foregrounded the romantic potential of immortality without its abject consequences' (227–8). Curiously, Meyer herself has described her debut novel as 'a vampire book for people who don't like vampires' (Margolis 2005). By divesting her series of most of the usual generic elements of vampire fiction, she was able to activate a huge audience of readers beyond those interested in the Gothic (Crawford 2014: 180). This loyal army of readers was then mainly responsible for making the film version of *Twilight* the tremendous success that it was (ibid.: 242). By the time the movie was released, the paranormal romance trend had become such an undeniable phenomenon that film studios and TV networks were willing to accept the involved risks in developing more and more vampire romance franchises for film and television (ibid.: 236).

The Vampire Diaries and *True Blood*, too, are based on popular paranormal romance book series. Similar to *Twilight*, these series reached the height of their popularity in the course of their adaptation to another medium. *The Vampire Diaries'* original text is a series of novels of the same name by L. J. Smith, published between 1991 and 1992; *True Blood*'s literary source is Charlaine Harris's bestselling book series *The Southern Vampire Mysteries* (also known as *The Sookie Stackhouse Novels*; 2001–13). In March 2017, the most recent of this book's primary texts came to a close. *The Vampire Diaries*, which was developed by Kevin Williamson and Julie Plec for the broadcast television network The CW, can look back on eight seasons or a total of 170 episodes. For much of its seven and a half year running time, it functioned as the network's flagship series, generating an enormous viewership and drawing in a myriad of fans. For instance, the number of viewers who watched the pilot episode of *The Vampire Diaries* surpassed that of any other series premiere on The CW since the network was launched in 2006 (MacKenzie 2010). Actors and actresses portraying the main characters on the show have garnered numerous nominations at the *People's Choice Awards* and *Teen Choice Awards*, which attests to the tremendous recognition it received from the general public and the teenage demographic in particular. A similar success story was *True Blood*, which was broadcast on the premium cable and satellite television network HBO between 2008 and 2014. Despite receiving a TV-MA rating and primarily addressing a mature audience, the show is related to *The Vampire Diaries* and the *Twilight* franchise in terms of genre and subject matter. *True Blood*, which was created by Alan Ball and ran for a total of seven seasons, has equally been a favourite by audiences and critics. Among other things, it won both an *Emmy* and a *Golden Globe* award and was chosen as 'Favourite TV Obsession' at the *People's Choice Awards* in 2010. Like *The Vampire Diaries* for The CW, *True Blood* was one of the most profitable shows for HBO, surpassed only by the hit series *Game of Thrones* in terms of ratings (Garofalo 2014).

As pointed out already, the *Twilight* film series, being in the works at roughly the same time as these two TV series, has contributed decisively to the growth in mainstream popularity of the paranormal romance genre (Crawford 2014: 159). Technically, *True Blood* was the first to enter the scene: the HBO series premiered in September 2008, two months before the first *Twilight* movie hit theatres. As Darryl Jones clarifies, 'the Stackhouse novels actually predate *Twilight*, but the success of *True Blood* is clearly a response to the [*Twilight*] phenomenon. . . . The *Twilight* phenomenon has defined the terms by which twenty-first-century vampires are understood' (2018: 36). Ní Fhlainn, too, acknowledges the central role played by the *Twilight* franchise in the flourishing of the paranormal romance genre by stating that *True Blood* was 'providing an alternate adult vampire narrative as a cultural response to the extreme media attention focused on the *Twilight* saga, its film adaptations, and its fandoms' (2019: 12). Alan Ball himself has been very open about how the idea for developing the series came about: according to him, in 2005 he acquired a copy of Charlaine Harris's first *Sookie Stackhouse* novel, *Dead until Dark*, and began reading it while waiting for a dentist appointment. After finishing his work on *Six Feet Under* (HBO, 2001–5), his then most recent critically acclaimed TV series, Ball was looking for a new project to develop for television and was instantly drawn to the *Sookie Stackhouse* material (Crawford 2014: 247). While Ball's discovery of the *Sookie Stackhouse* series roughly coincided with the publication and initial popularization of *Twilight* – the novel reached the shelves in October 2005 and quickly rose to number five on the *New York Times* Best Seller list within a month of its release (Kostihova 2012: 98) – the development period of *True Blood*, which began in late 2005 and ended in late 2008, was perfectly situated in the time frame in which the *Twilight* series came to achieve massive global fame (Crawford 2014: 247). As Crawford suggests, '[t]he rising tide of popularity which vampire media enjoyed in these years must go some way towards explaining HBO's decision to actually green-light *True Blood*' (ibid.: 247). The fact that the creators decided to centre the first season around a romance plot allows the assumption that the series aimed to join the ranks of the contemporary wave of paranormal romance fiction (ibid.: 248).

During its running time, *True Blood* was often framed as the racier, gorier, more mature alternative to the 'defanged' *Twilight* franchise. On the one hand, this framing was put forward by Ball himself (Gross 2010). On the other hand, Mellins has shown that this interpretation was indeed shared by audiences: '*True Blood* was frequently referred to as *Twilight* for grown-ups, as women frequently pitted these franchises against each other' (2013: 63).[3] It seems that many subsequent texts made an attempt to define themselves against the *Twilight* franchise in order to establish an identity of their own. Sam George and Bill Hughes refer to this phenomenon as 'the shadowy presence of *Twilight*' (2013a: 1) in fiction emerging in the decade after *Twilight*'s publication. As Hannah Priest argues in her essay 'Young Adults and the Contemporary Gothic', 'the ways in which later fiction and film reference the Twilight franchise establish Meyer's work as the *locus classicus* of contemporary teen Gothic. While some of the references are overt . . . many rely on "in-jokes," which only a reader/viewer will understand' (2014: 281; emphasis in original). A particularly interesting reference is cited by Ní Fhlainn, who describes a newborn vampire character in *What We Do in the Shadows* (2014) 'joyously shar[ing] his undead status with everyone he meets, yelling out "I'm a vampire! . . . I'm *Twilight*!" to random members of the public' (2019: 249). In a humorous way, *Twilight* is basically equated with the vampire genre as a whole here. Examples of references in other products' paratexts range from director Neil Jordan's *Byzantium* (2014) being marketed as "'the other Twilight', or "the alternative to Twilight'" (Jones 2018: 36) to the dismissal of Isaac Marion's debut young adult novel *Warm Bodies* (2010) as '*Twilight* with zombies' (Valby 2012). According to Priest, such references serve 'to preserve the status of Meyer's work within the genre, reifying Meyer's vampires as a model against which all others will be measured' (2014: 281). A second function of this kind of 'textual cannibalism' (ibid.) is the demonstration of 'a continuity with tradition' (ibid.: 280). This assessment is in line with Ken Gelder's well-known argument that vampire texts are particularly aware of their heritage and always draw on earlier texts within the genre (1994: 86).

Such self-referential positioning in the lineage – and hierarchy – of vampire texts occurs in *The Vampire Diaries* as well. In the first-season episode 'Family Ties' (1.4), Damon flicks through one of the *Twilight* novels (as is implied) and comments sceptically: 'What's so special about this Bella girl? Edward's so whipped. . . . I live in the real world where vampires burn in the sun. . . . This book . . . has it all wrong.' Most likely, *The Vampire Diaries* TV series was commissioned in the wake of success of both the *Twilight* franchise and *True Blood*. The large time gap between the release of the novels and the TV series suggests that the paranormal romance boom had something to do with the producers' decision to adapt the relatively 'old' source material. Crawford points out that *The Vampire Diaries* was originally conceptualized as a show that would 'tak[e] the middle route between the established successes of the *Twilight* and the *True Blood* franchises' (2014: 263). Because 'it is not as sexually explicit or gory as *True Blood* but is more "adult" than *Twilight*' (Williams 2013: 89), the series was typically positioned as '[s]omewhere in between' (Carlson, qtd. in ibid.) in on- and offline media. As Kevin Williamson has admitted, he was initially wary of becoming involved in developing the show together with Julie Plec because he 'felt it was a sort of Twilight rip-off, no matter which came first' (Hughes 2010). Needless to say, he eventually changed his mind about the material. Nevertheless, this quote by Williamson reveals, once again, the status of Meyer's franchise as the central popular cultural reference point in the paranormal romance genre of the period.

Not only has the *Twilight* franchise enabled the enormous expansion of vampire and paranormal romance genres, it has also had a tremendous cultural impact beyond these genres. The past decade has seen an explosion of female-led Hollywood blockbusters, including *The Hunger Games* tetralogy (2012–15), the *Divergent* series (2014–16), the *Fifty Shades* series (2015–18),[4] *Star Wars: Episode VIII – The Last Jedi* (2017), *Wonder Woman* (2017), *Wonder Woman 1984* (2020) and *Black Widow* (2021), to name only a few. The American film industry seems increasingly inclined to produce big-budget films featuring female protagonists and targeting a female demographic. This shift in the industry is not least a result of *Twilight*'s overwhelming success at the box office (Crawford 2014: 272). In an online article of *Entertainment Weekly*, Owen Gleiberman describes this ground-breaking shift:

> The ascendance of the *Twilight* saga represents an essential paradigm shift in youth-gender control of the pop marketplace. For the better part of two decades, teenage boys, and *overgrown* teenage boys, have essentially held sway over Hollywood, dictating, to a gargantuan degree, the varieties of movies that get made. . . . Sure, we have 'chick flicks,' but that (demeaning) term implies that they're an exception. . . . No more. With *New Moon*, the *Twilight* series is now officially . . . a juggernaut on the big screen. . . . And that gives the core audience it represents – teenage girls – a new power and prevalence. (2009; emphasis in original)

Their extraordinary popularity, scope and cultural impact alone are reasons to study the *Twilight* Saga, *The Vampire Diaries* and *True Blood*. As some of the most prominent examples of their kind, these media products have reached – and continue to reach – widespread audiences, transporting notions of gender norms, identities and relations, sexuality, race, class and age to a diverse group of consumers; it is then up to the latter to negotiate, accept, question or reject these notions. An analysis of these three texts is particularly worthwhile because all three of them come in the form of audio-visual media. As Kristopher Broyles contends, 'the visual medium facilitates more passive learning than do other forms of media. Therefore, the impact of ideas about femininity and masculinity may be more passively learned, accepted, or integrated into society' (2010). Considering the cultural power of these three paranormal romances, it is an especially valuable endeavour to uncover the subtle as well as naming the less subtle messages they contain. Besides the discursive and ideological power of these vampire romances, their pronounced emphasis on gender and sexuality makes them an instructive object of academic study from a gender studies perspective. The vampire is an overwhelmingly popular symbol for the erotic (Wisker 1998: 63), and according to Melissa Ames, 'the vampire narrative is a productive space to tease out problems of gender and sexuality' (2010: 45). Similarly, Catherine M. Roach describes 'romance . . . as a rich cultural site that yields much insight into critical issues of gender and sexuality in America today' (2010: 2). Thus, the hybrid genre of paranormal romance lends itself perfectly to the study of gender that is undertaken within the frame of this book.

Although there are a number of differences between the *Twilight Saga*, *The Vampire Diaries* and *True Blood*,[5] an obvious commonality of the three texts is that they all centre on a love story between a young female human protagonist and a male vampire, a narrative premise that apparently strikes a chord with the target audiences. The fact that women and girls are the intended primary consumers of all three series was/is unusual and partly accounts for these cultural products' tremendous success at the box office and within fan communities. As Stacey Abbott argues, '[p]art of [these fictions'] appeal is linked to how they have been used to explore women's desires and sexuality in rather provocative, at times controversial, ways' (2016a). Interestingly, although the *Twilight* franchise, in particular, has been favoured by many, it has also been widely castigated for its retrogressive gender politics by critics, scholars and audiences alike.[6] Considering the vampire's fascinating potential to 'break . . . down categories, transgress . . . boundaries, and upset . . . the very premises upon which systems of normality are structured' (Kane 2010: 103), it is striking that – in marked contrast – this contemporary vampire romance seems to introduce its vampires as reinforcing the dominant social order. Meyer has been criticized for crafting a group of vampires that do not disrupt the status quo but that 'align with a trend of non-heteronormative characters supporting heteronormativity' (ibid.: 104). Indeed, the franchise depicts a world in which heterosexual relations and marriage are granted centrality. However, despite the common criticism that the novels and movies (re-)stage 'gender roles that reflect the rigid social mores of a few centuries ago' (Hawes 2010: 174), the franchise has cultivated a massive fan following, especially among female fans of diverse ages (Dietz 2011: 104), including many 'self-described feminists' (Wagenseller Goletz 2012: 147). As I argue, the inconsistent reception of the *Twilight* franchise can be traced back to a range of internal contradictions and ambiguities inherent in the texts, which I relate to current discourses of postfeminism.

Although similarly paradoxical positions have not dominated the discourse surrounding *The Vampire Diaries* and *True Blood*, these series, too, are full of internal conflicts. *True Blood* may commonly be referred to as '*Twilight*'s ideological antithesis' (Ní Fhlainn 2019: 232), in which – in contrast to *Twilight*'s 'denial of blood and . . . denial of sexuality' (Donnelly 2011: 182) – 'blood and sexual fluids flow excessively' (Ní Fhlainn 2019: 232). In other words, the two series' antithetical positions may seem clear-cut. However, as Ní Fhlainn points out, 'political, social, and cultural complexities and contradictions emerge in both texts, whether it concerns social or sexual inclusion or a reaffirmation of conservative heterosexual idealism' (ibid.: 219). Meanwhile, *The Vampire Diaries*, with its characteristic 'breakdown of the fixed subject' (Bridgeman 2013: 17), provides its own brand of exploring cultural ambiguities. In the course of the fast-paced narrative that typically relies on numerous plot twists and turns per episode, '[s]tories of all kinds, historical, mythic, local, and personal, are frequently discovered as falsified or cover-ups. In this way the viewer is taught to question the validity of any story and the stability of every character' (ibid.: 12). As a result, moral ambiguities are emphasized.

Contradictoriness, as I contend, is at the core of these mid-aughts vampire romances, as they oscillate between the reinforcement and the disruption of conventional gender structures. One of my central arguments is that these texts are highly problematic in some instances, while they simultaneously offer spaces of subversion and the suspension of gendered power dynamics. This 'both/and' (Rutland 1999: 74) moment at the heart of these cultural products is one of postfeminism's essential features. Within this book, postfeminism is understood as 'the cultural formation that has become the dominant framework in western culture's discourses of gender' (Levine 2009: 137), a hybrid phenomenon emerging at the intersection of such varied influences as feminism, neoliberalism, consumer culture, individualism, postmodernism and mainstream media. While some scholars have called into question the continued relevance of postfeminism as a critical notion,[7] I maintain that it remains a highly useful analytical category capturing a range of contradictory but clearly identifiable patterns in contemporary culture(s). As scholars such as Angela McRobbie (2015), Tisha Dejmanee (2016), Rosalind Gill (2016; 2017), Stéphanie Genz (2017) and Sarah Banet-Weiser (2018) have convincingly argued, postfeminism still holds sway over the current era and therefore warrants continued scholarly attention. Although recent developments, such as the resurgence of popular feminism and feminist activism, the 2008 financial crash and the ensuing global economic crisis, have caused distinct shifts in postfeminist discourses, 'the postfeminist moment is far from over, and its contradictions continue to inform and displace current generations of young women' (Dejmanee 2016: 131). As a matter of fact, the transformations that postfeminist ideology has undergone in the past decade(s) attest to its 'cultural malleability and longevity' (ibid.: 120).

Essentially, I argue in this book that the *Twilight* Saga, *The Vampire Diaries* and *True Blood* both reflect and promote notions that are rooted in contemporary postfeminist culture. As I will demonstrate, the supernatural figure of the vampire functions as a trope that is ideal for the incorporation of postfeminist ideas on gender, sexuality, identity and the body. Thus, not only do vampire narratives lend themselves to affirm, explore and/or subvert power hierarchies, particularly relating to categories of sexuality, gender and race, but vampires also work as a projection surface for postfeminist discourses of subjectivation, self-discipline and the management of the body. Vampires, according to Crawford, 'whilst notionally outsiders, are actually perfectly suited to act as champions of mainstream (white, heterosexual) American culture and morality' (2014: 175). Thus, on the one hand, vampires are suitable vehicles through which to explore questions of Otherness as well as sexual, moral and social transgression based on their supernatural status. On the other hand, they can and do appear as perfectly ordinary citizens, attending the local high school (Edward Cullen in the *Twilight* Saga; Stefan Salvatore in *The Vampire Diaries*) or separating recyclable items from waste in their household (Bill Compton in *True Blood*). These vampires' 'structured and distinct . . . manner of *living* . . . is what distinguishes them from the other monsters providing horrific ambiance for the Gothic romance and places them, instead, in contention for the role of hero' (Mukherjea 2012: 115; emphasis in original). More so than werewolves, mummies or other supernatural beings, vampires have been of 'rich metaphorical usefulness' (Gordon and Hollinger 1997b: 3) in popular culture, standing in for a variety of issues, ranging from death and disease (AIDS in particular), homosexuality, capitalism, immigration, class warfare and others. Being an 'ambiguously coded figure' (Gordon and Hollinger 1997b: 1) straddling oppositional categories such as life and death, human and animal, danger and desire, the vampire is ideally suited to embody and explore the 'both/and' nature of postfeminist culture.

In investigating what characterizes the vampire figure portrayed in the selected paranormal romances, I build upon an extensive body of academic research on the popular cultural vampire motif. In particular, my study is based on Nina Auerbach's frequently cited argument that vampires are subjected to cultural change and that they tend to reflect issues at the centre of current debates within society. As Auerbach writes, 'vampires shape themselves to personal and national moods', and, '[b]ecause they are always changing, their appeal is dramatically generational' (1995: 5). Thus, a key research question explored in this book concerns the characteristics of the contemporary vampire figure and the ways in which it is represented in the examined narratives. This is important because, '[l]ike the pre-twentieth century Gothic, the appeal of today's "new" vampire tale is to do with its ability to represent what is disavowed, to speak to anxieties and desires that are difficult to name' (Williamson 2003: 105). Hence, I argue that, in conjunction with the vampire figure, the way in which gender and sexuality are represented in the three key texts is in fact a reflection of 'the plurality and contradictions of contemporary female (and male) experience' (Genz and Brabon 2009: 39). The fact that these media products address and negotiate a variety of aspects pertaining to the conflict-laden experience of individuals living in the postfeminist era explains their tremendous appeal to audiences. Rather than framing my analysis of the *Twilight* Saga, *The Vampire Diaries* and *True Blood* as an attempt to determine whether these texts are essentially feminist or anti-feminist, I draw on the work of Gill, who argues that postfeminist popular culture '*critiques as well as endorses*' (2007: 248; emphasis in original) gendered patriarchal strictures. Importantly, I understand postfeminism not solely as a retrogressive, anti-feminist backlash but as a dominating discursive system having emerged at the intersection of different cultural influences, including feminism, neoliberalist, consumerist ideology, individualism and postmodernism. Thus, a fundamental assumption of my work is that '[p]ostfeminist culture does not allow us to make straightforward distinctions between progressive and regressive texts' (Tasker and Negra 2007b: 22).

Studying vampire romance

I approach my leading questions by providing a discursive and ideological textual analysis of the *Twilight* film series and the television shows *The Vampire Diaries* and *True Blood*. Thus, I employ the theoretical strategy 'of "reading" cultural products, social practices, even institutions, as "texts"' (Turner 2002: 71). Through my meticulous close reading of the series,

I aim to uncover what kinds of meanings these paranormal romances hold for contemporary postfeminist audiences. To achieve this, I draw on genre theory, gender theory and psychoanalytic theory in the form of Laura Mulvey's concept of the male gaze as well as Joey Soloway's concept of the female gaze. In keeping with the established practice of supporting and developing textual analysis 'around a wider contextual or extratextual framework' (Creeber 2006a: 35), these approaches are coupled with an ideological analysis of the texts. Through this wide reading, I examine the ways in which the *Twilight* Saga, *The Vampire Diaries* and *True Blood* are both building blocks and products of postfeminist discourses surrounding gender, sexuality, identity and feminism.

Committing myself to critically examining representations of gender and sexuality in the narratives, I will scrutinize my own readings wherever possible. I acknowledge that the analyses carried out here predominantly revolve around representations of white, cis, heterosexual, middle-class femininities and masculinities. This focus is difficult to avoid, given that these cultural products favour the experiences of these demographics. The fact that the texts, for the most part, neglect to represent in any complexity the experiences of marginalized communities reveals 'the class, age, and racial exclusions that define postfeminism and its characteristic assumption that the themes, pleasures, values, and lifestyles with which it is associated are somehow universally shared and, perhaps more significant, universally accessible' (Tasker and Negra 2007b: 2). Throughout my analyses, I will take into account the intersectionality of subject categories, considering the ways in which gender is entangled with other axes of power regarding race, class, age and sexuality. Proceeding from the premise that gender should not be examined in isolation from other categories of difference that are fundamental to (popular) cultural constructions of identity and alterity, I will, for instance, discuss the role that Jacob Black's Native American heritage plays in his representation as sexualized object of Bella Swan's gaze in Chapter 3 of this book. Nevertheless, the examination of gender and sexuality in these three vampire romances will remain the focus of my analyses.

My work's discursive and ideological approach to textual analysis is rooted in a Foucaultian conceptualization of discourse and power. Michel Foucault has theorized discourses as processes through which meaning, knowledge and subjects are produced (Milestone and Meyer 2012: 25). According to Foucault, power is inscribed in and works through discourse, which is '(re)produced . . . across all social sites and practices' (ibid.: 26). Crucially, in this model, power is not understood as an inherently negative, coercive or restrictive force but as something that is 'simultaneously productive and repressive' (ibid.: 27). In Foucault's view, power is constantly being negotiated – a conceptualization that opens up positive possibilities of action and resistance (Pilcher and Whelehan [2004] 2011: 118). My book is informed by this idea of a constant struggle for the supremacy of certain discourses. Here, I will work with the Gramscian notion of hegemony. Similar to Foucault, Antonio Gramsci has theorized that, because a group's hegemonic position is always subject to potential challenges by non-leading groups and must therefore be continually struggled for, hegemony can be defined as 'a *condition in process*' (Storey 2011: 79; emphasis in original). Thus, Gramsci's notion of hegemony emphasizes precisely that there is always the possibility of awareness and change (Milestone and Meyer 2012: 17). Based on these theoretical frameworks, I will tease out which discourses are at work and battling for hegemony in the paranormal romances I am looking at. My analysis will focus on both old-fashioned and innovatory renditions of gender roles and relationships that can be found in these series.

Forming the backdrop of my work is Judith Butler's notion that gender is a performative construct and that identity categories in general are 'the *effects* of institutions, practices, discourses with multiple and diffuse points of origin' (1990: ix; emphasis in original). Thus, my work is based on the assumption that the differences between what is considered feminine and what is considered masculine are not causally linked to biological characteristics, but that gender is produced through social and cultural acts and is therefore a historically variable category.

Strongly influenced by Foucault's ideas, Butler considers gender 'an ongoing discursive practice... open to intervention and resignification' (ibid.: 33). Basing my study on this notion, I will explore what kinds of resignifications of femininities and masculinities can be found in this selection of paranormal romances.

Transferring Gramsci's concept of hegemony to my study of the *Twilight* Saga, *The Vampire Diaries* and *True Blood*, I perceive these popular cultural products as a political space in which competing interests and values are negotiated in contradictory ways (Storey 2011: 82). In this way, I follow Lorraine Gamman and Margaret Marshment, who argue that

> [p]opular culture is a site of struggle, where many... meanings are determined and debated. It is not enough to dismiss popular culture as merely serving the complementary systems of capitalism and patriarchy, peddling 'false consciousness' to the duped masses. It can also be seen as a site where meanings are contested and where dominant ideologies can be disturbed. ([1988] 1994a: 1)

It is this critical approach that I am indebted to. With the aid of this approach, I examine the ways in which the *Twilight* Saga, *The Vampire Diaries* and *True Blood* may – or may not – present alternative conceptions of gender and sexuality that break with 'traditional' or hegemonic ideological ideas of these concepts. The notion of ideology that I work with is one that defines ideology as 'a dynamic social practice, constantly in process, constantly reproducing itself' (Fiske 1992: 287–8) in institutionalized discourses such as religion, politics, the law, media and culture, for instance through the representation of 'certain characteristics and practices as "natural" and "typical" of men and women' (Milestone and Meyer 2012: 21). Following Stuart Hall, representation is understood here as 'an essential part of the process by which meaning is produced and exchanged between members of a culture' (1997c: 15). As Hall maintains, '[m]eaning has to be actively "read" or "interpreted"' (ibid.: 32); in this way, multiple interpretations on the part of audiences may be the consequence. Connecting with this idea, my study draws on Hall's concept of polysemic texts and the possibility of 'dominant'/hegemonic, 'negotiated' or 'oppositional' readings (Creeber 2006b: 50). My book, then, adheres to a Cultural Studies approach to issues of representation and mediated discourse. By conducting textual analyses of the *Twilight* Saga, *The Vampire Diaries* and *True Blood*, I will investigate how representations of femininities and masculinities in these narratives function within and impact wider cultural discourses surrounding gender, race, age, class and sexuality. As will become clear, these postfeminist texts are heavily characterized by the use of polysemy and double meanings, offering audiences numerous possibilities of constructing their own interpretations of the narratives.

Chapter overview

My introduction presents the vampire romance phenomenon that this book aims to tackle, elaborates on the context in which the *Twilight* Saga, *The Vampire Diaries* and *True Blood* were created, and locates these texts in the contemporary postfeminist landscape.

Chapter 1 introduces the intricacies of postfeminist culture and provides an overview of three perspectives on the phenomenon that are commonly differentiated in academia. These are the conception of postfeminism as a theoretical perspective, as a historical break and as anti-feminist backlash. After briefly elaborating on these perspectives, I develop my own understanding of postfeminism, which forms the basis of my book. Thus, I understand postfeminism as a distinct discursive formation. My book incorporates Stéphanie Genz's and Benjamin A. Brabon's contextualizing approach, which understands postfeminism as a hybrid phenomenon 'aris[ing] in a late twentieth-century Western context characterised by the proliferation of media images and communication technologies and a neo-liberal, consumerist ideology that replaces collective, activist politics with more individualistic assertions of (consumer) choice and self-rule' (2009: 8).

Chapter 2 looks at the *Twilight* Saga, *The Vampire Diaries* and *True Blood* from a genre-theoretical perspective. The chapter provides a definition of paranormal romance and delineates the complicated history of the genre, focusing on how it developed out of the entangled strands of the Gothic and the romance novel. This account of the way the precursors of contemporary paranormal romance coalesced to form a hybrid that emerged in the early 1990s as a niche genre forms the backdrop of my argument that due to its defining generic characteristics, paranormal romance works as a suitable backdrop for the complexities of postfeminist ideas. As will become clear, Gothic and romance are both inherently ambivalent genres torn between conservative generic conventions and feminist subtext. Similarly, paranormal romance texts like the *Twilight* Saga, *The Vampire Diaries* and *True Blood* cross boundaries in terms of genre, storytelling techniques, target audiences and subject matter. I argue that the genre's transgressive nature makes it particularly prone to registering and negotiating cultural tensions. Chapter 2 thus explores how the hybrid paranormal romance genre intersects with contemporary postfeminist discourses based on the ambivalence and liminality that characterizes both.

Chapter 3 investigates strategies of privileging heterosexual female desire and subjectivity in the *Twilight* Saga, *The Vampire Diaries* and *True Blood*. Making use of Mulvey's influential film-theoretical concept of the male gaze as well as Soloway's innovative manifesto on the female gaze, this chapter offers close readings of illustrative scenes, which are then related to postfeminist discourses surrounding sexual empowerment and self-determination. I argue that the texts stage instances not of a male but a heterosexual female gaze, thereby addressing straight female (teen) viewers and generating female subjectivity. For this purpose, the paranormal romances strategically employ the figure of the male vampire on a narrative as well as a visual level. Here, the vampire's supernaturally sexy body becomes the primary object of erotic gazing, blurring conventionally 'masculine' and 'feminine' positions in the process. As I contend, the female gaze found in these texts can be linked to contemporary postfeminist culture in which women are experiencing a 'shift from objectification to subjectification' (Gill 2007: 255). At the same time, female protagonists Bella Swan and Sookie Stackhouse share with viewers their experience of how it feels to become the sexualized object of a heterosexual male gaze, emphasizing both the constraining and violent, and the potentially empowering aspects of this experience. By foregrounding a (straight, white) female gaze, these series criticize, complicate and/or take advantage of conventional gaze dynamics as well as the sexist, patriarchal culture that has generated them. Meanwhile, the emergence of this straight, white female gaze is closely interrelated with postfeminist, neoliberal aspects of marketing and capitalizing on (post)feminism for economic reasons.

Chapter 4 interrogates the relationship between the selected paranormal romances and postfeminist discourses of individual empowerment, self-optimization and body maintenance. Through the close readings that I provide in this chapter, it will become clear how the *Twilight* Saga, *The Vampire Diaries* and *True Blood* use the figure of the female vampire to negotiate postfeminist/neoliberal ideas concerning the management and disciplinary shaping of body and self. Here, I read storylines of vampiric transformation as narratives of postfeminist makeovers, in the course of which the central female characters Bella Swan, Caroline Forbes and Jessica Hamby come to epitomize the paradox of the active/passive 'self-surveilling post-feminist subject' (Negra 2009: 119), which is individually empowered and simultaneously ruled by social norms. By relating the texts to discourses rooted in postfeminist/neoliberal consumer culture, I explore the ways in which paranormal romance both mirrors and constructs the contradictory nature of contemporary culture, which provides opportunities of subjectivation and reclamation of the self for women while simultaneously condemning female subjects to perpetual self-discipline and bodily control.

Chapter 5 examines the representation of masculinities in the *Twilight* Saga, *The Vampire Diaries* and *True Blood*. As I will show, the texts' humanized vampire romance heroes, Edward Cullen, Stefan Salvatore and Bill Compton, work as embodiments of contemporary postfeminist masculinity, which Genz and Brabon describe as the 'ongoing conglomeration of at times contradictory and conflicting masculinities' (2009: 142). An intrinsically contradictory formation, the postfeminist man both holds continuities with older, traditional forms of masculinity and offers a new conception of self-reflexive, potentially progressive masculinity in tune with feminist ideas. Here, I argue that discourses surrounding this hybrid masculinity, which is in the process of interrogating and challenging its own gendered dominance as well as responsibilities, are mapped onto the body of the male reluctant vampire. By centralizing this paradoxical masculinity in the form of their male vampire protagonists, the paranormal romances provide a highly attractive redefinition of hegemonic masculinity. Thus, I contend that what emerges here are transitional postfeminist masculinities that may still be hegemonic but simultaneously open to dismantling gender hierarchies.

In the concluding chapter, the different strands investigated in the preceding chapters will be brought together to paint a full picture of the relationship between the *Twilight* Saga, *The Vampire Diaries* and *True Blood* and the ideologies of postfeminism.

1

More than a backlash
The contradictions of postfeminist culture

Postfeminism's many faces

In the course of the past four decades, postfeminism has become established as a central critical term in feminist and cultural-theoretical discussions across the academe. As Gill points out in her relatively recent overview of the state of the critical debate, 'postfeminism has tightened its hold upon contemporary life and become hegemonic. . . . It has both spread out and intensified across contemporary culture' (2017: 606). Having emerged at the intersection of a number of cultural, academic and political contexts, postfeminism made its way into the popular consciousness in the early 1980s (Gamble [1998] 2009a: 43). Since then, it has continually developed and transformed, inspiring numerous disputes and analyses among scholars. Pinning down what exactly postfeminism is and what it constitutes has been a matter of heated discussion taking place in academic, political and cultural arenas. Even 'whether it exists at all as a valid phenomenon' (ibid.) has been challenged at times. The characteristic of intangibility is something postfeminism has in common with its semantic relative postmodernism. In fact, Sarah Gamble conceives of postfeminism as 'a pluralistic epistemology . . . capable of being aligned with postmodernism, poststructuralism and postcolonialism' (ibid.: 50), thereby taking into account two further important 'post'-discourses. Recognizing the defiance of being easily defined as one of the core features of the phenomenon, Genz maintains that perhaps 'rather than trying to immobilize postfeminism in a rigid structure of meaning, we should interpret its polysemy as an integral part of its cultural force' (2007: 70). Furthermore, Dejmanee, among others, has emphasized 'the malleability and corruptibility of postfeminist rhetoric' (2016: 120). Because of its ability to adapt flexibly to varying national contexts as well as changing political and cultural backdrops, postfeminist ideology has managed to 'become the new normal, a taken-for-granted common sense that operates as a kind of gendered neoliberalism' (Gill 2017: 609) in both Western and non-Western spaces. As Dejmanee finds, postfeminism's tenacity lies in its versatile applicability 'to any and all facets of feminine lifestyle according to the social trends and ideological demands of the moment' (2016: 131). In keeping with these observations about the phenomenon's nature, a monolithic definition of postfeminism is to be avoided here. Nevertheless, for the purposes of this book, a more extensive characterization of postfeminism is needed. This chapter can give neither a comprehensive nor a conclusive definition of the concept, but it aims to shed light on a number of essential aspects of postfeminism.

Postfeminism's 'post' prefix is a crucial element generating difficulties tied to the term, as it comprises several possible meanings and thereby allows for varying interpretations of the word (Gamble [1998] 2009a: 44). Misha Kavka has epitomized this issue in the title of her much-cited essay 'Feminism, Ethics, and History, or What Is the "Post" in Postfeminism?' (2002). At the same time, however, the prefix lends itself as a productive way of approaching the 'semantic confusion' (Genz and Brabon 2009: 2) surrounding postfeminism in order to conceptualize it and distinguish different versions of it. In academic writing, four perspectives on postfeminism are commonly differentiated. From the first perspective, postfeminism is conceived as an epistemological break (Gill 2007: 250), the 'post' being understood as 'part of a process of ongoing transformation' (Genz and Brabon 2009: 4). In this view, postfeminism is seen as 'a theoretical perspective concerned to emphasise diversity rather than commonality of experience amongst women (and men)' (Abbott, Wallace and Tyler 2005: 52). From the second perspective, the phenomenon is conceived as a historical shift (Gill 2007: 251), the 'post' thereby carrying the idea of 'after'. In this view, postfeminism is 'a cultural phenomenon, characterised by the emergence of an [*sic*] historical period "after" feminism' (Abbott, Wallace and Tyler 2005: 52). From the third perspective, postfeminism is most pessimistically perceived 'as a retrogressive, anti-feminist backlash that retracts and invalidates the gains and social transformations brought on by or through the feminist movement' (Genz and Brabon 2009: 5), again with an emphasis on 'post' meaning 'after'. The fourth perspective, then, understands postfeminism as 'a critical analytical term that refers to empirical regularities or patterns in contemporary cultural life' (Gill 2016: 4). This is the perspective that I adopt in my research. All four perspectives are elaborated further in this chapter.

Throughout this book, I use the feminist 'wave' analogy, which indicates shifts in key issues of feminist politics (Pilcher and Whelehan [2004] 2011: 52; 144), while acknowledging that there are/were feminist work, activism and achievements in between the waves. In the ensuing chapters, I will take into account recurring themes in feminist debates across the decades, and thereby address their cyclical reappearance. Innovative approaches to feminist historiography have made the case for a rethinking of Western feminist theory by challenging both the implied distinctions between what is commonly conceptualized as waves and the notion of a linear progress from one wave to another. For instance, Clare Hemmings has convincingly shown that the stories told about the history of Western feminist theory typically follow three consistent patterns: they are constructed 'as a series of interlocking narratives of progress, loss, and return that oversimplify this complex history' (2011: 3). Considering Hemmings's argument that the writing of history always involves 'politics that produce and sustain one version of history as more true than another' (15–16), I want to acknowledge that the recounting of feminist discussions in this chapter necessarily presents a condensed, broken down and partial view of the history of feminism from a decidedly Western point of view. Any summary of these debates that I am able to offer here is bound to be selective and will therefore likely reproduce certain chronologies and framings firmly established in Western historiography of feminist theory.

Feminism's 'coming of age': Postfeminism as theoretical perspective

As already pointed out, from the perspective that conceives postfeminism as a theoretical stance, the 'post' prefix makes reference to feminism by denoting 'a genealogy that entails revision or strong family resemblance' (Genz and Brabon 2009: 3–4). This position is typically taken up by those who stress the continuity of thought between feminism and postfeminism (ibid.: 4). In this chronological sense, postfeminism is thus read as 'a healthy rewriting of feminism, a sign that the women's movement is continuously in process, transforming and changing itself' (Gamble [1998] 2009a: 11). As Ann Brooks argues in *Postfeminisms: Feminism, Cultural Theory and Cultural Forms* (1997), since feminism's heyday in the 1960s and 1970s, it has been subject to a number of significant changes in ideas and focus, which can be attributed to its more recent intersection with cultural theory, in particular with postmodernist, poststructuralist and postcolonial theory ([1997] 1998: 5). In a crossing of postmodernism and feminism, for instance, postfeminism engages with the intersection of different subject categories, such as gender, race, class, age and sexuality. Displaying awareness of the multiple ways of oppression and privilege that people can be subjected to or enjoy, postfeminist theorists dismiss the notion of an essential female self (Genz and Brabon 2009: 28). Postfeminism thus critically engages with its own feminist theory and questions the ways in which it is/was based on dualistic thinking, for example in its reliance on separate opposing categories like 'women' and 'men', and totalizing concepts, such as 'patriarchy'. Gill points out that, combined with input from postmodern theory, postfeminism has 'risen partly as a result of critiques from black and Third World feminists which destabilized dominant feminist theorizing and interrogated the right of (predominantly) white Western (Northern) women to speak on behalf of all others' (2007: 250). Thus, postfeminism has also been shaped significantly by postcolonial theories.

Brooks refers to postfeminism as feminism's 'coming of age' ([1997] 1998: 1), taking into account its growth into a politics of pluralism and difference as well as its ability to reflect on its position in relation to other political and intellectual movements. This type of story about feminism's past and present has been identified by Hemmings as a 'Western feminist progress narrative' (2011: 36), which retroactively reads a clear chronology into historical events. As Hemmings points out, a progress narrative presents 'a positive account, one told with excitement and even relish. It is a narrative of success and accomplishment and positions feminist theory, and its subjects, as attentive and dynamic' (35). Going a step further and adding an evaluative commentary, Genz and Brabon contend that the 'definition of postfeminism as a self-critical, evaluative mode is simply too optimistic'. They instead suggest that postfeminism's politics are 'more complex and subtle than a simple rewriting or modernisation' (2009: 12) – a view which is supported by the analyses undertaken within this book.

The 'end' of feminism: Postfeminism as historical break

Diametrically opposed to the view of postfeminism as a theoretical stance are perspectives that conceive the phenomenon as a historical break. In these accounts, the 'post' prefix signifies a complete rupture, invoking a narrative of progression and thereby historicizing feminism (Genz and Brabon 2009: 3). Advocates of this standpoint assume that society has fully satisfied the demands of first and second-wave feminism, such as women's enfranchisement, the right to own property and sexual liberation (ibid.: 13–14). They therefore argue that feminism or feminist activism as such have become irrelevant for young women living today. Hardly any writers have claimed the label 'postfeminist' for themselves, but a number of them have been identified with the term (Gamble [1998] 2009a: 45). Some of the most prominent American names among them are Naomi Wolf, Katie Roiphe and Rene Denfeld. Although these writers have not expressed a great deal of solidarity between one another (Siegel 1997: 59), they have a number of argumentational strategies in common. They may usually appreciate their feminist 'heritage', but they collectively argue for the replacement of a supposedly dull, restrictive, anti-sex, backward and ultimately ineffective feminism by a new feminist movement with a focus on strength, pleasure, individualism and consumerism.

Naomi Wolf's *Fire with Fire: The New Female Power and How It Will Change the 21st Century* (1993) is exemplary of this perspective. In her book, Wolf starts from the premise that a so-called 'genderquake' ([1993] 1994: xiv) has taken place in the twentieth century, thereby acknowledging and welcoming the achievements of feminism. At the same time, she denies feminism in the second wave sense the right to exist for much longer (Gamble [1998] 2009a: 48). In Wolf's opinion, women could easily take over authority from men and claim their power, but they are standing in their own way by identifying as victims of patriarchy (Genz and Brabon 2009: 68). This 'outdated' version of feminism is what Wolf refers to as 'victim feminism' ([1993] 1994: 147). Stressing the importance of 'identifying with other women through shared pleasures and strengths, rather than shared vulnerability and pain' (Genz and Brabon 2009: 69), what she sets against this supposedly unstylish, rigid, anti-sex tradition of feminism is her version of so-called power feminism. Convinced that feminism can benefit from working within the patriarchal, capitalist system, with women seizing their individual 'power as consumers' ([1993] 1994: 325), Wolf assumes a decidedly media-friendly stance. She believes that 'victim feminism' is counterproductive to the feminist cause and needs to be replaced by 'power feminism' in order to sustain the women's movement.

Developing a simplistic vision of 'power feminism' while ignoring institutionalized power structures that constrain women's ambitions of gaining equality (Genz and Brabon 2009: 70), Wolf has been criticized for imagining an 'impossibly utopian' (Gamble [1998] 2009a: 49) world.

Thus, Wolf tends to neglect that she speaks from a privileged position, failing to consider the cultural and material conditions of marginality experienced, for example, by Black and poor women. Not surprisingly, Wolf's 'power feminism' tends to be rejected by Black and postcolonial feminists for being 'exclusionary and ethnocentric' (Abbott, Wallace and Tyler 2005: 54). Essentially, Wolf advocates a vision of feminism that can be seen as oppositional to that suggested by Audre Lorde, whose identity as a 'Black lesbian feminist' (Lorde 1984b: 110) allowed her insights into the intersectionality of socio-cultural categories like race, gender and sexuality. In her famous speech at the Second Sex Conference at the New York University Institute for the Humanities in 1979, Lorde argued that 'racism, sexism, and homophobia are inseparable' (ibid.). According to Lorde, by ignoring the differences between women and thereby shutting non-white, nonheterosexual women's voices out of feminist discourse, (white) feminism avails itself of 'the tools of a racist patriarchy' (ibid.) that it is essentially trying to abolish: '*For the master's tools will never dismantle the master's house.* They may allow us temporarily to beat him at his own game, but they will never enable us to bring about genuine change' (ibid.: 112; emphasis in original). In contrast, Wolf turns Lorde's famous dictum on its head by asserting that 'it is *only* the master's tools that can dismantle the master's house, for he hardly bothers to notice anyone else's' ([1993] 1994: 59; emphasis in original).

Turning back the clock: Postfeminism as backlash

In turn, the notion of the contemporary era as a postfeminist age (an age in which feminism has been superseded) has been denounced by some scholars and critics as being 'part of a comprehensive backlash, a conservative counterassault on feminism' (Spieler 2012: 123). On the part of these scholars, postfeminism is interpreted as a betrayal of the feminist project and as intending a relapse to a former, pre-feminist state of society (Gamble [1998] 2009a: 44). Crucial ideas and arguments employed by these 'anti-postfeminist critics' (Genz and Brabon 2009: 15), among them Susan Faludi, Ann Braithwaite and Angela McRobbie, will be touched upon in the following. In Hemmings's schema of the historiography of Western feminist theory, these could be subsumed under the rubric of 'loss narratives' (2011: 24), which posit that 'the generational popularity of "postfeminism" [is an] empty parod[y] of a feminist social movement that has incontrovertibly passed' (ibid.: 4).

Faludi's book *Backlash: The Undeclared War Against American Women* (1991) is one of the most extensive analyses of what has come to be referred to in academia and elsewhere as the backlash, and is also one of the most popular positions against it. To document her thesis that postfeminism is nothing but an anti-feminist reaction on the part of the male-dominated establishment in defence of the status quo (Genz and Brabon 2009: 54), Faludi cites examples from film and television, the health care and beauty industries, politics and advertising. These are typically based on the assumption that women, instead of thriving under the new living conditions brought about by feminism since the late 1960s, are in fact miserable and depressed. According to Faludi, the 1980s and early 1990s media ascribe various sufferings to women: they are said to be troubled because they are increasingly childless, 'hysterical' because they may still be unwed at an advanced age, living in poverty because they are more often divorced, complaining about bad health due to the stress of their working lives – in short, women allegedly 'suffer from a new identity crisis'. Faludi addresses the paradoxical nature of backlash discourses in a sarcastic tone: '[I]t must be all that equality that's causing all that pain. Women are unhappy precisely *because* they are free. Women are enslaved by their own liberation' ([1991] 1992: x; emphasis in original).

While Faludi frames the late twentieth-century media discourse as a purely anti-feminist backlash, Braithwaite advocates for a more nuanced understanding of the described phenomenon, arguing that it involves more than a repudiation of anything feminist. As she contends, the 'backlash . . . works not by rejecting ideas about equality and women's "rights," but instead by acknowledging those at the same time as identifying feminism as the cause of women's current miseries' (2004: 22). McRobbie, too, stresses this 'double-entanglement' (2007: 29) contained in postfeminist/backlash discourses. Analysing a cultural situation in which feminism has become 'common sense' and is simultaneously dismissed, McRobbie observes 'the coexistence of neoconservative values in relation to gender, sexuality, and family life ... with processes of liberalization ... in domestic, sexual, and kinship relations' (ibid.: 28). What these conflicting discourses seem to have in common is their emphasis on the concept of choice.

In the case of (neo)liberal strands of postfeminist discourses, contemporary life is understood as a 'postfeminist utopia' (Genz and Brabon 2009: 37) or 'choiceoisie' (Probyn 1990: 152) that treats major life decisions as individual options while disregarding cultural or political influences. The notion of 'choiceoisie' is closely linked to the concept of the American Dream, which is similarly seen to be available to every individual who works hard enough (Genz and Brabon 2009: 37). In the postfeminist logic, it becomes every woman's own responsibility to fulfil her individual dreams. Because this 'postfeminist utopia' is seen to understand 'oppression and structural disadvantage as personal suffering while reframing success as an individual accomplishment, faith and self-determination' (ibid.: 38), there exists considerable scepticism about this particular strand of postfeminist discourses among critics. The neoconservative fraction of postfeminist discourses, on the other hand, is 'much more overtly antifeminist' (Spieler 2012: 126). Elspeth Probyn refers to this fraction as 'new traditionalism [which] naturalizes the home into a fundamental and unchanging site of love and fulfilment' (1990: 152). Instead of considering female domesticity a patriarchal strategy to exclude women from participation in public life and political arenas, new traditionalists romanticize domesticity as 'an idyllic space of personal satisfaction and freedom from the shackles of working life' (Genz and Brabon 2009: 58), reinforcing the dichotomy between the 'feminine' domestic and the 'masculine' public sphere. New traditionalism, too, is grounded on the notion of choice, as the vision of the home is one 'to which women have "freely" chosen to return' (Probyn 1990: 149). As Sophie Spieler puts it: 'Now that feminism has liberated women from the confines of patriarchy, they can freely choose to reenter them' (2012: 126). Both neoliberal versions of postfeminism and new traditionalist strands employ feminism as a justification: both 'claim to be facilitated by feminism while, at the same time, they covertly and overtly undermine it' (ibid.). Braithwaite points out that in this way, 'feminism is "written in" precisely so it can be "written out"; it is included and excluded, acknowledged and paid tribute to, and accepted and refuted, all at the same time' (2004: 25).

A constructionist and contextualizing approach to postfeminism

As Hemmings has demonstrated, progress and loss narratives provide opposite framings of one 'common storyline' (2011: 61), each interpreting the recent past of feminist theory and activism differently and claiming to tell the 'true story' (ibid.: 5) about it. The result is a variety of different understandings of postfeminism. In this book, I avail myself of postfeminist theoretical notions in order to analyse the cultural phenomenon of postfeminism. Thus, I work with the notion of the pluralistic, unstable subject constructed through the discourses around it, and I acknowledge the intersection of different socio-cultural subject categories that individuals are subjected to, such as gender, race, class, age and sexuality. Following Gill, I conceive of postfeminism as an 'analytical category' (2016: 3) or 'sensibility' (2007: 254) entailing a range of traits distinctive to representations of gender, race, class and other identity categories in twenty-first-century popular culture. Gill's approach circumvents the dichotomous notions of feminism and postfeminism, and it does not require any pledges for or against one of the two. Instead, it 'is informed by postmodernist and constructionist perspectives' (ibid.: 255), understanding postfeminism as a discursive system or construct. A second advantage is that it can easily take into account different intersecting discourses that play a central role in the phenomenon. Thirdly, by establishing postfeminist media culture as a 'critical object; the phenomenon which analysts must inquire into and interrogate' (ibid.: 254), this approach is indebted to ideas from Cultural Studies, such as Hall's cultural theory. The latter posits that 'culture is concerned with the production and the exchange of meanings... between the members of a society or group' (Hall 1997a: 2), and that these meanings can be studied by analysing '"regime[s]" of representation' (ibid.: 6). Gill's observations about postfeminist media culture can be summarized as a range of themes that keep recurring across popular media texts:

> the notion that femininity is a bodily property; the shift from objectification to subjectification; the emphasis upon self-surveillance, monitoring and discipline; a focus upon individualism, choice and empowerment; the dominance of a makeover paradigm; the articulation or entanglement of feminist and anti-feminist ideas; a resurgence in ideas of natural sexual difference; a marked sexualization of culture; and an emphasis upon consumerism and the commodification of difference. (2007: 255)

Throughout my analyses of the *Twilight* Saga, *The Vampire Diaries* and *True Blood*, a number of these themes will keep resurfacing, which confirms their centrality in contemporary postfeminist culture. In the course of the running time of these three paranormal romances (2008 to 2017), postfeminism has undergone a number of discernible shifts, which has prompted questions as to whether we are still living in a postfeminist culture (Gill 2016: 2). While postfeminist ideology may manifest itself differently towards the end of *The Vampire Diaries*' broadcast in 2017, compared to the time frame of the initial releases of the *Twilight* Saga and *True Blood* in 2008, I contend that the current era is still very much informed by postfeminist discourses and that postfeminism therefore continues to be highly useful as an analytical category. Indeed, a conclusion of recent scholarship on the subject has been that postfeminism/neoliberalism has actually 'intensified' (Gill 2017: 606; Genz 2017: 28) over the course of the past two to three decades. Tracing 'a qualitative shift in the expression of postfeminist values' (2016: 121) between the mid-1990s and the mid-2010s, Dejmanee points out that notions of work, consumption and femininity appear slightly differently in popular culture nowadays than they did twenty years ago, but that they have remained constants in postfeminist discourse. If the female body was at the centre of postfeminist makeover culture in early twenty-first-century culture, it is now being held to even more extreme standards, namely to what McRobbie terms the 'idea of "the perfect"' (2015: 4). Emphasizing the intensifying regulatory effects of postfeminist/neoliberalist discourses, Gill points out that current forms of postfeminism use 'a psychological register built around cultivating the "right" kinds of dispositions for surviving in neoliberal society: confidence, resilience and positive mental attitude' (2017: 606). These kinds of dispositions have come to play a key role in responding to and supposedly successfully navigating a variety of crises, ranging from the global financial crisis in 2008, to the European migrant crisis in the 2010s, to the increasingly devastating effects of global warming and climate change (ibid.: 608). In the context of persisting social injustice, media messages calling upon women to be confident and resilient are also remarkable for their being exceptionally 'capitalism, neoliberalism and patriarchy-friendly' (ibid.: 618): by telling women to focus on thinking optimistically and building their self-esteem, postfeminist culture asks them to work on themselves rather than engage the structural inequalities they are facing. It is here that postfeminism's 'relentless individualism . . . that exculpates the institutions of patriarchal capitalism and blames women for their disadvantaged positions' (ibid.: 609) is revealed to be still at the heart of the phenomenon.

Curiously, in current postfeminist culture, 'this "can do and must do better" ethos . . . is . . . made compatible with being a modern day young feminist who will excel at school and make her way to the boardroom in years to come', as McRobbie puts it (2015: 16). That is, in the course of the past fifteen years, feminism has made a definite comeback in terms of visibility across popular and social media. For instance, the issues of sexism and sexual violence have occupied the news, with feminist activism such as Laura Bates's Everyday Sexism project (launched in 2012), Emma Sulkowicz's performance artwork Carry That Weight (2014–15) and the Me Too movement (initiated in 2006 by activist Tarana Burke and spreading virally on Twitter from 2017 onwards) achieving a profound impact. If considering oneself a feminist was not in vogue at the turn of the century, a feminist identity has since become fashionable and attractive (Gill 2016: 2). Interestingly, as Banet-Weiser has argued, '[w]hile postfeminism and popular feminism are oppositional on the surface, they are actually mutually sustaining. Indeed, the feminist visions that come into dominant view in the current moment are shaped by the same affective politics that shape postfeminism: entrepreneurial spirit, resilience, gumption' (2018: 20). In other words, feminism as a positively coded project has been incorporated into postfeminist discourse, demonstrating 'the sensibility's dynamism and adaptability' (Gill 2017: 611). As a number of scholars have pointed out, this postfeminist variety of popular feminism coexists with a rise in overt misogyny in public discourse and popular media (Gill 2017: 611; Rivers 2017: 134; Banet-Weiser 2018: xi).

Instead of only looking at postfeminism in relation to (popular) feminism(s), I start from the premise that postfeminism emerges at the intersection of a number of cultural phenomena: 'mainstream media, consumer culture, neo-liberal politics, postmodern theory and . . . feminism' (Genz and Brabon 2009: 5). Thus, I conceive postfeminism as a hybrid phenomenon. Gill emphasizes that an informed approach to postfeminism must go beyond understanding it solely as a backlash against feminism but ought to take into account neoliberalism as a closely related discursive phenomenon (2007: 254). Genz's and Brabon's contextualizing approach is therefore taken as a leading example for this book. Postfeminism's position at the 'junction between a number of often competing discourses and interests' (Genz and Brabon 2009: 6) is responsible for its 'double movement' (ibid.: 8), which makes postfeminist texts neither undoubtedly 'progressive or regressive, liberating or containing' (Tasker and Negra 2007b: 21).

Furthermore, my approach to postfeminist media culture is characterized by contemporary media theories. While Faludi assures her readers that '[t]he backlash is not a conspiracy' ([1991] 1992: xxi), she refers to the backlash as 'outright propaganda' (ibid.: xxiii) and to the media as a 'backlash collaborator and publicist' (ibid.: 78) aiming to 'dictate trends and determine social attitudes' (ibid.: 79). Rather than attributing the backlash to a male-dominated establishment, I follow Foucault's analytics of power and focus on elements of backlash as they manifest in cultural discourses. Besides, I work with the notion of an active audience, conceptualizing media audiences as critically thinking about cultural texts and being 'actively involved in the process of meaning production' (Milestone and Meyer 2012: 154). This is in contrast to Faludi's *Backlash*, which seems attached to the hypodermic syringe model, an early theoretical model positing that the media directly affect entirely passive audiences. It is within this frame that popular culture was seen in a highly pessimistic light, suspected of being an 'instrument of mass deception' (ibid.: 152) and offering no choice for viewers but to uncritically take in whatever is presented to them. This hostility towards the media has meanwhile given way to a more relaxed and positive attitude in (post)feminist circles and media theories. Popular culture is now considered a more complex site of meaning-making, and 'notions of consumer agency and popular resistance' (Genz and Brabon 2009: 24) have become firmly established in the academe. Consumers are recognized as active, aware and using the media to construct their (gender) identities. It is from these notions that I take my cue.

2

Paranormal romance

A quintessentially postfeminist genre?

This chapter examines paranormal romance's relationship with postfeminism with the help of genre and transmedia theory. First, a short definition of the paranormal romance genre will be given. The delineation of some of paranormal romance's defining features seems worthwhile, considering that the genre is a relatively young one. As this chapter will illustrate, paranormal romance crosses boundaries in virtually every respect: it transgresses genre boundaries due to its hybrid status, destabilizes binaries of reality/fantasy and self/Other with its narratives of human-monstrous alliances, appeals to different audiences and age groups at the same time and uses more than just one medium to narrate its stories. The chapter will first zoom in on the genre's hybrid nature as well as its use of the figure of the sympathetic/reluctant vampire. Because it is important to focus not only on textual conventions but also on practices of production, distribution and consumption when analysing genres (Gelder 2004: 2), I will also take into account the transmedia storytelling techniques used in paranormal romance. These are not only an important aspect of the creation and the marketing of the genre, but also offer participatory possibilities on the part of audiences. Furthermore, I will look at the overall public reception of the *Twilight* franchise among American audiences as exemplary for paranormal romance. Finally, this chapter will elaborate on paranormal romance's relation to contemporary postfeminist discourses. Based on its ambivalent, liminal nature in terms of formal and textual features, I tie the genre to postfeminism's double movement between progression and regression and relate it to the 'contradictions at the core of postfeminist culture' (Tasker and Negra 2007b: 8).

Defining paranormal romance

Broadly speaking, genre can be described as a way of 'grouping or framing texts' (Branston and Stafford 2010: 74). Most genre theorists now agree that genres change over time, that they may overlap and that mixtures or hybrids of different genres are increasingly common. As Gill Branston and Roy Stafford point out, genres 'are seen no longer as sets of fixed elements, constantly repeated and occasionally innovated within, but as working with "repertoires of elements", fluid systems of learnt conventions and expectations. These are shared by makers and audiences, who are *both* active on *both* sides of meaning-making' (2010: 83; emphases in original). For audiences, the classification of popular cultural products into genres is a means of understanding texts (Neale 2008b: 3). For media companies, it can be a way of 'minimis[ing] risk by grouping, marketing and distributing their products via well-established expectations' (Branston and Stafford 2010: 79). In order to appeal to as many audience segments as possible, they have increasingly relied on cross-generic or hybrid media forms (ibid.: 81–3). Combining elements from a number of different genres, the *Twilight* Saga, *The Vampire Diaries* and *True Blood* doubtlessly represent the trend to hybridity in popular fiction. Both the *Twilight* Saga and *The Vampire Diaries* can be classified as teen paranormal romances, while *True Blood* is similar but leans more towards horror and predominantly addresses a mature rather than adolescent audience. Leigh M. McLennon argues that paranormal romance 'transgresses traditional boundaries of genre by simultaneously hybridising, cannibalising and parodying generic structures from other numerous genres' (2014). Thus, it may borrow the element of the star-crossed lovers from romance, the convention of the antiquated, haunted setting from the Gothic and the element of sexual non-conformity from the Southern Gothic in particular. Important to note is that the conception of paranormal romance as a subgenre of romance is likely to result in the idea that paranormal romance has only ever been influenced by one single parent genre (romance), which is historically not the case. Thus, understanding paranormal romance as a subgenre involves the risk of neglecting other significant influences, for example from crime fiction or fantasy (ibid.).[1] The concept of a hybrid with a 'complex generic interplay' (ibid.) is therefore a more favourable way of approaching paranormal romance. Concerning the transgression of generic boundaries, an interesting core feature is the amalgamation of two genres in particular which show fascinating parallels. Thus, paranormal romance primarily hybridizes two so-called 'women's genres (women-targeted mass cultural forms)' (Dines and Humez 1995a: 161), Gothic and romance.

Before delving into the entangled histories of Gothic and romance, I want to briefly expand the definition of paranormal romance given earlier. Paranormal romance narratives, which are typically set in fictional worlds that 'closely mimic our contemporary reality' (McLennon 2014), additionally incorporate paranormal, fantastic and monstrous creatures and/or components. The protagonist – usually female and narrating the story from her perspective – strives to resolve a conflict, investigate a crime or deal with a mysterious event that may turn out to be supernatural in nature. Within the frame of this adventure, she typically forms an alliance with a supernatural being, which often leads to a romantic bond between her and the monster; in the case of the *Twilight* Saga, *The Vampire Diaries* and *True Blood*, this creature is a vampire. As the narrative progresses, boundaries between reality and the fantastic as well as those between human self and monstrous Other become increasingly blurred and indistinguishable (ibid.). McLennon explicitly rejects the distinction between urban fantasy and paranormal romance that is often undertaken in critical definitions. Instead, she proposes the conception of both genres as occupying two ends of a broader generic continuum, since definitions of urban fantasy and paranormal romance as two distinct genres 'obscure the complex generic interplay which actually constitutes' them (ibid.).[2] As I contend, due to the central position of a love story, its development and consummation in the *Twilight* Saga, *The Vampire Diaries* and *True Blood*, these texts can be located closer to the paranormal romance end of the proposed continuum.[3] The *Twilight* Saga centres on the relationship between the human Bella Swan (Kristen Stewart) and the vampire Edward Cullen (Robert Pattinson); the main storyline in *The Vampire Diaries* is concerned with the love triangle between the human Elena Gilbert (Nina Dobrev) and the vampire brothers Stefan (Paul Wesley) and Damon Salvatore (Ian Somerhalder); and *True Blood* follows the romantic adventures of human–faerie hybrid Sookie Stackhouse (Anna Paquin) with the vampires Bill Compton (Stephen Moyer) and Eric Northman (Alexander Skarsgård), the werewolf Alcide Herveaux (Joe Manganiello) and the faerie–vampire hybrid Ben Flynn/Warlow (Robert Kazinsky). The term 'paranormal romance' will therefore be used when referring to the genre of the texts discussed here.

Like all genre products, the *Twilight* Saga, *The Vampire Diaries* and *True Blood* involve both repetition and difference (Branston and Stafford 2010: 77). Crucially, audiences may derive pleasure from both processes. On the one hand, they 'understandably seek the pleasures of the familiar. We enjoy the ritual and reassurance involved in knowing *broadly* what "might happen" in a particular media text' (ibid.: 77; emphasis in original). On the other hand, it can be exciting to find out how exactly connections between the well-known elements of a genre will play out in one particular text. Furthermore, after a genre has become established, its conventions can be played with (ibid.: 75). Part of the viewing pleasure can be recognizing and understanding not only references to but also deliberate breaks with genre conventions. The latter are especially interesting for studying genres as cultural categories. Rachel Blau DuPlessis emphasizes that '[a]ny . . . convention – plots, narrative sequences, characters . . . – as an instrument that claims to depict experience, also interprets it. No convention is neutral, purely mimetic, or purely aesthetic' (1985: 2). Implied in this statement is the assumption that television and film represent reality by constructing it from a particular ideological point of view. It will be interesting, then, to examine where the *Twilight* Saga, *The Vampire Diaries* and *True Blood* deviate from established genre conventions and what effect this break with viewing expectations may have for audiences.

Since this book is concerned with one film and two television texts, a brief discussion of genre in terms of these two media is warranted. When it comes to differences between film and television, it is noteworthy that television is particularly prone to the use of stereotypes 'because the medium often needs to establish character almost instantly before an audience loses interest and switches over or off' (Creeber 2006a: 47–8). Thus, due to certain preconditions of the medium, television texts are likely to rely on generic conventions more extensively than film narratives. This renders an analysis of *The Vampire Diaries* and *True Blood* vis-à-vis their adherence to genre conventions especially urgent and fruitful. Steve Neale predicts that genre will indeed remain central to television and its consumers in the future because of these reasons (2008a: 6). Another aspect that distinguishes television from film genres is that they are more heavily influenced by market pressures, which may shape the structure and development of the respective texts (Turner 2008b: 7). Since many TV shows are produced in relatively close proximity to their screening dates, audience reactions may have an impact on the content or even the running time of the shows, which stresses the active position of TV audiences. Even more so than film genres, television genres and programming formats are 'notoriously hybridised and becoming more so' (ibid.: 8). In fact, one single series may tap into different genres from season to season or even from episode to episode, because in television, 'genre is not a static system' (Banks 2004: 20). For film and television alike, it remains true that 'genre plays a major role in how . . . texts are classified, selected and understood' (Turner 2008b: 7). Here, it is essential to keep in mind that the formation of genres is an 'ongoing process' (Altman [1999] 2000: 70), with genres changing and developing over time – a factor whose significance will become much clearer in the following subsection.

Gothic, romance and their convoluted histories

In order to gain a deeper insight into the hybrid genre of paranormal romance, it is crucial to look at its origins, namely the way it developed out of the entangled strands of the Gothic and the romance novel. As Crawford points out, 'the histories of those genres which we now call "Gothic" and "romantic" fiction have always been heavily interlinked; indeed, for most of their history, the single word "romance" has served to denote them both' (2014: 5). Here, Crawford is referencing the Gothic romance of the eighteenth and nineteenth centuries as well as contemporary romance fiction.

Having emerged in the 1100s as a form of fantastic narrative poetry and gradually been superseded by the narrative form of the novel, the romance re-emerged towards the end of the eighteenth century in the form of what we now refer to as the 'Gothic novel'. Within the frame of the so-called Gothic revival, writers of Gothic romances sought to imitate the romance tradition of the seventeenth century by including supernatural or fantastic elements in their stories and setting the latter in historical rather than contemporary spaces (ibid.: 17). By putting psychologically 'realistic' characters into extraordinary, magical situations (Chaplin 2014: 200), these authors strove to distance themselves from the relatively young novel tradition and instead emphasized their ambition to employ impulses from both the novel and the romance. One of these authors was Horace Walpole, who published the earliest and one of the most influential Gothic romances in 1764, *The Castle of Otranto*. In the second preface of his work, he described *Otranto* as 'an attempt to blend the two kinds of romance, the ancient and the modern' ([1764] 1994: 11). This Gothic romance, a hybrid par excellence, then, was mother to both the genres of the Gothic and romance fiction that are popular today (Crawford 2014: 16).

From the beginnings of Gothic romance to the paranormal romance of today, the genre has changed in significant ways. Crawford describes the evolution of the dark and powerful male protagonist, who transformed from an evil villain into a figure of simultaneous danger and (sexual) appeal. Three texts that were foundational for this evolution are Jane Austen's *Pride and Prejudice* (1813), Charlotte Brontë's *Jane Eyre* (1847) and Emily Brontë's *Wuthering Heights* (1847) (2014: 37). Not coincidentally, the latter is referenced and quoted repeatedly in the *Twilight* and *Eclipse* novels as well as the first season of *The Vampire Diaries*, which confirms its significance within the historical development of contemporary paranormal romance.[4] In the run-up to the Brontë sisters' success, Jane Austen had popularized the novel of mutual education, most clearly in *Pride and Prejudice*, as a story of two 'lovers who must educate and reshape each other, overcoming one another's initial failures, misunderstandings and character flaws in order to establish the basis for a successful subsequent marriage' (ibid.: 22). This element of mutual education was essential for the further development of Gothic romance, as it marked a departure from the polarized figures of the evil villain and the morally pure hero/love interest. Instead, it opened up the possibility of the heroine finding herself with a hero–villain she must redeem. The hero–villain figure – an ambiguous character defined by violence and cruelty but also passionate and tortured by his actions (Crawford 2014: 23) – was already established in Gothic fiction before it was taken up and made commercially viable by Charlotte Brontë's *Jane Eyre* (ibid.: 23). This is the 'Byronic hero', which was popularized by Lord Byron and satirized in John Polidori's *The Vampyre* (1819). Lord Ruthven, *The Vampyre*'s Byronic vampire, was an outcast living on the fringes of society, 'yearning for redemption and ultimately finding none' (Aquilina 2013: 28), but nevertheless a nobleman, intelligent and with irresistible powers of seduction. Deeply intertwined with Lord Byron's carefully cultivated public persona as a brooding and melancholic aristocratic wanderer, the Byronic hero played a significant role in the shift from understanding the vampire as a grave-haunting revenant to its portrayal as an irresistibly seductive hero–villain, an archetype still dominant today (ibid.: 27; 35). As Crawford suggests, the commercial success of Brontë's *Jane Eyre* 'marks the point at which the Byronic hero, already so prominent in Gothic fiction, crossed decisively over into the English love story' (2014: 30). Similar to Austen's heroines, Brontë's protagonist Jane finds herself entrapped in a large, dark house, Thornfield Hall, which scares her; her life story is filled with violence and the threat of death. However, instead of replacing the villain residing in the eerie place with a suitable husband, Jane 'will purge Thornfield by saving Mr Rochester, the flawed, embittered, but still redeemable Byronic hero who owns it, through the redemptive power of her love' (ibid.: 32). Brontë thereby established a narrative template that has persisted in romance texts throughout the centuries: the trope of the hero's redemption through the romantic love of the heroine is one of the core features of contemporary popular romance narratives, as – in the logic of the genre – the heroine's redeeming of the hero demonstrates her power over him: 'It is the true and selfless love of the "good" woman (or "true female of worth"), who proves understanding, reliable and supportive, which helps her mate come to terms with his dark nature that stems from a traumatic past' (Șerban 2012: 107–8). Charlotte Brontë's sister Emily's *Wuthering Heights* equally features a monstrous, powerful hero. However, contrary to Mr Rochester, Heathcliff is not redeemed in the course of the narrative, which renders *Wuthering Heights* a much darker and more controversial novel, compared to *Jane Eyre*. Nevertheless, as Crawford explains, what both authors explored in their books was 'the potential attractiveness of the Byronic hero' (2014: 37), which makes both novels important cornerstones in the history of twentieth- and twenty-first-century romance narratives.

The narrative templates that Jane Austen and Charlotte Brontë provided were picked up by a range of authors almost a century later, in the 1920s and 1930s (ibid.: 41). This was when the modern romance genre started to form a generic identity of its own (ibid.: 38). The emergence of the popular romance proper was closely linked to British and American women's increasing employment in the white-collar workforce. The lucrative possibilities that came with this new audience were quickly recognized by publishers, and the romantic love story as a specifically female-directed narrative was rendered 'a viable commercial category' (ibid.: 39). In contemporary understanding, romance is usually seen as a type of formulaic fiction 'where the plot focuses on the development of a romantic relationship between two people that is resolved happily' (Ryder 2005: 508). Crucially, male protagonists in romance texts of the 1930s and beyond were largely modelled after the figure of the Byronic hero. As Crawford suggests, 'such masterful heroes would become virtually obligatory', since guidelines to depict the hero as 'an "Alphaman": tall, strong, powerful, handsome and socially dominant' (2014: 41) were fixed, for example, in the editorial policy of romance publisher Mills and Boon. The interwar period, as 'an epoch saturated with both the physical violence of modern warfare and the ideological violence of authoritarian politics' (ibid.: 45), produced narratives of accepted and welcomed male violence in a number of genres.[5] Hence, the romance genre went on to feature powerful, violent men, who were increasingly seen as desirable. Indeed, as we will see in Chapter 5, the popularity of physically violent, yet benevolent masculinities in contemporary postfeminist culture can equally be linked to post-9/11 times of cultural turmoil.

In the course of the 1970s, romance and Gothic genres became more and more similar and almost converged. On the one hand, portrayals of male lovers in romance fiction fused the Gothic villain with the romantic hero. On the other hand, villains in Gothic fiction, such as vampires, became more and more humanized (ibid.: 50). This development in the depiction of vampire characters in particular is frequently traced back to broader cultural shifts concerning society's attitude towards outsiders (ibid.: 52; Senf 1988: 150). Having witnessed the rise and successes of the feminist, civil and gay rights movements, American audiences were more likely to express an appreciation for characters refusing to conform to socially prescribed notions of normality. While a character's vampire nature had previously been something that may have impeded audiences' sympathizing with that character, it could now serve as precisely the feature that audiences found engaging (Carter 1997: 27). The vampire came to represent attraction, rather than threat: 'As rebellious outsider, as persecuted minority, as endangered species, and as member of a different "race"

... the vampire makes a fitting hero for late twentieth-century popular fiction' (ibid.: 29). This shift in representation was accompanied on a formal level by the introduction of the vampire as viewpoint character or even narrator (ibid.: 27).

As McLennon emphasizes, this figure of the humanized or 'good' vampire is a trope through which paranormal romance explores the destabilization of boundaries between reality and fantasy as well as self and Other (2014). Besides generic hybridity, the thematic transgression of these cultural categories is another defining feature of paranormal romance. The Gothic, as Botting points out, has always had a 'fascination with transgression and the anxiety over cultural limits and boundaries' (1995: 1). The figure of the humanized vampire upholds this trend. Here, it is important to differentiate between reluctant and sympathetic vampires – two terms that are often used interchangeably (Abbott 2014). Abbott defines the reluctant vampire as 'a figure who seeks to deny its vampire identity in favour of a desire to live a human-like life' (ibid.). In order to become a member of the human community, this type of 'vampire has become socialized and humanized, as well as secularized' (Zanger 1997: 22). One of the key characteristics of reluctant vampires is their abstaining from human blood and their desire not to hurt or kill people. Their self-loathing and struggle to control their physical impulses render them noble and facilitates audiences' sympathy for these characters (Abbott 2014). In *The Vampire Diaries*, it is Stefan Salvatore who represents the reluctant vampire type; *True Blood* has Bill Compton; and the *Twilight* Saga features the Cullen family, most of all Edward, as so-called vegetarian vampires. Sympathetic vampires, on the other hand, are figures who are 'sympathetic without being reluctant, embracing their vampirism and urging audiences to negotiate a tightrope walk between attraction and repulsion' (ibid.). Damon Salvatore, Stefan's brother, embodies the features of the sympathetic vampire most clearly in *The Vampire Diaries*; in *True Blood*, it is Eric Northman who represents this type. Both are cast in the role of 'the ultimate "bad boy"' (Wilson Overstreet 2006: 25) who regularly 'giv[es] in to his darker nature and wallow[s] in the kill' (Abbott 2014). However, especially Damon oscillates between both reluctant and sympathetic vampire types, depending on the respective season and on whether he is currently in a relationship with Elena, his true love. Similarly, there are periods in which Stefan gives in to his vampire needs and turns into a ripper,[6] thus shedding his usual reluctant vampire identity.

In general, characters of both types nowadays typically appear in 'the context of everyday life' (Kane 2006: 88) and are portrayed 'no longer [as] exotic and aristocratic intruders, but rather [as] average people, such as neighbors, family, and friends' (Abbott 2007: 9). This is why vampires in contemporary popular culture are frequently described as having undergone a process of 'domestication' (Gordon and Hollinger 1997b: 2). However, Stacey Abbott and Lorna Jowett provide a more differentiated perspective by arguing that vampires appearing in serial texts may be sympathetic/reluctant but are precisely not defanged. According to Abbott and Jowett, 'the sympathetic or reluctant vampire, while not exclusive to TV, is a recurring trope in series' (2013: 202).[7] In long-running serial dramas, vampire characters can be developed in complex ways. Against this backdrop, their malevolent actions become more complicated, and moral ambiguity is emphasized (Abbott 2013). Through the sense of intimacy that is established between audiences and vampires by means of televisual seriality, audiences become complicit in their favourite characters' crimes (Abbott and Jowett 2013: 202). As a consequence, 'the assumed connections between monstrosity, evil and Otherness' (McLennon 2014) are challenged and destabilized. At the same time, '[t]he seriality and suspense of each series . . . is built around the potential that [the vampires] will give in to their bloodlust – which each of them do [sic] at some point. Their inevitable downfall makes their crimes all the more horrific and disturbing' (Abbott 2014). Interestingly, it is often deeply human flaws like revenge, grief or jealousy that incite the vampires' monstrosity (ibid.). Again, the consequence is ambiguity and a blurring of social–cultural binaries of good/evil and self/Other.

One early example of this trend towards the complex, boundary-blurring, humanized TV vampire is Barnabas Collins, who was introduced to the Gothic soap opera *Dark Shadows* (ABC, 1966–71) as a vampiric antagonist in 1967. Vampire Barnabas was depicted as a mysterious stranger, isolated from the rest of the characters not only due to his potential dangerousness but also because he had just entered the contemporary world after having been confined to a chained coffin for about two centuries. Due to these characteristics, Barnabas was interpreted by viewers not as a monstrous villain, but as a redeemable Byronic hero (Crawford 2014: 52). This interpretation does not come as a surprise, considering that *Dark Shadows* was 'established as a classic female Gothic narrative from the outset (young woman, relocated from her home, arrives in a threatening house)' (2006: 147), as Helen Wheatley underlines. It seems plausible that viewers were reading the show's vampire character within the established conventions of the Gothic romance genre. Owing to the positive audience response, Barnabas was endowed with greater complexity in subsequent episodes and was kept on the show despite initial plans to the contrary. The character's shift from Gothic villain to romantic lead, or rather his simultaneous embodiment of both roles, confirms that, by the 1970s, 'it was possible for one to be mistaken for the other' (Crawford 2014: 52).

Having been brought to a mass audience by Anne Rice in her *Vampire Chronicles* book series (1976–2018), the figure of the humanized, conflicted vampire anti-hero became increasingly popular as a potential romantic love interest towards the end of the twentieth century. The *Buffy the Vampire Slayer* TV series (The WB/UPN, 1997–2003) had its human female protagonist Buffy engage in complicated relationships with two male vampires, Angel and Spike. As Crawford explicates, Buffy's affair with Spike became 'an interpretative battleground between the writers of the show and a vocal (and mostly female) sub-section of its viewers' (2014: 129). Similar to what happened with Barnabas Collins in the 1960s, this group of viewers was reading in terms of post-1970s romance conventions what was intended by the writers as a clearly abusive relationship. Crawford argues that it may have been precisely the lack of a conventional, happily resolved romance narrative in *Buffy* that generated a huge demand for similar narratives in the new millennium (2014: 144). This ultimately created the circumstances in which paranormal romance would transition from a lesser known genre to a more mainstream one, and achieve the immense success it had with the *Twilight* Saga, *The Vampire Diaries* and *True Blood*.

Teen vampires, teen audiences?

The great popularity of the aforementioned *Buffy*, which began in the late 1990s, was indicative of an important trend in the American media industries: the rapidly growing and increasingly diversified sector of young adult fiction (Crawford 2014: 89). By the 1980s, 'teenagers had become demanding "arch-consumers"' (Waller 2009: 194) and young adult literature enjoyed tremendous commercial success – a trend that spread to screen media in the course of the subsequent decades (Smith and Moruzi 2020: 610). The *Twilight* Saga and *The Vampire Diaries* (the TV series) – to a lesser extent also *True Blood* – function as successors of these late twentieth-century teen-focused narratives. As Timothy Shary writes, the teen genre 'is defined not so much by its narrative characteristics (although there are considerable generic similarities among teen films) as it is by the population that the films are about and to whom they are directed' (1997: 38). Both the *Twilight* Saga and *The Vampire Diaries* centre on the lives of teenaged characters, and their intended primary audience is arguably the teenage demographic. As Catherine Spooner notes, 'Gothic has always had a strong link with adolescence'. The heroines of classic Gothic texts, like Ann Radcliffe's and her contemporaries', were typically 'young women on the verge of adulthood' (Spooner 2006: 88). Teenagers might be the ideal protagonists of Gothic narratives, given the status between child and grown-up that is culturally ascribed to them: 'Subject to physiological change and occupying a liminal space between past and future, adolescence would seem a particularly viable subject position in which to explore anxieties about the return of the past, and the preoccupations with excess, limits and transgression'

(McLennan 2012: 86), which are, of course, core themes of the Gothic. Conversely, the figure of the vampire is linked to the teenager in its boundary-crossing nature, since the 'inherent liminality of the . . . vampire provides an ideal site, or focus, of transition' (Bacon 2011: 152). Indeed, transition has been a central concept when it comes to defining adolescence in psycho-social discourses (Waller 2009: 30). Since the 1920s, the dominant perception of adolescence has been that it is a liminal stage 'defined by its "in-between-ness", its transitory position between childhood and adulthood' (ibid.: 6).[8]

In the course of the frequently lengthy period of transition from childhood to adulthood, teenagers 'straddle . . . a huge and often incommensurate set of situations' (Davis and Dickinson 2004a: 11). On the one hand, they increasingly gain rights and mobility, and are addressed as subjects by consumerism; on the other hand, they are not allowed to vote, drink alcohol or earn more than the minimum wage (if such a thing exists where they live). Thus, the life stage of adolescence is actually 'heavily monitored' (ibid.: 10). Increasing independence from parental and institutional authority and the discovery of one's sexual identity are processes that may not always go smoothly. In this context, teen fantasy/horror 'offers excellent possibilities for creating situations in which young people's dilemmas can be represented and tested' (Hilton and Nikolajeva 2012b: 15). Thus, teen paranormal romance 'tackles real adolescent problems, sometimes disguised in metaphorical ways' (Rogobete 2012: 116) and allows teenage audiences, who are in the midst of establishing their identities, to experiment and try on transgressive roles that may otherwise be unacceptable (Wilson Overstreet 2006: 13). *Buffy* is an often-cited example of this kind of exploration of typical teen issues in the form of supernatural metaphors – creator Joss Whedon himself has defined the show as 'a horror story about high school, and that's exactly what high school life is like . . . both literally and metaphorically' (qtd. in Campbell and Campbell 2001: par. 9). Among the vampire romances examined in this book, *The Vampire Diaries* most obviously dramatizes issues surrounding adolescence and high school life with the help of supernatural metaphors, thereby following in *Buffy*'s footsteps. For example, the series' metaphorical explorations touch on the topics of romantic love, homosexuality and homophobia; the changing pubescent body; the management of grief and loss; and the difficult navigation of the high school environment with its very own social system and hierarchies.

However, while the *Twilight* Saga, *The Vampire Diaries* and *True Blood* successfully address teen issues, it is striking that they do have a cross-generational appeal. Rachel Moseley points out that '[g]iven the intense nostalgia that surrounds the teenager and teenageness in contemporary culture, the audience for the teen drama may exceed the teenage years' (2008: 54). Thus, although the target audience of the *Twilight* franchise is generally presumed to be 'largely teen and tween girls' (Roth 2011), there were/are also huge *Twilight* fan communities of adult women like the 'Twilight Moms' (Em & Lo 2009). Their existence demonstrates that teenagers are definitely not the only demographic enjoying contemporary (teen) paranormal romance. Similarly, although the channel The CW, which broadcasts *The Vampire Diaries*, maintains a teen-centric brand identity with its focus on shows like *Riverdale* (2017–) and *Stargirl* (2020–), its official overall target audience is '18- to 34-year-old women' (Dana 2008). Moving 'within the boundaries of acceptable broadcast material, broadcasting regulations, and generic expectation' (Williams 2013: 95), *The Vampire Diaries* balances both horror and teen genres. In contrast, *True Blood* predominantly addresses a mature audience, while also leaving a backdoor open for younger viewers, for example by foregrounding teen character Jessica Hamby (Deborah Ann Woll). Jessica's character is absent in the book versions of *True Blood*, Harris's *The Southern Vampire Mysteries*. Arguably, it was added to the TV series because it adds a teenage point of view to the narrative and may thereby draw in younger viewers. Being new to the vampire world, Jessica also provides the possibility for writers to introduce audiences to the basic rules of the vampire society in *True Blood*. Thanks to its position at the pay TV channel HBO, the series is not subject to the same FCC regulations that series broadcast on other channels are bound to

(Jowett and Abbott 2013: 11). As a result of HBO's greater freedom from certain restrictions, its shows are frequently 'stylistically, generically and narratively provocative and transgressive, often breaking social, cultural and televisual taboos' (ibid.), which makes them less suitable for t(w)een audiences.[9]

Possible reasons for the fact that teen narratives have a cross-generational appeal in contemporary society may include 'a complicated but generally increased accessibility to higher or further education; the social pressure to grow up quickly and then to stay young for longer . . .; and the current decay of the notion of the "job-for-life" whose acquisition was so often a marker of adult maturity in the past' (Davis and Dickinson 2004a: 11). In other words, the crossover phenomenon may be linked to social changes that have occurred over the course of the twentieth century, particularly the expansion of the phase of adolescence and the de-standardization and individualization of markers of transition into adulthood (Hurrelmann 2003: 115; 122). These changes could explain (young) adult viewers' interest in teen narratives, since these demographics continue to have an adolescent status despite their early autonomy in cultural, consumer-related and private spheres of life (ibid.). Furthermore, as mentioned earlier, it is beneficial for media industries to cater to different consumer tastes in one product. *The Vampire Diaries* in particular contains a high level of self-reflexivity and self-irony, which may especially draw in older viewers. Through a knowing make-up, the series can 'deliberately court such [mature] audiences with [its] intelligence and intertextuality' (Davis and Dickinson 2004a: 11).[10] By including a range of different features, a teen series like *The Vampire Diaries* thus aims to attract as many audience segments as possible.

Transmedia storytelling and the transgression of media boundaries

Besides its generic and thematic blurring of boundaries and its addressing of cross-generational audiences, a further defining feature of paranormal romance is that it functions as a transmedia genre, thereby additionally transgressing media boundaries (McLennon 2014). Henry Jenkins has theorized transmedia storytelling as 'a process where integral elements of a fiction get dispersed systematically across multiple delivery channels for the purpose of creating a unified and coordinated entertainment experience' (2007). This means that a given story is not only told within the frame of a single movie or television series, but instead spreads across multiple media platforms; every part of the story which is added 'enhance[s] or expand[s] the source material' (Anyiwo 2012: 161). Although the concept of transmedial representation is not a new one, it can be considered a growing phenomenon in contemporary popular culture. Using a range of different media platforms and multiple ways of narration, media companies aim to attract as many audiences as possible 'by creating different points of entry for different audience segments'. Hence, transmedia storytelling has almost become 'an economic imperative' (Jenkins 2007) among modern media industries. However, it also serves a number of other important functions.

Transmedia storytelling can facilitate a more immersive experience: since audiences are already familiar with a given storyworld and its main characters, they may instantly delve into the narrative when consuming a sequel, prequel or any other extension of the original work (Ryan and Thon 2014a: 1). Furthermore, transmedia storytelling techniques can add to a story's sense of realism, provide further background information about certain characters and explain or delve into different elements of a narrative (Jenkins 2007). Most importantly, transmedia texts are 'both participatory and performative' (McLennon 2014). As U. Melissa Anyiwo argues, they rely 'on the active participation of an audience willing to go far beyond the initial source – the television show or film – to find and engage in a wealth of additional and enhanced content'. In this way, consumers are able to exert influence on what kind of content is produced by media companies and thereby to 'drive the narrative in real ways' (2012: 158). Not least, transmedia storytelling is also a means of building and maintaining audience loyalty (Jowett and Abbott 2013: 204). Significantly, transmedia narratives are based on elaborate fictional worlds, rather than individual characters or specific storylines

(Jenkins 2007). This makes sense because an interesting world can always generate more stories and explore new interrelations between different characters (Ryan and Thon 2014a: 19). Due to their depth, the resulting multi-layered worlds resemble our experience of real life much more than any simple movie or TV show could (Anyiwo 2012: 158). Jenkins argues that the 'process of world-building encourages an encyclopedic impulse in both readers and writers' (2007). Since different consumers may notice different story elements and interpret them in different ways, they may draw on each other's expertise in order to reach a more comprehensive picture of the narrative. Transmedia texts encourage this kind of active audience participation in meaning-making processes by consciously and consistently fuelling audience speculation and discussion, and by motivating consumers to convene on social media like Twitter, Facebook, YouTube and Tumblr (McLennon 2014). In online as well as offline conversations, audience members are invited to analyse and dissect the 'multi-layered world that can be peeled away to reveal layer upon layer of depth' (Anyiwo 2012: 160). Drawing pleasure from their interaction with the text(s), consumers become 'puzzle solvers' (Ndalianis 2012: 12) or 'hunters and gatherers moving back across the various narratives trying to stitch together a coherent picture from the dispersed information' (Jenkins 2007). Gaps and discrepancies within the transmedia narrative invite readers or viewers to engage with the text in an array of active ways, for instance by producing fan fictions presenting alternative turns of events or filling in the perceived gaps. Fan fiction can be considered 'an unauthorized expansion of . . . media franchises' (ibid.), with fanfic authors 'tak[ing] the story imaginatively in another direction' (Lindgren Leavenworth 2014: 320).

True Blood in particular has been discussed as an excellent example of a transmedia narrative.[11] As already established, the TV series is based on Charlaine Harris's *The Southern Vampire Mysteries* novel series, but it is more than that: the *True Blood* universe extends across novellas, short stories, companion world guides, a graphic novel prequel as well as tie-in graphic novels presenting spin-off narratives of specific characters, bonus scene material released online and on DVD, and character webisodes. The series was also publicized through a transmedia marketing campaign that expanded 'beyond the boundaries of traditional narrative media' (McLennon 2014). Thus, in the run-up to the airing of the first *True Blood* episode on 7 September 2008, HBO drew in potential audiences through a number of marketing measures blurring the boundary between reality and fiction. Part of this global marketing strategy was the placement of billboards advertising a new synthetic blood drink called 'Tru Blood' (Anyiwo 2012: 163). Not providing any context, the campaign spurred the curiosity of horror fans and bloggers. In June 2008, before the official announcement of the series, a number of videos that appeared to show footage of vampires revealing their existence to the public went viral. Here, HBO was able to 'capitalize on new media and the evolving technologies of the Internet' (ibid.: 165) in a clever manner. Since the vampire community's 'coming out of the coffin' is a central event in the first season of *True Blood*, the viral marketing campaign can be seen as the starting point of the series' transmedia narrative (ibid.: 167).

The boundary between reality and fiction then continued to be blurred during the broadcast of the series. For instance, the narrative explored the existence of a number of religious communities and hate groups targeting vampires, such as the Fellowship of the Sun, a church devoted to the extinction of all 'creatures of the night'. During the series' airtime, viewers could access these hate groups' websites online.[12] Another companion website created by HBO was BabyVamp-Jessica.com, a recurring video blog and online journal created for the teenage vampire Jessica Hamby. The blog was updated after each episode and provided additional insight into Jessica's interior life as well as the opportunity to comment on her blog entries. Viewers were thereby invited to personally interact with the *True Blood* narrative. Besides, this blog was also 'a great marketing tool allowing fans to click on the sidebar links to Jessica's favourite stores which just happen[ed] to sell HBO-themed products' (Anyiwo 2012: 168). Besides traditional merchandise like t-shirts, books and posters, fans were able to buy items that also existed in the series, such as the Merlotte's waitress uniform and specific characters' jewellery.[13] Anyiwo, drawing on Matt Hills's concept of performative consumption, argues that these products could be 'used to replicate a *True Blood* experience or role play' (2012: 167). Here, too, the marketing concept of the series facilitated a more immersive experience for viewers and complicated the boundaries between fiction and reality.

Transmedia storytelling techniques can also be found in the *Twilight* Saga and *The Vampire Diaries*. For instance, active engagement with the narratives was spurred and fan investment was invited by the creators in a number of ways. *The Vampire Diaries* carefully cultivated a certain ambivalence towards Elena's relationship with the Salvatore brothers, which was presented as a perpetual love triangle. While the relationship between Stefan and Elena was initially foregrounded within the narrative, a reading that privileges the Damon-Elena pairing was also possible. Through this openness to alternative readings, viewers were encouraged to choose which of the romances they wanted to support. In this way, they were prompted to actively engage with the text and discuss their position with other fans (Williams 2013: 93). Viewers were also invited to process their alternative readings in fan fiction. The *Twilight* franchise is well known for its encouragement of 'Team Edward'/'Team Jacob' affiliations; it has also spawned an unusually large number of fan fictions offering alternative constructions and subversions of elements of the original text (Lindgren Leavenworth 2011: 69). E. L. James's *Fifty Shades of Grey* trilogy (published in novel form between 2011 and 2012) actually originated as *Twilight* fan fiction and has by now become a phenomenon of its own. Thus, besides transgressing boundaries of genre and media, paranormal romance also complicates mutually exclusive definitions of producers and consumers. Strikingly, '[t]he varied fan-created products (fan fiction, fan films, and fan art) and the different approaches to the canon suggest that readers are both active and critical' (ibid.: 69), which disproves popular views on paranormal romance consumers that I explore in the following subsection.

Conflicting consumer reactions

The visceral public reaction to paranormal romance as well as its fans can hardly be overlooked in a discussion of the genre; it can be illustrated particularly well through the example of the *Twilight* franchise. Particularly the novels, but also the film versions of the series, were received with a tremendous amount of hostility, scorn and mockery in cultural (and partly also in academic) arenas. As Anne Morey argues, '[b]ecause Meyer is working with a combination of low-status genres – the vampire tale, the romance, the female coming-of-age story – the political aspects of the Saga's genre are both prominent and inextricable from gender' (2012c: 2). Thus, the public discourse failed to take the *Twilight* narratives seriously and followed 'a familiar pattern of degrading media that girls and women find appealing' (Click, Stevens Aubrey and Behm-Morawitz 2010b: 5). In short, the novels were typically judged for Meyer's poor style of writing, their formulaic structure and their focus on melodrama and interpersonal conflict. An additional criticism was that they supposedly taught 'dangerous life lessons and unhealthy sexual attitudes' (Crawford 2014: 183) to young girls.

As for the *Twilight* franchise's female audiences, the public discourse framed them as 'somehow mentally inferior, if not crazy' (Siebert 2011: 220). The vocabulary that mainstream media used to describe 'Twi-Hards' (passionate *Twilight* fans) is telling: a lot of 'Victorian era gendered words like "fever," "madness," "hysteria," and "obsession"' (Click, Stevens Aubrey and Behm-Morawitz 2010b: 6) were dominating the discourse. Here, the audience of girls and women, which was thought of as a homogeneous group,[14] was perceived as irrational and out of control. As Mark Jancovich puts it, instead of 'engaging in cerebral forms of aesthetic appreciation', which would presumably be a way of consuming cultural products associated with rationality/'masculinity', fangirls were 'depicted as consuming wantonly' (2014: 27). Strikingly, the physical enjoyment and sexual desire that was rather openly displayed by female *Twilight* lovers was met with incomprehension and even disgust (ibid.: 28).

Maria Verena Siebert argues that the aim of these kinds of critiques of Twi-Hards's passionate reactions was to inspire shame and to prompt fans to hide or give up their consumption of the *Twilight* narratives altogether (2011: 222). Furthermore, these female fans were commonly considered passive, mindless consumers (Click, Stevens Aubrey and Behm-Morawitz 2010b: 8) so 'entranced' by their favourite media franchise that they could not differentiate between reality and fiction (Jancovich 2014: 27). McRobbie has shed light on such assumptions about female fans in her influential work *Feminism and Youth Culture* (1991). In her book, she examined how girls were either completely ignored or treated with contempt in academic research on subcultures because they were seen as non-rebellious and conformist cultural consumers (1; 12). Objecting to the assumption that female consumers are uncritical, McRobbie argued that '[g]irls negotiate a different leisure space and different personal spaces from those inhabited by boys. These in turn offer them different possibilities for "resistance"' (1991: 14). Fifteen years later, the public commentary surrounding the *Twilight* franchise still frequently positioned girls and women 'as unexpected and unwelcome media fans' (Click, Stevens Aubrey and Behm-Morawitz 2010b: 6). Not only was the franchise scorned for expanding male consumers' previously (supposed) exclusive access to fan culture, but it was also accused of having '"ruined" vampires and/or vampire fiction' (Crawford 2014: 223) in general. Thus, Meyer was frequently derided by her critics for departing from established vampire lore (ibid.: 179): vampires in the *Twilight* series are, quite literally, 'defanged' (they do not possess fangs but have unbreakable teeth with razor-sharp edges), and instead of burning in the sun, their skin scintillates in it. A web campaign launched in 2010 called 'Real Vampires Don't Sparkle' is illustrative of the often ostentatious opposition against Meyer's vampire mythology (Spooner 2017: 83).

One may interpret the strong resistance to the *Twilight* narratives within the frame of generic expectation. Thus, Nia Edwards-Behi traces the widespread critical attacks back to the Saga's hybrid generic categorization, which raises certain expectations that may then not be met, consequently disappointing readers/viewers (2014: 42). Crawford also argues that 'the *Twilight* debate was, at base, primarily a debate over the legitimacy of different reading strategies' (2014: 221): *Twilight* fans were consuming the texts with established romance conventions in mind, while its critics were referring back to the standards of horror, consequently judging the books and films as 'failed horror products' (Edwards-Behi 2014: 42). This clearly echoes debates around *Dark Shadows*'s Barnabas Collins and *Buffy*'s Spike mentioned earlier. Thus, the *Twilight* Saga's generic hybridity may be both a blessing and a curse, since each of the movie adaptations 'can appeal individually to different segments of its audience, and simultaneously frustrate spectators by undermining what they anticipate in a viewing experience' (Clayton and Harman 2014a: 4). However, gender also plays into the understanding of these different genres: horror is still seen as a 'masculine' genre (Edwards-Behi 2014: 44), while the *Twilight* Saga is consistently gendered feminine, which 'can of course be attributed to the high visibility of its female fans' (Harman 2014: 51) as well as its reliance on romance conventions. As a feminine-gendered text employing elements from 'masculine' genres like horror and action, the *Twilight* franchise oversteps gender-based boundaries. Viewed in this light, the harsh rejection of *Twilight* can be considered 'an attempt to restore order to gender and genre hierarchies' (Larsson and Steiner 2011b: 16), in the sense that boundaries are re-emphasized and *Twilight* is intentionally pushed out of the realm of 'real' horror. Furthermore, the dismissal of the 'glittering' (Meyer 2005: 228) vampire is also gendered: Priest suggests that '"glitter" is highly symbolic of teen female sexuality' (2011). Thus, the mocking of sparkly vampires is also an indirect devalorization of 'femininity' and young adult women's sexuality. These dynamics reveal that the *Twilight* Saga and, by extension, paranormal romance, are deeply involved in contemporary politics of gender. *The Vampire Diaries* and *True Blood* are equally subject to the culturally constructed gender and genre order. In reviews and online commentaries, *The Vampire Diaries* is commonly located in between the *Twilight* franchise and *True Blood*. Since it addresses a more mature audience than the former but a younger one than the latter, *The Vampire Diaries* is described as occupying the 'perfect middle ground' (Hughes 2010). As Rebecca Williams points out, '*Diaries*' less graphic depictions of sexuality and violence, coupled with its status as a teen drama, make it less likely to appeal to male audiences and, relatedly, less likely [to] be constructed and viewed as quality television' (2013: 90). In contrast, *True Blood* enjoys a higher cultural status because of its position at the pay TV channel HBO, which is usually associated with critical acclaim due to positively loaded features such as aesthetics, narrative ambiguity, a pushing of boundaries and depth (Jowett and Abbott 2013: 11).

The gendered dismissal of teen paranormal romances like the *Twilight* franchise and *The Vampire Diaries* echoes reactions to its forerunner genres, Gothic romance and twentieth-century popular romance. Both have been associated with predominantly female readers and writers, and commented upon in very similar ways. As is well documented, throughout the eighteenth and nineteenth centuries, Gothic romance was viewed as entertainment for (mostly white) middle-class female readers (Vargo 2004: 233). Texts belonging to the genre were often female-authored, a fact that led Ellen Moers to refer to them as 'Female Gothic' ([1976] 1977: 90) texts. As a literary genre, Gothic romance was 'downgraded in the cultural hierarchy of the day because of the association with femininity, the irrational and the supernatural' (Williamson 2014: 79). Lacking literary credibility, these novels were often subject to ridicule but also caused serious concern among contemporary thinkers as to their supposedly morally corrupting effect on the minds of readers, especially young female ones. For instance, in the *Monthly Review*, a doctor wrote in 1773: 'a young girl, instead of running about and playing, *reads*, perpetually reads, and at twenty becomes full of vapours, instead of becoming qualified for the duties of a good wife, or nurse' (qtd. in Ferguson Ellis 1989: 15; emphasis in original). Here, it becomes clear that the fear that women might neglect their 'proper female duties' played a significant role in the denigration of Gothic romance as a genre. Unlikely as it may seem, the same accusations were levelled at adult female fans of the *Twilight* franchise over two centuries later: for instance, an entry in the online Urban Dictionary described '*Twilight* moms' as a 'group of 40 something pre-menopausal women who have been neglecting their children, spouses, jobs since 2008 to post their ramblings about a dazzling 107 year old vampire' (qtd. in Siebert 2011: 222).

When it comes to the popular romance genre, similar criticisms have been the norm. Considering the widespread popularity of romance fiction across the decades of the twentieth and twenty-first centuries, it is perhaps surprising how little acceptance and respect it is awarded in the larger culture (Regis 2003: xi). Joanne Hollows summarizes the most frequent points that make up the romance genre's poor reputation: 'It has become part of contemporary "common sense" that romantic fiction is a "formulaic" "trivial" and "escapist" form read by "addicted" women' (2000: 70). Many of these derogatory views may be traced back to mass culture criticism, which considers popular culture to be standardized and formulaic, and therefore easily consumed by passive audiences who cannot tell the difference between reality and fantasy. It is exactly these assumptions that are commonly made about romance audiences as well as women in general (ibid.: 70–1). As can be concluded, paranormal romance's hybrid history and generic forerunners have significantly shaped this relatively recent genre. The fact that its texts are so fiercely contested and inspire such heated debates around issues like gender, sexuality, genre and fan culture indicates that there is something larger going on here. If anything, these debates confirm that paranormal romance's cultural politics are worth studying.

Linking paranormal romance and postfeminism

So what are paranormal romance's cultural politics and what is the genre's link to postfeminism? As became clear throughout this chapter, paranormal romance is, historically speaking, an inherently hybrid genre, merging elements of the Gothic, popular romance and other genres. Thematically speaking, it tends to be concerned with destabilizing boundaries by deconstructing binary configurations. Through transmedia storytelling techniques, it blurs the distinction between reality and fiction. Addressing cross-generational audiences and making it a point to invite consumers to actively participate in the narrative expansion of the storyworld, these genre texts also complicate simplified and clear-cut notions of their audience. By taking into account these formal and textual defining features of paranormal romance, 'it becomes possible to consider how this genre might register real, contemporary social anxieties about unstable boundaries' (McLennon 2014). Thus, due to its defining characteristics, paranormal romance is particularly prone to incorporating and negotiating fears around the destabilization of modern binary categories. This is why it ideally lends itself to carrying postfeminist ideas. In its plurality and liminality, postfeminism is a typical 'post-discourse': 'Post-discourses', developing out of the 'deconstruction of current hegemonic systems' (de Toro 1999a: 16), essentially create 'a transitory space, a space other, a third space that is not here/there, but both' (ibid.: 20).

In cultural studies research, the intersection of postfeminism and the Gothic is not a new area of study: in 2007, Brabon and Genz coined the critical category of the 'postfeminist Gothic' (a: 5). Their edited volume by the same name, which explores 'the future of Gothic and its connections with (post)feminism', points out conspicuous parallels between the two concepts, namely 'the evasiveness and multiplicity of meaning exhibited by both terms' (2007a: 1). According to Genz, '[p]ostfeminism and Gothic are . . . worthy companions as they both eschew easy categorization and definition' (2007: 70). Ambivalence is at the core of both phenomena, which may explain the twenty-first-century proliferation of postfeminist paranormal romance narratives. As Carole Veldman-Genz puts it, Gothic as a liminal discourse 'provides a particularly fitting backdrop for twenty-first-century feminisms' muddled politics of contradictions' (2011: 46). Interestingly, Claire Knowles has suggested that the simultaneous rise of female-authored Gothic romance and 'the emergence of what we now recognize as modern-day feminism' (2007: 141) in the 1790s is hardly a coincidence.

As she notes, there was an affinity between the two movements in terms of emerging discourses and targeted audiences (ibid.: 142). Transferring Knowles's observation to the contemporary context, this raises questions as to which quintessentially postfeminist discourses may materialize in the twenty-first-century Gothic fictions examined in this book.

Building on previous scholarship on the links between feminism and the Gothic, Brabon and Genz proposed the category of postfeminist Gothic as a 'new critical space' with reference to the term 'Female Gothic (and its ghosts of essentialism and universalism)' (2007a: 7). As briefly mentioned earlier, the notion of the Female Gothic was first brought up by Moers in her influential study *Literary Women* (1976).[15] Following Moers's lead, feminist readings of Gothic romance novels have elaborated on the genre's function as an articulation of female experience and oppression in a male-dominated society – contrary to the genre's seeming preoccupation with the terrorization and victimization of its female protagonists. For instance, Kate Ferguson Ellis has demonstrated how the typical Gothic setting, the dark and haunted castle, functions as a symbolic representation of the actual social and domestic spaces that contemporary privileged female readers were confined to. The supposedly safe castle can easily turn into a prison exposing the Gothic heroine to violence without any opportunity of escape (Ferguson Ellis 1989: 45). Ghosts of a concealed past may haunt the place, and in the hands of the villain, 'the home becomes not a sanctuary from terror but a source of it' (ibid.: 46). As Ferguson Ellis suggests, the 'subversive nature' of the Gothic novel 'may best be understood . . . if we see in it a way of resolving, in fiction, problems and tensions in the world of the reader arising from the polarization of work and home' (1989: 51). These feminist analyses of the ways in which Gothic romance addresses gender inequalities are still insightful for the examination of paranormal romance today. As Brabon and Genz point out, 'gender and the relationships between the two sexes remain important issues that postfeminist Gothic engages with' (2007a: 8). Rather than focusing on women's confinement to the domestic sphere assigned to them by patriarchal society, I argue that contemporary paranormal romance gives voice to the contradictory aspects of living in a postfeminist culture. Contemporary gender roles under postfeminism are impacted by feminist ideas of gender equality as well as neoliberalist ideas of consumer capitalism. What exactly these ambivalent postfeminist gender configurations look like in the *Twilight Saga*, *The Vampire Diaries* and *True Blood* is the subject of this research.

The antithetical nature inherent in postfeminist culture and politics also finds its equivalent in the ideological thrust of contemporary romance narratives. Thus, the postfeminist move 'from the exclusionary logic of either/or to the inclusionary logic of both/and' (Rutland 1999: 74) is paralleled in the conflicting messages about gender and sexuality that are typically ascribed to the popular romance genre by scholars. For instance, Kathleen Therrien argues that '[t]he heterosexual romance narrative is . . . frequently a site where competing ideologies . . . are brought into conflict. But it is also a place where these conflicts may be ultimately, if only imaginatively, negotiated out "safely." . . . Romances are therefore ultimately "both/and" texts' (2012: 165). Setting a precedent for the interpretation of romance as a deeply contradictory genre was the work of Tania Modleski and Janice A. Radway, from which I both take my cue and intend to set myself apart in my research. Modleski's *Loving with a Vengeance* (1982) and Radway's *Reading the Romance* (1984) insisted on taking the romance genre as well as popular culture in general seriously (Gill 2007: 221). While differing in terms of methodology – Modleski performed textual analyses of exemplary romance texts and Radway primarily relied on reader-response criticism – both scholars set out to determine what kinds of pleasures these texts offer to their largely female readership. Their conclusions were similar: Modleski suggested that romance texts 'speak to very real problems and tensions in women's lives' (1982: 14), for which the narratives offer symbolic solutions. Similarly, Radway concluded that the typical romance narrative 'represents real female needs within the story' ([1984] 1991: 138), which are thereby acknowledged and taken care of.

Although Modleski and Radway took seriously the reasons why female readers would seek out fantasy solutions in the form of romance narratives, they criticized the ways the genre supposedly eases women into accepting patriarchy. For instance, Radway noted that the consumption of romance can be conceived of as 'an activity of mild protest and longing for reform' ([1984] 1991: 213) – a necessary reform since patriarchal institutions fail to satisfy the emotional needs of women. On the other hand, she suggested that the narrative structure of romance essentially does not challenge the hierarchy of control upon which patriarchal society is built (ibid.: 216); on the contrary, it is indicative of romance's 'conservative ideology' (ibid.: 186). Ultimately, both scholars therefore ended up disapproving of romance fans' reading strategies, considering the fantasy solutions that the genre offers inadequate. In repeatedly referring to romance readers' pleasure as 'vicarious', Radway positioned it as 'only temporary' and 'somehow not really real' (Ang 1996: 104). As Ien Ang puts it, Radway seemed to be arguing that '"[r]eal" social change can only be brought about . . . if romance readers would stop reading romances and become feminists instead' (1996: 103). Implicit in this argument is the existence of 'two parties with fixed identities: that of a researcher/feminist and that of interviewees/romance fans' (ibid.: 101). This oversimplification suggests that one person's identity can only ever be composed of one facet, it denies individual and micro-level everyday practices that may open up agency positions for women outside of political arenas, and it unquestioningly poses feminism 'as the superior solution for all women's problems, as if feminism automatically possessed the relevant and effective formulas for all women to change their lives and acquire happiness' (ibid.: 103). Modleski and Radway essentially distanced themselves from romance consumers because they 'implicitly framed their work as an updated, feminist version of a very old, patently moralizing question: "Are these books good or bad for their readers?"' (Selinger and Frantz 2012: 5) – a fallacy I explicitly aim to avoid in my work. Despite this fallacy, these 1980s analyses of the romance genre put forward the convincing argument that romances provide reassuring and pleasurable fantasies that address important cultural and societal issues. It is this assumption, which mirrors the aforementioned feminist studies of the Gothic, that I want to start from. Rather than attempting to ascertain whether the *Twilight* Saga, *The Vampire Diaries* and *True Blood* are 'good or bad' texts, I agree with Ann Rosalind Jones, who argues that '[i]t seems . . . so difficult to assess any of these [romance] novels as regressive or progressive in its [*sic*] totality that I've concluded such judgments aren't the point' (1986: 214). In her essay 'Mills & Boon meets feminism' (1986), Jones examines the ways in which romance novels of the early 1980s incorporate feminist ideology, and finds that different kinds of contradictions on the story level occur as a result of the 'conflict between feminism as emergent ideology and romance as residual genre' (204). Although Jones does not use the term 'postfeminist' to characterize these newly emerging ambivalent features, the advent of postfeminism might be exactly what she was observing. In fact, I suggest that the contradictory make-up of the paranormal romances I set out to examine in this book is related to postfeminist hybridity. The crucial point is that contemporary (paranormal) romance narratives are characterized by conventional formulas but also by an engagement with feminist ideas (Gill 2007: 5), which is what marks them as distinctively postfeminist. The 'entanglement of feminist and anti-feminist ideas' (ibid.: 269) in romance echoes postfeminism's double movement between utopia and backlash.

Due to its ambiguous, liminal nature and its refusal to decide between utopia and backlash, postfeminism has been referred to by Shelley Budgeon as a 'politics of becoming' (2001: 22). This is particularly interesting because it may present a link to the centrality of female teenaged protagonists in the *Twilight* Saga, *The Vampire Diaries* and *True Blood*. These teenaged protagonists are equally in a state of becoming – sometimes, they are 'simply' becoming more mature, sometimes they are on the verge of becoming vampires. As discussed earlier, '[t]eenageness is a significant "in-between" period' (Moseley 2008: 54). Strikingly, 'the ideal postfeminist subject is seen to be a . . . girl' (Genz and Brabon 2009: 7). Postfeminism's occupation with girlness and youthful femininity is most obviously expressed in the 1990s Girl Power movement (ibid.: 42), the theme of 'time anxiety' (Negra 2009: 47) linked to the ageing female body and the centrality of generational metaphors in postfeminist discourses (Tasker and Negra 2007: 18). Sarah Projansky even argues that 'postfeminism depends on girlness, is defined by it in fact' (2007: 43). As she explains, 'girlness – particularly adolescent girlness – epitomizes postfeminism. If the postfeminist woman is always in process, always using the freedom and equality handed to her by feminism in pursuit of having it all (including discovering her sexuality) but never quite managing to reach full adulthood, to fully have it all, one could say that the postfeminist woman is quintessentially adolescent' (ibid.: 45).

This chapter has sought to make sense of the ubiquitous presence of (teen) paranormal romance in contemporary postfeminist culture. Media texts like the *Twilight* Saga, *The Vampire Diaries* and *True Blood* respond to and mirror current postfeminist discourses, which are characterized by their simultaneous potential for liberation and backlash. As we have seen, Gothic and romance, the historical precursors of contemporary paranormal romance, are both inherently ambivalent genres torn between conservative generic conventions and feminist subtext. Displaying a tendency to transgress boundaries of genre, media, audiences and content, paranormal romance has a particularly great 'potential to register and reflect contemporary sociocultural anxieties' (McLennon 2014). The latter are negotiated by the genre in complex and sometimes conflicting ways. The result is a genre that is neither progressive nor regressive, with a style of politics that reflects the complexity of the contemporary cultural moment.

3

The politics of looking
Female protagonists between subject and object

In the previous chapter, I discussed the exceptional amount of derision, ridicule and disdain that the *Twilight* Saga has faced on the part of critics and self-declared anti-fans. The strikingly polarized media discourse around *Twilight* provides an excellent segue into an investigation of its gender politics. As I suggest, one of the reasons for both the immense popularity and the simultaneous widespread dismissal of the *Twilight* Saga in the public arena is its privileging of a heterosexual female gaze, by which the film series manages to address female (teen) viewers and to complicate, maybe even subvert, patriarchal power structures. Similarly, *The Vampire Diaries* and *True Blood* turn the tables when it comes to the power dynamics of looking: these shows, too, refrain from (exclusively) representing straight male desire through a conventional male gaze but instead stage instances in which the male vampire body is displayed as visual spectacle. At the same time, the texts recount the experience of being gazed at from the perspective of the female subject – a narrative feat that works to further complicate conventional binaries of the gazer and the person-to-be-looked-at. This chapter, then, investigates how postfeminist discourses surrounding sex-positivity, female pleasure and sexual empowerment are appropriated and negotiated in the *Twilight* Saga, *The Vampire Diaries* and *True Blood*.

Beyond the male gaze: Conceptualizing a female gaze

The study of the male gaze begins in 1970s feminist film theory. In her influential essay 'Visual Pleasure and Narrative Cinema', first published in 1975, Laura Mulvey suggests that our fascination with Hollywood cinema is traceable to the pleasure in looking (scopophilia). Basing her analysis of cinema on psychoanalysis, Mulvey claims that in a patriarchal society, 'pleasure in looking has been split between active/male and passive/female'. In this configuration, women present an 'element of spectacle', 'hold[ing] the look, and play[ing] to and signif[ying] male desire' ([1975] 1989: 19). Meanwhile, the man is the 'bearer of the look' (ibid.: 20), and cinema, as a whole, functions as a site of patriarchal power. Thinking about ways of undermining the structures of male-centred Hollywood cinema, Mulvey altogether disavows the possibility of a genuine female gaze, claiming that 'the male figure cannot bear the burden of sexual objectification' (ibid.: 20). Because the whole cinematic apparatus is assumed to be fundamentally patriarchal, for Mulvey, the only solution of dismantling the prevailing male gaze can be to 'engage in experimental practice: thus, women's cinema should be a counter-cinema' (Smelik 2007: 492). The result would be a self-aware avant-garde film that 'destroys the satisfaction, pleasure and privilege' (Mulvey [1975] 1989: 26) of the (male) spectator. The conclusion that women can never assume the position of desiring subject in Hollywood cinema was shared by feminist film theorists of the 1980s and beyond. For instance, Ann Kaplan argues in *Women and Film* (1983) that a female gaze cannot exist as the equivalent of the male gaze since patriarchal culture ensures that 'the woman does not own the desire, even when she watches' (27). Likewise, Mary Ann Doane suggests that woman, due to her marginalized position in society, is only allowed a passive look, rather than an active gaze (Paul 2014: par. 6). There is no other choice for women but to desire to desire, a conclusion which Doane captures in her book title *The Desire to Desire: The Woman's Film of the 1940s* (1987).

In the course of the decades, feminist film theory has received much criticism for its use of essentialist psychoanalytic theory and its recourse to the heteronormative binary model of male/female as the sole category of difference. One of its often-observed gaps is the representation of gay, lesbian and bisexual desire. Furthermore, spectators have almost exclusively been imagined as white (Smelik 2007: 497). Drawing attention to the fact that the male gaze is also informed by race and class factors, Jane Gaines problematizes Mulvey's central hypothesis that all men objectify all women on screen by pointing towards 'the less privileged black male gaze' (1999: 408). Invoking the historical construction of Black men as rapists as well as their castration and lynching as a punishment for (supposedly) sexually desiring white women during slavery times and long after, Gaines emphasizes that 'some groups have historically had the license to "look" openly while other groups have "looked" illicitly' (1999: 409). All in all, Gaines's work drives the point home that feminist film theory must expand its horizon and take into account intersections between gender, race and class categories. In this book, then, I seek to avoid the fallacies of Mulvey's original essay by taking into account the ethnicity and class affiliation of the characters that I examine. More precisely, in this chapter, I discuss the differences in the portrayal of the white, affluent character Edward Cullen and the non-white, working-class character Jacob Black in the *Twilight* Saga, and investigate the role which Jacob's Native American heritage plays in his representation as a sexualized object of Bella Swan's gaze. My research acknowledges and problematizes the fact that the *Twilight* Saga, *The Vampire Diaries* and *True Blood* all centre on white, heterosexual, cis experiences. Nevertheless, despite its shortcomings, Mulvey's theory simply cannot be disregarded in a scholarly analysis of the gaze in media texts, as it remains a standard and useful framework to analyse film texts in terms of their form and content. As Wheatley has shown, the concept of scopophilia can equally be applied to the medium of television (2015: 896–8). In fact, according to Wheatley, 'television is particularly adept at articulating the female gaze and female desire' (2015: 898), which my analyses do confirm.

Besides critically engaging with Mulvey's theory, I draw on an additional contemporary gaze theory for my analysis. Thus, I will complement Mulvey's theory with American writer and director Joey Soloway's theory of the female gaze, which does not differentiate between TV and film media. Soloway[1] has made a case that a female gaze does exist and that it encompasses three aspects, namely what they term 'the feel with me gaze, the being seen gaze [and] the I SEE YOU gaze truth gaze [sic]' (2016). In a keynote at the Toronto Film Festival in 2016, Soloway presented their vision of the female gaze, which is conceived as 'a political platform'. First, this gaze requires embodied camera work inviting viewers to identify and empathize with a female protagonist, for instance through the use of subjective or point of view (POV) shots. Second, Soloway argues that the female gaze conveys to viewers the experience of being gazed at, as this experience structures and affects most women's lives to a greater or lesser degree.[2] This part of the gaze also extends to the narrative level; Soloway gives the example of a coming-of-age narrative that might trace a young female character's process of entering adulthood. Along the way, the female protagonist would invite viewers to 'come feel with me specifically how I become . . . what men see'. Third, the female gaze entails the reversal of gendered object and subject positions by allowing women to return the gaze – as Soloway puts it, '[i]t's not the gazed gaze. It's the gaze on the gazers' (2016). Through combining the portrayal of what it feels like to be the object of the gaze with the experience of gazing, the female gaze, in Soloway's conception, illustrates 'how women are frequently put in the position of experiencing their bodily-self as both object and subject' (Vera-Gray 2017: 154) at the same time. Soloway, emphasizing the impact of popular media products on broader cultural discourses, understands this female gaze as a socio-political 'justice-demanding way of art making [sic]'. By rendering women the protagonists of their own stories and relaying their experience, the gaze creates empathy on the part of audiences and ultimately works as a 'privilege generator' (2016) for women.

Indeed, the question of whose stories are told and whose gaze is privileged in media texts revolves around the issue of subjectivity (Smelik 2007: 496). According to Mulvey's theory, men are regularly granted subject status when it comes to Hollywood cinema, but this is also true of American culture in general: men 'are taught that it is their birthright to *do* things (run, jump, desire, look) while women remain relatively immobile in order to be the object of the male gaze' (Benshoff and Griffin 2009: 240; emphasis in original). The significance of texts privileging a female gaze becomes clear if one considers that 'subjectivity is not a fixed entity but a constant process of self-production. Narration is one of the ways of reproducing subjectivity' (Smelik 2007: 496). With reference to Sigmund Freud, Teresa de Lauretis sees the traditional narrative as 'prompted by men's desire for woman, and by men's desire to know' (1984: 111) – much like Mulvey describes the process of the hero subjecting the heroine to sadistic voyeurism in Hollywood film ([1975] 1989: 21). In this configuration, woman is both the riddle that man tries to solve and the object he desires (Smelik 2007: 496). If the desire to know and the desire to see, both pleasures provided by cinema and television, are dependent on 'an engagement of the spectator's subjectivity, and the possibility of identification' (de Lauretis 1984: 136), it is of utmost importance that the *Twilight* Saga, *The Vampire Diaries* and *True Blood* all feature female protagonists whose perspectives shape the stories that are told in these series. The existence of female protagonists offers an opportunity of identification for female (teen) viewers in particular. As de Lauretis suggests, '[t]o identify . . . is to be actively involved as subject' (1984: 141). Thus, texts that privilege a (heterosexual) female gaze and thereby invite identification with a female character participate in the construction of (straight, mostly white) female subjectivity.

'We'll be watching you': The *Twilight Saga*, *True Blood* and the function of the 'gazed gaze'

Bella Swan being watched by men

The first instalment of the *Twilight* film series is conspicuous for its preoccupation with the act of looking, particularly in scenes set at school. Bella Swan, our protagonist, has recently moved to Forks and is therefore new to Forks High School, a fact that draws attention to her when she joins classes in the middle of the school year. Being shy and socially as well as physically awkward, Bella is made uncomfortable by being the centre of a vast number of looks, some of them merely curious, some judgmental, some favourable or even impressed. When she is approached by Eric (Justin Chon), who introduces himself as 'the eyes and ears of this place' (*Twilight* 2008) and wants to write a front-page story about Bella for the school newspaper, she adamantly refuses. During her first day at school, Bella manages to attract no less than three male suitors whose gazes linger on her while she is walking through the school hallways, taking part in gym class and sitting down to have lunch at the cafeteria. Besides, she also becomes the object of Angela's (Christian Serratos) 'professional' look. Like Eric, Angela works for the school newspaper as a photographer and startles Bella by taking a photo of her before even introducing herself: 'Sorry, I needed a candid for the feature' (*Twilight* 2008). Soloway's conception of the female gaze can be drawn on to make sense of what *Twilight* is doing here. First, the film employs the subjective camera to narrate events from Bella's point of view. This is in keeping with Soloway's assertion that the female gaze 'uses the frame to share and evoke a feeling of being in feeling, rather than seeing – the characters' (2016). Second, the film shows us what it feels like to become the object of the gaze by making Bella the focus of a variety of gazes, mostly male ones.

These male gazes function as the embodiment of a paternalistic attitude that aims to govern Bella's actions and, more precisely, her sexuality. Thus, in the course of the Saga, Bella's romantic and sexual relationship with Edward, a vampire, is continuously policed by a number of male characters. These include her father Charlie (Billy Burke); Billy Black (Gil Birmingham), who is an elder of the Quileute tribal council and therefore a representative of the werewolves; Jacob (Taylor Lautner), Edward's romantic rival; and Mike (Michael Welch), a classmate of Bella's who is also romantically interested in her. Because the story is narrated from Bella's perspective, we experience with her what it feels like to be at the centre of this much uninvited attention. Without being asked, Mike lets Bella know that he does not approve of her dating Edward: 'So, you and Cullen, huh? That's . . . I don't like it' (*Twilight* 2008). Over the course of the film series, Jacob, too, barges into Bella's life decisions a number of times. In *Twilight*, he still acts as a mouthpiece for his father Billy, who is bothered by Bella being with a vampire and wants to persuade her to end her entanglement with Edward. Otherwise, she is told, she will be under surveillance from the Quileute shapeshifters. 'We'll be watching you', is the message Billy has Jacob deliver to Bella. This comment makes the paternalistic gaze directed towards Bella explicit. Later, Jacob develops his own romantic interest in Bella. When he realizes in *Breaking Dawn – Part 2* that Bella intends to consummate her marriage with Edward during their honeymoon while she is still human, he is infuriated and even becomes physically aggressive. Moreover, in a number of scenes, Bella's father Charlie ostensibly performs his dislike of Edward because the latter might have a sexual relationship with his daughter. While this functions as comic relief within the films, the set-up drives home the point that Bella's sexuality is monitored by a variety of male characters in the Saga.

Three further scenes in *Twilight* allow audiences to experience with Bella how she becomes the sexualized object of the male gaze and (almost) the victim of assault in connection with this gaze. The first incident takes place in Port Angeles, where Bella spends a day out shopping with two of her friends from school. While Angela and Jessica (Anna Kendrick) are trying on prom dresses in a shop, a group of young men walk by the window. They stare at the young women's bodies, make objectifying comments and draw attention to themselves by knocking on the glass (see Figure 3.1). Angela and Jessica are visibly embarrassed, as the men's unsolicited gazes and comments are not welcome. Angela awkwardly turns her back to the window, Jessica voices that 'that is uncomfortable' and Bella remarks: 'That's disgusting' (*Twilight* 2008). By including this scene that is absent in the novel, the *Twilight* film puts particular emphasis on the way the bodies of these three female characters become the sexualized object of the male gaze in the public arena, and how they feel about this objectification. Strikingly, the film seems intent on underlining that although Bella's friends are shopping

Figure 3.1 Bella and her friends becoming objects of the male gaze. *Twilight*, directed by Catherine Hardwicke © Summit Entertainment 2008. All rights reserved.

for dresses that enhance their sexual attractiveness – right before the men walk by, Jessica has found a dress she likes because it 'makes my boobs look good' (*Twilight* 2008) – this is not the kind of attention and sexualization they desire or deserve. Later that day, Bella runs into the same group of men once again in a deserted street after dark. When they circle and start to encroach on her despite her telling them to stay away, it is clear that Bella is in serious danger of being sexually assaulted. In the scene, the camera cuts back and forth quickly between the perpetrators' perspective on Bella and her own point of view. In a number of subjective shots, we experience Bella's view of some of the men looking at her, with the camera shifting from one man to the next. The perpetrators are looking straight into the camera, with provocative grins, leering and yelling (see Figure 3.2). The close-up shots are cut together in a way that conveys Bella's feeling of being trapped in this circle of sexually aggressive gazes, with her stumbling and looking frantically from one face to the other. Edward coming to Bella's rescue then interrupts the scene.

As Kim Edwards observes, this near-rape scene is later 'paralleled visually' (2009: 30) in Bella's confrontation with James (Cam Gigandet), an evil vampire who has lured her to a deserted ballet studio. James takes a perverse pleasure in emotionally and physically torturing Bella; part of his pleasure is to watch her suffer. As Edwards points

Figure 3.2 POV shot from Bella's perspective. *Twilight*, directed by Catherine Hardwicke © Summit Entertainment 2008. All rights reserved.

Figure 3.3 James staring at Bella/the viewer. *Twilight*, directed by Catherine Hardwicke © Summit Entertainment 2008. All rights reserved.

out, James's 'climactic attack is deliberately sexualised and encoded as another attempted rape. Bella is pushed against the wall as James leers lasciviously at her, she turns away her face as he whispers in her ear, she shrinks from the horror of a camera's eye as he begins filming her, porn-style' (2009: 30–1). Again, a range of POV shots relays Bella's experience of being gazed at, with James looking directly into the camera (see Figure 3.3). His gaze is multiplied by the mirrors in the ballet studio, which makes it even more powerful and threatening. It is also underlined by his use of a portable camera with which he films the violence he inflicts on Bella 'to make things more entertaining . . . and action!' (*Twilight* 2008). Karen Backstein contends that the vampire's use of a camera 'is one of *Twilight*'s several interesting and negative references to still and movie cameras in relation to women' (2009: 40). By referring to Bella as '[b]eautiful. Very visually dynamic' (*Twilight* 2008), James aims to reinforce her '*to-be-looked-at-ness*' (Mulvey [1975] 1989: 19; emphasis in original) on a verbal level. Meanwhile, audiences are invited to empathize with Bella, fearing for her and being relieved when Edward suddenly enters the scene and saves her life.

The *Twilight* film adaptation thus demonstrates in a number of instances how Bella experiences herself as an object exposed to a controlling male gaze, while simultaneously emphasizing her subjectivity through the representation of her individual perspective. To speak with Soloway, '[t]he camera talks out at you from its position as the receiver of the gaze. This piece of the triangle rep[resent]s the Gazed gaze. This is how it feels to be seen' (2016).

Sookie Stackhouse managing the patriarchal gaze

Similar to *Twilight*, *True Blood* uses the strategy of the female gaze to make audiences empathetic to Sookie's experience of being gazed at, particularly at Merlotte's Bar and Grill, where she works as a waitress. Being a public space in which the townsfolk of Bon Temps meet up regularly and in which '[t]he classes mix' (Amador 2012: 130), the bar is a site where social conflict plays out, gossip is shared and the social standing of individuals is negotiated and determined. All this finds expression in the vast array of gazes being cast, directed, held and avoided in the large room of the Bar and Grill, which thereby mirrors the social space of Forks High School. In this context, *True Blood* provides a portrayal of Bon Temps's rural Southern community that is exaggerated and satirical. The series' grotesque depiction of both 'good country people and white/trailer trash' (ibid.: 124) can be tied back to its generic entanglement with Southern Gothic (Ruddell and Cherry 2012: 39). Thus, the population of the small town is represented as largely small-minded, misogynistic, racist, xenophobic and homophobic.

As we learn in the first episode, Sookie is under constant suspicious observation by the townsfolk due to her telepathy because her gift disturbs people. In addition to this, she is often the object of a male/patriarchal gaze in particular: in her daily work routine, she is confronted with sexist judgment concerning her appearance and (sexual) behaviour, both from her customers, and her boss and co-workers. Sookie is well aware of the patriarchal gaze that lingers on her both literally and metaphorically. Her first scene shows her waitressing at Merlotte's; right before she enters the public section of the bar, she adjusts her facial expression to form a fake but pleasant smile. This short introductory scene reveals that Sookie knows that she is the object of a variety of gazes and that she makes the conscious decision to model her behaviour to people's expectations. Sookie navigates the difficult working environment she faces by trying to work it to her best advantage: 'When I wear make-up, I get bigger tips. . . . And I get even bigger tips when I act like I don't have a brain in my head. But if I don't, they're all scared of me' ('Strange Love', 1.1). Sookie's strategy to conform to gendered expectations by grooming herself and exhibiting a pleasing, non-threatening attitude in order to gain financial and social benefit can be referred to as a 'patriarchal bargain' (Kandiyoti 1988: 282). The term was coined by Deniz Kandiyoti, who argues that '[d]ifferent forms of patriarchy present women with distinct "rules of the game" and call for different strategies to maximize security and optimize life options with varying potential for active or passive resistance in the face of oppression' (1988: 274; italics in original). Sookie's readiness to actively bargain with patriarchy marks her as an agent of postfeminism, which focuses on individual women's (momentary) reward while simultaneously reinforcing a system that oppresses all women – some more and some less, depending on differences in race, socioeconomic class, and so on.

In other situations, Sookie is shown to be less accommodating and less willing to be policed by the constantly present male gaze. At her workplace, her conversations with Bill are monitored by her boss, colleagues and customers, but Sookie nevertheless seeks Bill's company.

When Bill draws her attention to the fact that 'every person in this establishment is staring at us right now', she brushes off his concern: 'Who cares what they think?' ('Strange Love', 1.1). Time and again, Sookie must defend herself for her choice to build a social and, later, a romantic relationship with Bill, a vampire. With the exception of her grandmother, everyone around her lets her know that they disapprove of her choices; these people include her friend Tara (Rutina Wesley), her boss and friend Sam (Sam Trammell), her co-worker Arlene (Carrie Preston), her brother Jason (Ryan Kwanten), funeral home director and coroner Mike Spencer (John Billingsley) and the local sheriff Bud Dearborne (William Sanderson). For most of these people, Sookie has quick-witted retorts. When Sam intrudes himself into her affairs and demands to know whether she kissed Bill and possibly went even further with him, Sookie does not allow him to shame her; she reminds him: 'That's really none of your business' ('Sparks Fly Out', 1.5). Strikingly, Sam uses the collective gaze that rests on Sookie at Merlotte's to make her comply with his patriarchal ideas concerning her 'appropriate' conduct with men in general and vampire men in particular. Thus, more than once, he puts Sookie in situations where she is under the pressure of the townsfolk's gazes in order to compel her to act according to what he perceives as 'best' for her. For instance, in 'Burning House of Love' (1.7), while she is waitressing at the crowded bar, Sam rips down Sookie's scarf in an aggressive gesture to expose her vampire bite wounds, which Sookie acquired in the frame of her sexual relationship with Bill. Through this action, he not only demonstrates that he feels entitled to uncover a part of Sookie's body that she herself chose to conceal, but he also aims to expose her sexual relationship with Bill to everyone at the bar – a relationship which she had kept private so far. After all, Sam knows very well that Sookie will be judged negatively by the prejudiced townspeople. As expected, she is ogled at by the whole community because Sam's attack happens at the very centre of the bar. Here, the camera captures the critical looks of a number of men as the scene attracts their attention. As conversations pause, the music stops and everyone turns their head towards the conflict, Sam has managed to relegate Sookie to her 'rightful' place of being the spectacle of the gaze. In this moment, Sookie's 'visual presence . . . freeze[s] the flow of action' (Mulvey [1975] 1989: 19), without her choosing to do so in the first place. While Sam's physical attack in front of the eyes of the whole community is meant to shame and intimidate Sookie, she is not willing to accept his abuse: 'Hey, you keep your hands to yourself, Sam Merlotte, you have no right to touch me. . . . What I do on my own time is no concern of yours, or any of y'all's. Yes, I had sex with Bill. And since every one of y'all is too chicken to ask, it was great' ('Burning House of Love', 1.7).

This physical assault by Sam is not the only assault Sookie experiences in the course of the season(s). In season one, her grandmother is killed in her stead because she happens to be at home when the killer strikes; Sookie is inconsolable. In this situation, her brother Jason slaps her across the face and blames her for their grandmother's murder: 'It's your fault! Gran's dead 'cause of you. It should have been you! . . . She's screwing a vampire. . . . A fucking vampire' ('Cold Ground', 1.6). Here, Jason brings up Sookie's supposedly transgressive sexual activity for which, as he implies, Sookie essentially deserves a punishment such as murder. Although he tries to apologize for his attack later, Jason maintains a judgmental and condescending attitude towards his sister and her sexual choices throughout the following episodes: 'My own sister. Nothing but a damn fangbanger. What, you saved it all these years for a fucking vampire?' Sookie does not give in to Jason's patronizing attitude and rebukes him for his hypocrisy: 'Bill is a gentleman. . . . He doesn't hit me, which is more than I can say for you' ('Burning House of Love', 1.7). Sookie is also familiar with sexualized violence. In 'The First Taste' (1.2), a young male customer at Merlotte's feels entitled to grab her bottom. In 'Release Me' (2.7), Sookie is almost raped while being on an undercover mission to help her vampire business partners. Besides, as we learn in 'Burning House of Love' (1.7), Sookie was sexually abused by her uncle as a child.

By inviting viewers to empathize with protagonist Sookie in situations in which she feels – and fights – the pressure and judgement of the male gaze, *True Blood* strengthens a female perspective, not only through subjective shots but also through narrative devices. As I argue, throughout its first season, the series frames the male gaze, which Sookie is subjected to, as part of a continuum of actions, attitudes and ideas that allow sexualized violence and/or misogynistic violence to occur. In this way, the show portrays the male gaze as an expression of the larger issue of sexism. In fact, *True Blood* makes misogyny a distinct theme running through the first season. Not only do viewers experience how Sookie is forced to handle situations in which she is treated in discriminatory ways due to her gender, but the murder mystery, which structures the whole season, is revealed to be rooted in male fear and hatred of women's sexual autonomy. As it turns out in the last episode, Drew Marshall (Michael Raymond-James) murdered several women, including his own sister, because he wanted to punish them for maintaining sexual relationships with vampires. As Kimberly A. Frohreich observes, Marshall 'does not attack vampires (the racial other); nor does he attack human men who "mix" with vampires' (2013: 41) – his victims are exclusively human women. In the finale, he attempts to kill Sookie as well but fails. The attempted murder, which is based on Marshall's contempt of Sookie's relationship with vampire Bill, reads like the extreme end of a continuum of sexist constraints and assaults that Sookie deals with on a daily basis. By illustrating the ways in which Sookie is confronted with a variety of actions situated along this continuum, *True Blood* addresses 'both the ordinary and extraordinary practices evidencing men's entitlement to act on women' (Vera-Gray 2017: 10).

To address and to illustrate issues of sexism, male structural power and the sexual objectification of women within patriarchal spaces, *True Blood* employs two elements of the supernatural, namely the figure of the vampire and Sookie's telepathy. Thus, throughout the first season, women who associate and/or have sex with vampires face particular disdain as well as verbal and physical threats by the human population of Bon Temps in general and the male citizens, including Drew Marshall, in particular. By using the figure of the vampire, the show manages to dramatize and criticize the dynamics of a sexist culture which demands that young women be sexually attractive and sexually available while at the same time punishing them for (certain forms of) sexual activity. Convoluted with these issues is a critical comment on issues of race and miscegenation, as Frohreich points out (2013: 33). As already hinted at, through Sookie's telepathic abilities, the pervasiveness of sexism is brought to light to a degree that would not be possible without this supernatural element. Sookie's abilities are simultaneously her gift and her curse. On the one hand, her telepathy allows her to discover clues about the identity of the killer and to know when he is approaching to kill her, so she can take measures to defend herself. On the other hand, due to her gift, she has not been able to get close to any of the men she has dated because she was involuntarily exposed to their deepest secrets; she also implies that she had to quit all her previous jobs because each of her bosses' thoughts were tantamount to workplace harassment for her. From the male coroner who muses about a female murder victim's 'fine pair of perfect, natural breasts' ('Escape from Dragon House', 1.4) to Sookie's date who thinks about the fact that he 'can't wait to see her naked. I wonder if she's a natural blonde. Nothing worse than a blonde with a big, black bush' ('The First Taste', 1.2) – audiences encounter the casual sexualization and dehumanization of female characters everywhere. It is normally hidden under the surface but is dragged forth by Sookie's power. The voice-over that represents a particular person's thoughts often accompanies and amplifies the male gaze that Sookie experiences. For instance, this is evident in the second episode, when – or right before – a young male customer non-consensually touches her body (this is the scene referenced earlier). Here, the objectifying gaze that the customer fixes on Sookie's body is complemented by his obnoxious train of thoughts. While he looks her up and down with a salacious grin on his face, we hear what he is thinking: 'If you could serve them nachos off them perfect titties, we'd all be mighty obliged. Ain't nothing I like more than licking food off a girl's tits. And that's a fine ass, too' ('The First Taste', 1.2). By employing Sookie's telepathy to reinforce the way the man looks at her, *True Blood* represents the issues underpinning the male gaze in a particularly graphic and striking way. All the while, Sookie is the subject whose perspective and supernatural ability allow viewers to experience being the object of the gaze. Following Soloway, this female gaze that *True Blood* orchestrates here 'says WE SEE YOU, SEEING US' (2016; emphasis in original).

Having examined how the *Twilight* Saga and *True Blood* employ a female gaze conveying to audiences the experience of being gazed at, I now want to turn to the ways in which *Twilight*, *The Vampire Diaries* and *True Blood* make their female protagonists the bearers of a desiring and investigative gaze, which implies their status as active agents in their own story.

'I know what I saw': Strategies of subjectivity and the reversal of the gaze in the *Twilight Saga* and *True Blood*

Gazing at Edward Cullen and Jacob Black

As already pointed out, particularly the first instalment of the *Twilight* film series privileges Bella's perspective. The way the film achieves this is first and foremost by POV shots and voice-overs, which are both techniques creating interiority and encouraging viewers to identify with the character on-screen. In POV shots, 'the character is shown and then the camera occupies his or her (approximate!) position' (Branigan 1984: 73); this is how subjectivity is created in film. Essentially, a character becomes a subject 'through an act of vision directed toward an object' (ibid.: 77). In *Twilight*, Edward is the primary object at which Bella gazes. It is through her eyes that we see Edward and his family for the first time. When they first meet, Edward behaves in an extremely unfriendly way and acts dismissively towards Bella. His inexplicable behaviour is what drives her to find out what this mysterious stranger's secret is. She decides to 'confront him and demand to know what his problem was' (*Twilight* 2008), as the voice-over tells us. Thus, Bella assumes an '"active investigative gaze" normally reserved for males and punished in females when they assume it themselves' (Clover 1992: 48). In this way, *Twilight* provides an interesting counter-example to the sadistic voyeurism that Mulvey identifies as one strategy of asserting power over female characters in traditional Hollywood film ([1975] 1989: 22). As Harry M. Benshoff and Sean Griffin elaborate, 'attempts to "figure out" and thus control the dangerously beautiful woman have structured many Hollywood movies. . . . Men stare harder at these mysterious women in the hope that the power of the male gaze will penetrate the female's beautiful armor. At times, once her shell is cracked by the male gaze, the woman can then be reclaimed by the hero' (2009: 256). *Twilight* reverses this paradigm, putting Bella in the powerful position to gaze at Edward in order to figure out his mysterious allure. Edward's secret is, of course, that he is a supernatural creature. Here, the figure of the vampire serves as the 'dangerously beautiful' man's secret identity and is employed to elicit and justify the investigative/desiring female gaze. Following de Lauretis, *Twilight*'s narrative is generated by Bella's desire to know Edward; her narration is based on her quest for knowledge and the fulfilment of her desires.

At first, Bella's investigative gaze comes to nothing: she searches for Edward at school every day, her gaze wandering across the schoolyard and the cafeteria, but he is absent. When he returns, he is like a different person: polite, accommodating, chatty. During their first conversation, both Edward and Bella look at each other attentively. While reciprocal POV shots are used in this scene, Bella's perspective is nevertheless foregrounded by close-ups and extreme close-ups of Edward's face, especially his eyes (see Figure 3.4). Interestingly, this first conversation between Bella and Edward takes place during biology class. The setting not only alludes to the budding teenage sexuality in this scene, but also provides the opportunity for another reference to the realm of looking: in their first lesson, Bella and Edward were 'observing the behaviour of planaria aka flatworms' (*Twilight* 2008); in the second one, they are looking at onion root tip cells under the microscope and labelling them into phases of mitosis – a task both of them master easily. Bella's expertise in recognizing prophase and anaphase is mirrored in her

Figure 3.4 Extreme close-up of Edward's eyes. *Twilight*, directed by Catherine Hardwicke © Summit Entertainment 2008. All rights reserved.

ability to look closely at Edward. While nobody else seems to notice, she sees that Edward's eye colour has changed since their last encounter – a phenomenon having to do with his vampire nature. When Edward saves Bella's life by stopping a car from crushing her with his bare hands, she trusts her perception despite his attempts to deny what happened: 'I know what I saw' (*Twilight* 2008). Bella's 'unexpected power in looking (at him) disturbs Edward, and he tries on various occasions to undermine her ability to believe her eyes and interpret what she sees' (Edwards 2009: 29), but Bella is not deterred. Despite Edward's attempts to make Bella distrust her vision, she continues to investigate him. Here, it is important to note that the camera is 'reproducing and thus validating her gaze', so that Bella's perception 'is supported by the audience's own viewing experience' (ibid.). Having followed a hunch and done some research in books and online, Bella puts the pieces together. Alongside her, viewers come to the realization that Edward must be a vampire.

Besides the investigative gaze driven by the quest for knowledge, the *Twilight* Saga also indulges in a heterosexual female gaze that is more distinctly offering viewers the pleasure of looking at male characters in a desiring way. In numerous instances in the film, Bella gazes at Edward, simply being fascinated and enjoying looking at him. In addition, Jacob's body is frequently put on visual display throughout the series. In the scenes involving Edward, it is worth noting that *Twilight* is indebted to a rather traditional approach, focusing on Edward's face and eyes rather than his body. As Natalie Perfetti-Oates writes, the focus of the desiring female gaze in romantic comedies and romantic dramas used to be not on the protagonist's abs or buttocks, but on his handsome face. She argues that this pattern was replaced at the beginning of the new millennium by a proliferation of 'scenes which position the male lead's body as a source of visual pleasure for his spectators' (2015: par. 4). Seen in this light, it is interesting – and perhaps a little anachronistic – that *Twilight* regularly shows close-ups of Edward's eyes but his body is usually concealed under his elegant, classic clothes. As I will elaborate later, this choice in the presentation of Edward's body may be tied back to his whiteness and higher social class. Nevertheless, there are a number of scenes putting Edward's vampire body on display.

After Bella has confronted Edward with her knowledge about his secret, he tries to convince her that she should not be pursuing him because he is dangerous. In order to demonstrate his Otherness, he steps into a clearance in the forest, revealing that his vampire skin glistens and sparkles in the sun: 'This is why we don't show ourselves in the sunlight. People would know we're different. This is what I am' (*Twilight* 2008). While Bella is staring at him with gaping mouth, Edward turns around to face her, his shirt unbuttoned. In a medium shot, the camera first shows his sparkling face and neck. Another shot of Bella gasping reminds us that she is gazing at Edward's body (see Figure 3.5). The fact that her face is shown in a close-up emphasizes the importance of her emotions at this moment: as Frank E. Beaver points out, '[e]motions, feelings, and nuances can be suggested by the close-up by merely magnifying and isolating an individual in an intensely dramatic moment' (1994: 70). While Bella is visibly trying to wrap her head around what she is seeing, the camera slowly pans upwards over Edward's naked torso, signifying Bella's desiring gaze (see Figure 3.6). Bella then proceeds to put her desire into words by commenting on Edward's attractiveness: 'You're beautiful' (*Twilight* 2008). The representation of Bella's sexually desiring gaze at Edward's vampire body is a feature that was particularly

Figure 3.5 Close-up of Bella gazing at Edward. *Twilight*, directed by Catherine Hardwicke © Summit Entertainment 2008. All rights reserved.

Figure 3.6 Close-up of Edward's sparkling torso. *Twilight*, directed by Catherine Hardwicke © Summit Entertainment 2008. All rights reserved.

appealing to viewers at the time of the movie's release, as Ananya Mukherjea's quantitative research has revealed: in her survey of self-identified American *Twilight* fans, she found that '[g]azing upon the men . . . was a central feature of the pleasure all the respondents took in *Twilight*' (2011b: 76). Looking at the male supernatural characters 'allowed these fans to be desiring subjects' (ibid.: 78) and gave them the opportunity to engage in a 'social bonding activity' (ibid.: 77) by talking about their experience with others. It stands to reason that the extent and/or visibility of fans' exchanges about Edward's (and Jacob's) bodies was closely related to the social media boom that occurred around the same time as the release of the earlier *Twilight* movie adaptations (Kheraj 2018). Although fandom had previously played out online, the advent of platforms such as Facebook, Twitter and Tumblr facilitated, spurred and made particularly visible a collective acknowledgement and discussion of the Saga's sexualized portrayal of its male supernatural bodies. Indeed, *Twilight* was the first movie to reach 1 million followers on Twitter (Dugan 2012), and the hashtags #TeamEdward and #TeamJacob allowed fans to lead 'almost real-time discussions' (Kheraj 2018) about their experiences as gazing subjects.

As already pointed out, in *Twilight*, Edward's vampire nature functions as a catalyst for Bella's investigative gaze. His mysterious allure and his strange behaviour, which are rooted in his being a vampire, drive her to look at him more closely. In the scene described earlier, it becomes clear that the vampire body expressly invites the female gaze: it is for the purpose of demonstrating his vampire nature that Edward presents his naked upper body to Bella. The fact that his skin sparkles 'like diamonds' (*Twilight* 2008) in the sunlight explicitly marks his body as visual spectacle. Furthermore, through the use of dramatic lighting, Edward's body is positioned as connoting *to-be-looked-at-ness* in the same way that female bodies have been positioned in Hollywood film. Traditionally, the technique of three-point lighting has been used to guide viewers' gazes and enhance actresses' visual appeal. This technique includes the employment of three sources of light, key light, fill light and back light, which serve to illuminate the body of the female star (Benshoff and Griffin 2009: 245). In the forest scene in *Twilight*, the use of the back light creates a so-called '"halo effect" – a glowing outline around the star's hair and body, as if the light was radiating directly out of them' (ibid.), which makes Edward more attractive to the camera's gaze. The lighting technique also emphasizes his sparkling skin. Thus, Edward, based on his vampire nature, occupies the position of erotic object in *Twilight*. Strikingly, this finding is in accord with arguments that Marcus Recht and Alison McCracken have made in their respective studies of the visual construction of masculinities in *Buffy the Vampire Slayer*. According to Recht, the vampire characters Angel and Spike are able to break the gender binary based on their vampire status and their position as Others (2011: 41). Their Otherness as vampires links them to 'femininity', which has traditionally been referred to as the Other, on a visual level. Thus, vampire Edward Cullen takes up a position that is traditionally seen as synonymous with 'femininity' in *Twilight*. In a similar vein, McCracken argues that Angel, by excessively performing the role of the 'eroticized body' in *Buffy*, 'reverses the usual spectacularization of the female body' that is so ingrained in 'the gendered conventions of the classical Hollywood narrative model (to which most television series also subscribe)' (2007: 120). The portrayal of the male vampire body as visual spectacle, then, is one defining characteristic that *Twilight* inherits from *Buffy*. What it strengthens even further is the gaze of its female protagonist, Bella, whose experience the *Twilight* Saga almost exclusively revolves around.

As briefly mentioned earlier, the body of another supernatural character is regularly put on display for the visual pleasure of audiences in the *Twilight* Saga. Here, the camera does not reproduce Bella's gaze but rather incidentally presents the muscular torso of Jacob Black, Edward's rival for Bella's affection, at various points throughout the Saga.[3] The sexualization of Jacob's body is an aspect the *Twilight* films are both notorious for and very self-aware of. In the Saga, the circumstance that Jacob is frequently shown shirtless is narratively attributed to the fact that he is a werewolf/shapeshifter. As George and Hughes contend, werewolves – following vampires – have emerged as a close second among the 'supernatural species [that] have been found in the arms and beds of humankind' (2020b: 6) in contemporary media texts. For one thing, as a shapeshifter, Jacob can transform into a wolf at any time. As is established in *New Moon*, members of the pack may suddenly take wolf form either intentionally or if they lose their temper; their transformation is not dependent on the presence of the full moon. In the process, they naturally shred their clothes into pieces, which is assumably why they are not wearing much clothing in the first place. For another thing, the Quileute shapeshifters are characterized by a heightened body temperature. Due to this bodily feature, Jacob is portrayed as 'naturally' not needing any overgarments. Thus, in a similar way that the vampire body is used as a focal point of the female gaze in *Twilight*, Jacob's presentation for the visual pleasure of (female) audiences is justified by his supernatural status as a werewolf.

A troubling aspect that comes in here is the way werewolf mythology is conflated in the *Twilight* series with the real Quileute guardian spirit mythology. The Quileute are not Meyer's invention but a Native American people living in Washington State, whose mythology Meyer has appropriated in her novels. As several scholars have noted, the Quileute characters and myths in the *Twilight* books are 'a product of . . . the romantic and patronizing Western stereotype of the "Noble Savage"' (Jensen 2010: 92). The *Twilight* film adaptations transfer this problematic depiction to a different medium and continue it on a narrative as well as visual level. Thus, Jacob's representation as being in a constant state of undress is in keeping with historical portrayals of Native Americans in American film and literature (Wilson 2010: 65). These portrayals dictated that Native Americans' 'power derives not from their intellect but from their bodies or their closeness to nature' (ibid.: 63). In contrast to Edward, whose whiter-than-white body is usually hidden under clothing, Jacob's non-white and nude body is portrayed as less 'civilized', more animalistic and having a greater potential for violence and loss of control. Needless to say, Jacob's last name is 'Black', he literally turns into a wolf and, as Natalie Wilson puts it, 'the werewolves' lack of clothing . . . emphasizes their status *as* bodies' (2010: 64; emphasis in original).

While the Cullens are associated with high culture and can be read as revealing 'the links between white privilege and class privilege' (ibid.: 58), Jacob is working class, his 'non-whiteness [associated] with physicality and manual labor' (ibid.: 59). This is the case, for example, in the scenes in which Jacob repairs two motorcycles for himself and Bella in *New Moon*. Yvonne Tasker points out that 'the kinds of male body – black and white working class – that have traditionally been displayed within western culture are those that are *already sexualised*, perceived through an accumulated history of sexual myths and stereotypes' ([1993] 2004: 79; emphasis in original). Seen in this light, it must be taken into account that while the *Twilight* Saga provides potentially subversive spaces for the application of a female gaze onto male sexualized objects, it simultaneously stands in the harmful and discriminatory tradition of representing the Native American man as a Romantic Savage: 'passionate, *always* attractive, . . . and yet, still exotic, still at one with nature, and still – if threatened – capable of savage violence' (Burke 2011: 208; emphasis in original). The fact that Jacob is both non-white and working class explains why his body is more overtly sexualized throughout the film series than Edward's body is. The latter is a character who enjoys a variety of race and class privileges and who is the one whom Bella finally chooses as her romantic partner.

Sookie Stackhouse, sexual subject

True Blood, too, represents its female protagonist's active desiring gaze primarily in the first season. Here, vampire Bill becomes the object of Sookie's sexual and romantic desire. Although Sookie is depicted as a (sexual) subject here, in other, more ambivalent scenes, she is portrayed as sexually empowered while her sexualized body is simultaneously presented as visual spectacle. These different variations of sexual 'empowerment' shall be examined in the following. Generally speaking, *True Blood* regularly depicts both female and male bodies in overtly sexualized ways. This phenomenon is likely due to *True Blood*'s being affiliated with the subscription-only cable channel *HBO*, which 'has a reputation for cutting-edge, in-your-face television that employs liberal amounts of sex, violence and swearing as well as serious or adult themes in an artful and stylistic package' (Cherry 2012a: 3). The fact that the show includes hyper-masculine bodies in this excessive process of eroticization, however, was unusual and differentiated *True Blood* from other TV series on both network and pay TV channels.

A scene in 'Mine' (1.3) is representative of the series' way of putting Sookie's sexual desire for Bill in the foreground. At this point in the narrative, Sookie and Bill have become acquainted with one another and have already shared their first kiss. The scene begins with the subjective camera perspective of a person or creature approaching the Compton mansion, opening the front door and moving into the living room. There we spot Bill, poring over a book. The unnerving soundtrack adds to the fact that the camera has not identified whose perspective we are sharing; equipped with knowledge about the horror genre, we are led to believe that this is the point of view of a predator sneaking into Bill's house, about to attack him. When the presumed creature approaches Bill from behind to look over his shoulder, he jumps to his feet and assumes a defensive position. It is then revealed that the intruder is Sookie. Tellingly, Sookie is placed in the active position of the attacker and/or predator here. The scene continues with her articulating that she would like to be intimate with Bill. Voicing her wish to share her first sexual experience with him, Sookie takes an active role in the pursuit of her desires. The scene then cuts from Sookie's and Bill's naked moving bodies to Sookie's bedroom. At this point, it turns out that we were actually part of one of Sookie's sexual fantasies. A medium shot shows her lying in bed, eyes closed, one hand under her blanket, masturbating. With the help of this narrative ploy, *True Blood* visualizes Sookie's sexual desire through the representation of her straight female gaze. Viewers are able to experience her active desire first hand by sharing an intimate fantasy with her.

Other scenes presenting Sookie's sexual subjecthood are more ambivalent, and the frequency of these contradictory scenes increases in later seasons. A striking example is another elongated dream sequence by Sookie that is dramatized in the episode 'Let's Get Out of Here' (4.9). In this dream, Sookie articulates her desire for Bill as well as Eric, with both of whom she has previously had sexual and romantic entanglements. Both vampires star prominently in her dream. Here, Sookie renounces both men's possessiveness towards her, which finds expression in their constant bickering, fighting and posturing: 'Sookie is mine' – 'Bullshit. She's mine' – 'I'm 10 times your age' – 'And I love her 20 times as much'. In her dream, which ridicules Bill's and Eric's trials of strength and 'masculinity', Sookie refuses to be at the mercy of their dominating behaviour: 'This is my dream, so both of y'all need to shut up and listen to me'. Instead, Sookie dictates the conditions of her relationship with both men on her own terms. In her speech, she puts her own desire at the centre and proposes a polyamorous relationship, in the frame of which she would be able to act out her feelings for Eric as well as Bill:

> Sookie: 'I think I'm in love with both of you. . . . I've always been this self-conscious, good little girl who was too scared to think outside the box, especially when it comes to love and sex. But as of right now, I'm putting that little girl behind me. . . . I can love both of you. . . . I don't have to be yours, or yours. I'm proposing that the two of you be mine . . .'
> Eric: 'You have to choose.'
> Sookie: 'This is such a double standard! When it's two women and one guy, everyone's hunky-dory with it, even if they barely know each other. But when a woman tries to have her way with two men she is totally and completely in love with, everyone's hemming and hawing. . . . It's either both of you or nothing at all. Take it or leave it.' ('Let's Get Out of Here', 4.9)

Sookie's ultimatum comes with the reference to a sexist double standard in contemporary culture that allows men the free expression of their sexuality while it forbids the same to women, which Sookie intends to break with. Prioritizing her own desires and ideas and making clear that she would rather abdicate both men than compromise her beliefs once again, Sookie presents herself in an assertive position of power in this dream sequence. Interestingly, she seems to derive her power not least from her sexual appeal and her positioning herself for the male gaze, which originates not only from Bill and Eric but also from the camera. Thus, while the male vampires are dressed in their usual clothes and sitting casually on the couch, Sookie is presented as posing in sexy lingerie in order to persuade them to agree to her conditions (see Figure 3.7). From the start of the dream sequence, Sookie's face and body are emphasized through lighting techniques as well as the

Figure 3.7 Sookie posing in sexy lingerie (4.9). *True Blood* © Home Box Office Inc. 2008–14. All rights reserved.

sexualized poses she assumes. Her outfit consists of a red, short robe with a deep neckline and high heels, her movements are directed in slow motion, and a lascivious saxophone soundtrack is playing in the background.[4] Through all of these measures, Sookie is put in the spotlight of the camera's gaze. When she takes off her robe coquettishly to reinforce her argument, a shot of both Bill and Eric gazing lustfully at Sookie underlines for whose gaze she poses here in her own sexual fantasy. In this fantasy sequence, Sookie is successful in the sense that both men seem to accept her conditions, as the three of them start to engage in passionate sex before Sookie wakes up in her bed.

Later in the series, Sookie once again relies on her sexual attractiveness to achieve her goals. This time, the representation of Sookie using her 'feminine wiles' for the purpose of deception and distraction draws heavily on the trope of the *femme fatale*. However, the show does not portray her approach as rooted in the agenda to pursue selfish interests or wreak havoc and corruption. Instead, Sookie essentially chooses her strategy, which is taking advantage of the male gaze, as a way of defending herself and gaining the upper hand in a conflict in which she is hitherto powerless. Towards the end of season five, she had found out that her ancestors promised her to the immortal faerie–vampire hybrid Warlow. Not long after the seemingly sympathetic Ben Flynn enters her life in season six, Sookie figures out that he is using a false identity and that he is in fact Warlow, who has escaped the prison realm he was trapped in and wants to collect the debt he is owed. Sookie then goes on the offensive: planning to kill Warlow with her faerie light once he is caught off-guard, she sets him up for a honey trap by inviting Ben to dinner under the pretence of wanting to take their newly formed relationship to the next level ('At Last', 6.4). Sookie lures him in by flirting coquettishly, then dresses up in a tight lace dress and starts to seduce him to get him into a defenceless position. The camera follows Sookie during her preparations, including her process of grooming herself, which consists of shaving, applying lipstick and checking her cleavage in the mirror, wearing nothing but a see-through lace bra and a light robe. Here, Sookie not only chooses to make herself the object of Warlow's gaze in order to distract him, but she also becomes the sexualized object of the camera's and the audiences' gazes. In classic male gaze fashion, her body is fragmented through an extreme close-up of her lower leg. Thus, while Sookie manages to take advantage of the dynamic of the male gaze for the purpose of seizing power in a situation in which she is treated as the possession of men – the plan works out and Warlow falls for the ruse – the series in turn takes advantage of Sookie by casually rendering her body the sexualized object of the gaze. *True Blood*'s season six in particular is conspicuous for the way it constantly represents female characters as using their sexuality as a tool to manipulate, persuade or bargain for advantages.[5]

Two episodes later, the series once again emphasizes that Sookie is taking charge of her sexuality while it simultaneously objectifies her body gratuitously for the visual pleasure of (heterosexual male) audiences. Having found out some disturbing truths about her family and subsequently changed her mind about Warlow, Sookie decides to have her way with him. In the scene, which is set in the faerie realm, Warlow is handcuffed to a pole and Sookie takes charge of the situation. The accompanying dialogue provides a specific context in which viewers are set up to interpret her actions. Here, once again, it is suggested that

Sookie is reclaiming her sexuality in the face of a sexist and sexually repressive culture: 'There's a town consensus about what kind of girl I am. . . . They call me a danger whore. . . . maybe it's time I just started accepting this about myself. . . . I may be a whore' ('Don't You Feel Me', 6.6). Thus, Sookie responds to the misogynistic language she encounters by appropriating and reclaiming it. She then proceeds to rip Warlow's shirt open for her own visual pleasure and to initiate sexual contact. After the mutual sharing of blood, Sookie strips off her clothes in front of Warlow, who watches her intently. The camera takes full advantage of the strip, showing her naked body down to her waist in a medium shot. The subsequent sex scene is fairly explicit as well; here we see more of Sookie's naked body exposed than of Warlow's, who continues to be strapped to the pole and lounging on the ground. Like the other two scenes analysed earlier, this scene can be read both as challenging and reinforcing the patriarchal order. In fact, both readings are deeply intertwined. Sookie's strategy of reclaiming a sexist slur that was meant to degrade her recalls recent attempts of taking back words such as 'bitch', 'slut' and 'cunt' in (post)feminist circles. Most recently, the global SlutWalk movement set out to 'challeng[e] harmful, victim-blaming language' ('About'), taking ownership of and giving it new meaning. Having erupted as a reaction to a police officer's statement at Toronto's York University in 2011 that if women wanted to avoid sexual assault, they should stop dressing as 'sluts' ('WHY'), SlutWalk rallies drew in masses of protesters across the globe. By representing Sookie as re-appropriating the pejorative label 'whore' in an assertive way, *True Blood* ties in with these (post)feminist approaches that try to re-signify discriminatory language and deal with the oppressive patriarchal culture by changing it from within.

'Are you staying for the show?' Damon Salvatore and the art of camp in *The Vampire Diaries*

How does *The Vampire Diaries* deal with the themes of female sexual subjectivity and the spectacularization of the male vampire body?

Initially, the series shares a number of similarities with the *Twilight* Saga regarding the portrayal of a desiring female gaze and the evolution of the central romance. Here, too, we accompany a female teen protagonist, Elena Gilbert, whose subjectivity is generated through the representation of her voice-over and her desiring gaze at a much older vampire, Stefan Salvatore. Several scenes in the first episodes set the tone for the rest of the show by establishing the pleasures of gazing as central. The pilot follows Elena navigating the high school environment at the beginning of a new term. While Stefan, who has transferred to the school as a new student, is first noticed by Elena's friends Bonnie (Katerina Graham) and Caroline (Candice King, née Accola), it is only when Stefan bumps into Elena that viewers get to see what his face looks like. Thus, audiences are explicitly invited to share Elena's perspective when it comes to looking at Stefan. In the first two episodes, Elena and Stefan playfully exchange looks during class, with Elena being the one initiating the exchange. At the same time, their nonverbal communication is observed not only by Matt (Zach Roerig), Elena's ex-boyfriend, but also by Bonnie, who informs Elena in a private text message: 'HAWT-E STARING @ U' ('Pilot', 1.1). The prevalence of gazes and looks at Mystic Falls High School is reminiscent of the conspicuous focus on who is looking and being looked at within the high school culture depicted in *Twilight* as well as the public space of Merlotte's Bar and Grill in *True Blood*. By characterizing Stefan as having 'that romance novel stare' (ibid.), *The Vampire Diaries* deliberately locates itself within the romance genre from the start.

Like Bella, Elena turns both a desiring and an active, investigative gaze towards Stefan, whose secret vampire identity she is initially not aware of. For instance, 'Friday Night Bites' (1.3) features a scene in which Elena is allowed to secretly gaze at Stefan's body while he is playing football (see Figure 3.8). Having taken a break from her own cheerleading practice, Elena picks a hidden spot next to the bleachers to admire Stefan's athletic abilities. Besides foregrounding Elena's desiring gaze, the scene establishes Stefan as being in excellent physical shape; the rock tune playing in the background characterizes him as

Figure 3.8 Elena secretly gazing at Stefan (1.3). *The Vampire Diaries* © Warner Bros. Entertainment Inc. 2009-17. All rights reserved.

cool and attractive. The fact that he is unaware of being the object of Elena's desiring gaze at this moment is striking: as Elena is standing in a spot in which she remains hidden from the men on the field, they are unable to return her gaze. In this way, Elena is able to occupy the position of the desiring subject without in turn becoming the object of Stefan's gaze, which was the case in the scenes taking place in class. When inexplicable phenomena pile up, Elena's quest for knowledge is triggered. In the same episode, she witnesses how Stefan cuts his hand trying to accommodate a quarrel between two of his fellow students. What Elena does not know is that Stefan's wound heals instantly due to his vampire nature. When he tries to convince her that he was not injured at all, she insists: 'No, no, no, I saw it. The glass cut your hand' ('Friday Night Bites', 1.3). Furthermore, she repeatedly notices that Stefan's eyes change when he is around blood (in *The Vampire Diaries*, when vampires feel the urge to feed on humans, their eyes turn red, dark veins become visible around their eyes and cheekbones, and their elongated fangs pop out). Stefan attempts to hide from Elena's look but he is unsuccessful. Elena's perceptiveness parallels Bella's acumen and tendency to be exceptionally observant when it comes to Edward in

Twilight. Interestingly, as discussed earlier, it is also a change in Edward's eye colour that Bella notices and that brings her closer to unravelling his vampire identity. In 'You're Undead to Me' (1.5), after interviewing an elderly citizen of Mystic Falls who believes he recognizes Stefan as someone he met in the 1950s, Elena taps her resources to access the archives of the local TV station to gather evidence of a supposed animal attack at the Salvatore boarding house in 1953. In the meantime, Stefan is given some advice about Elena, one of whose characteristics Matt describes as her active and relentless investigative drive and her strong motivation to see through people: 'She's big on trust. So whatever you're holding back from her, the more you try to hide it, the more she won't stop 'till she figures it out' ('You're Undead to Me', 1.5). A striking detail is that it is through the visual medium of a video report from the 1950s that Elena figures out Stefan's secret. She spots his blurry face in the background of a black-and-white video and zooms in on the detail on screen – a process that can be considered a literal representation of the active investigative gaze she directs at the boy she desires (see Figure 3.9). Elena comes to the conclusion that Stefan is a vampire. Through the power of her gaze and her insistence on knowing

Figure 3.9 Elena zooming in on Stefan (1.5). *The Vampire Diaries* © Warner Bros. Entertainment Inc. 2009–17. All rights reserved.

the person who has become important to her, she has figured out her 'dangerously beautiful' man's secret identity.

Over the course of the seasons, Elena becomes more and more infatuated with Stefan's brother, Damon, who is also a vampire. Her sexual and romantic interest in both brothers is an aspect the series continually plays with, sometimes very openly, sometimes more subtly. The love triangle is carefully cultivated by the showrunners, as it invites and fuels the involvement of viewers and strengthens the latter's relationship to characters. By setting up this male/female/male triangle, *The Vampire Diaries* offers a 'romance scenario [in which] the heroine is . . . an independently desiring subject whose desire propels most action and whose point of view governs [viewer] identification. . . . Her choice expresses a confident and determining female gaze and a knowing, autonomous subjectivity' (Veldman-Genz 2012: 111). Across the seasons, it is Damon's body that is most frequently and most markedly objectified. Although Stefan is also regularly presented as an erotic visual object, Damon provides a particularly interesting example because he is frequently displayed as deliberately and openly offering himself up to either Elena's or the camera's gaze. A fascinating aspect of Damon's representation as the object of the gaze in *The Vampire Diaries* is that it can be located within Damon's performance of camp. This aspect is particularly worth investigating because it underscores the subversive potential of Damon's body as visual spectacle.

As defined in the *Encyclopedia of Gender and Society* (2009), camp 'refers to styles, attitudes, and behaviors that are exaggerated, overstated and ironic. . . . the term now refers to self-conscious acts of subversion and parody in the context of society's gender norms. . . . Camp performances . . . can often destabilize norms and beliefs surrounding regulations that govern masculinity and femininity' (Purvis and Longstaff: 104). By exaggerating and/or contorting specific elements, camp draws attention to the constructedness of, for instance, gender roles. In this way, it may playfully disrupt the gender order. The roots of camp lie in gay culture and are based on what Jack Babuscio terms a 'gay sensibility' ([1977] 1999: 118). According to Babuscio, based on their stigmatization in society and 'a heightened awareness and appreciation for . . . the distinctions to be made between instinctive and theatrical behaviour' (ibid.: 124), which arise from the mechanism of passing as heterosexual, gays have developed a particular view of the world, in which camp often functions as a way of dealing with marginalization (ibid.: 133). However, people who deliver camp performances need not necessarily be gay (ibid.: 119). Thus, although Damon is portrayed as straight within *The Vampire Diaries* narrative, his character combines several features that constitute campness. Besides, as a vampire in a paranormal romance text, he disrupts several binaries, for instance those of life/death, attractiveness/repulsiveness, youth/old age, human/monster and hero/villain. The liminal position he occupies mirrors the status of queer people in society; as Babuscio writes (in the 1970s), '[s]ex/love between two men or two women is regarded by society as incongruous – out of keeping with the "normal", "natural", "healthy", heterosexual order of things' (ibid.). Because Damon exists on the margins, his character is ideally suited to be open to a camp sensibility.

According to Babuscio, '[f]our features are basic to camp: irony, aestheticism, theatricality, and humour' (ibid.). When it comes to *The Vampire Diaries*, it is striking that Damon incarnates these camp features within the show in general, and with respect to his performance for the straight female gaze in particular. Words that have been used to define camp, 'such as *affected*, . . . *exaggerated*, *ostentatious*, and *theatrical*' (Purvis and Longstaff 2009: 104; emphasis in original), also function as descriptions of Ian Somerhalder's performance of Damon Salvatore. In the pilot, Damon announces his presence by conjuring smoke and black crows to make a dramatic entrance. Stefan comments on his brother's extravagant performance: 'Crow's a bit much, don't you think?' (1.1). Here, the series draws on tropes established in early cinematic adaptations of *Dracula* and plays with these associations by exaggerating and verbally drawing attention to them. Interestingly, Babuscio argues that '[t]he horror genre, in particular, is susceptible to a camp interpretation'. This can be tied back to the emphasis on outrageous sentiments and excess that horror and camp share ([1977] 1999: 121). The strategy of linking horror tropes with camp is often made use of in the show; this serves a variety of functions. For instance, in 'Growing Pains' (4.1), Damon attacks Matt in order to lure Pastor Young (Michael Reilly Burke) out of his home; he does so to gain access to the house in which Stefan and Elena are being held captive. In a deliberately affected manner, he calls the Pastor: 'Yoo-hoo! Anybody home? Big bad vampire out here!' The fact that Damon's role as a dangerous predator is a performance is foregrounded in this scene. At the same time, although he has not killed Matt, Damon has not hesitated to sacrifice the latter's wellbeing in order to achieve his own goals. The kind of self-parodying he engages in here is fairly camp. As Babuscio argues, '[t]o appreciate camp in things or persons is to perceive the notion of life-as-theatre, being versus role-playing' ([1977] 1999: 123). Furthermore, theatricality and humour serve as strategies that allow us 'to witness "serious" issues with temporary detachment, so that only later, after the event, are we struck by the emotional and moral implications of what we have almost passively absorbed' (ibid.: 128). Thus, camp is frequently deployed in *The Vampire Diaries* to mitigate the horrors of Damon's actions. It is not by coincidence that he is the character with the campest performance; he is also the one who commits the most atrocities over the course of the seasons – all while remaining a vampire that is meant to be understood as sympathetic by audiences.

By introducing Damon as a camp vampire character, *The Vampire Diaries* (once again) follows in the footsteps of *Buffy the Vampire Slayer*. As Cynthia Masson and Marni Stanley argue, vampire Spike from *Buffy* is characterized by a camp sensibility, which 'is predominantly evident in the sarcastic humour he brings to his focus on the aesthetics of others. Spike's humour is often cruel – *biting* we could say – and this too is an inherent quality of camp' (2006: par. 16; emphasis in original). Bitter-wit, defined by Babuscio as typically camp ([1977] 1999: 126), is the main component of Spike's humour, which he usually directs at other characters to mock them. Similarly, Damon's humour is a sarcastic, arrogant one. Within the series, he frequently provides snarky and derisive commentary on situations as well as behaviour and looks of other characters. Damon's snarky commentary contributes significantly to the overall tone of the show. One frequent victim of his commentary is Elena's younger brother Jeremy (Steven R. McQueen), whom Damon mocks in season one for being a stereotypical adolescent troubled by drugs and alcohol: 'I have so many emotions, but I don't have any way to express them. Being a teenager is so hard' ('Founder's Day', 1.22). Another target of his derision is Stefan, who is ridiculed by Damon on a regular basis for his emotional and morally upright attitude, which is presented as contrary to Damon's personality: 'Stefan is different. He wants to be human. He wants to feel every episode of *How I Met Your Mother*' ('Isobel', 1.21).

The preceding quote also illustrates another aspect of Damon's camp commentary: popular cultural references and intertextuality. Thus, in the highly self-referential *Vampire Diaries*, references to other TV programmes and movies are in large part dropped by Damon. Damon's continual intertextual references as well as the self-conscious irony with which he addresses and thwarts genre tropes are part of his camp persona. Both are strategies that draw attention to the fictionality of the show. Like Spike, Damon points towards the constructedness of the TV series as a whole and the artifice of other characters. As Masson and Stanley write: 'Gods, superheroes, and vampires should not be concerned with their hair – but in *Buffy* they are, and Spike is the one to point out the artifice of these aesthetic details while sporting the most artificial looking hair of all' (2006: par. 16). Curiously, in *The Vampire Diaries*, Damon is equally concerned with mocking his brother's hairdo, for example in 'Daddy Issues' (2.13): 'You better watch your back. Because I may just have to go get a hero hairdo of my own and steal your thunder.' Interestingly, Damon also mirrors Spike's way of ridiculing other male characters for not being 'masculine' enough. Because Spike is insecure in terms of his own gender, he adopts a defensive attitude and mocks other men's performances of masculinity (Masson and Stanley 2006: par. 17). The effect is striking: 'the more he critiques masculine performance in others, the more the audience is aware of Spike's own performance of masculinity' (ibid.: par. 18). Accordingly, in *The Vampire Diaries*, the effect of Damon's camp commentary is a drawing of attention to the artificiality of gender roles. Thus, Damon's comments about Jeremy's emotionality as well as Stefan's sentimentality and beauty routine can be understood as mockeries of these characters' performances of masculinity. At the same time, the comments clash with Damon's own 'flawed' performance of traditional masculinity; he, too, often acts extremely emotionally and is known for his careful cultivation of an elegant clothing style.

Even more routinely than Spike, Damon performs for the straight female gaze in a deliberately camp manner. As I suggest, *The Vampire Diaries* manages to expose the constructedness of the category of gender through Damon's camp performance. Thus, prominent aspects of many scenes that present Damon's body as an erotic spectacle are the humour and theatricality involved. This is important because, as Babuscio argues, '[h]umour constitutes the strategy of camp'. According to Babuscio, this humour 'results from an identification of a strong incongruity between an object, person, or situation and its context' ([1977] 1999: 126). In the case of *The Vampire Diaries*, the incongruity that is the basis of Damon's camp consists of him occupying the conventionally 'feminine' position of being the sexualized object of the gaze. By taking a campy and playful approach to Damon's sexual objectification, the show indicates an awareness of traditional gaze paradigms and deliberately destabilizes dominant notions of what the object of the gaze should and can look like. A scene that comes to mind in this context takes place in the episode 'The Birthday' (3.1). Here, Damon is enjoying a bubble bath and sipping champagne with visible pleasure. While his female partner, Andie Star (Dawn Olivieri), is getting ready for work, Damon relaxes in the bathtub, having a dreamy, contented expression on his face. The fact that he engages in the stereotypically female endeavour of taking a bubble bath is further amplified by his intentional performance for the heterosexual female gaze. After realizing that the bottle of champagne is empty, Damon stands up in the bathtub, his naked body covered in bath foam. While – judging from his smug, provocative smile – he clearly enjoys his girlfriend's gaze, the camera makes an effort to shield the lower part of his body by moving behind different objects, like a table in the bathroom. Damon then prances through the hall and into the living room, with the camera continuing to conveniently position itself in ways ensuring that his private parts are never exposed. This seemingly random, yet very obviously strategic use of different camera angles has a comedic effect. The humour that accompanies this nude scene adds a campy undertone to the already comic situation of Damon relaxing in a bubble bath. The latter is comic because it presents Damon in a stereotypically female position; the bubble bath is usually associated with the 'feminine' realm of beauty treatments and self-care in a romantic atmosphere involving rose petals and romantic candle light. In Babuscio's terms, this scene could be characterized as ironic. As he writes, '[c]amp is ironic insofar as an incongruous contrast can be drawn between an individual/thing and its context/association. The most common of incongruous contrasts is that of masculine/feminine' ([1977] 1999: 119). When Damon enters the living room, he walks into Elena, who just arrived at the Salvatore house. Not surprisingly, he visibly relishes the moment she turns around to find him naked and covered in bath foam (see Figure 3.10). Damon's exhibitionism and extravagant self-presentation are integral parts of his theatrical performance. Moreover, the scene is based on the circumstance of Damon entering the living room just a few seconds after Elena's arrival, so he can deliberately tease her. According to Babuscio, '[t]he art of camp ... relies largely upon arrangement, timing, and tone' (ibid.: 120). Thus, the timing, which is crucial to the functioning of the scene, is a further aspect that marks this scene as camp.

Notably, *True Blood* features a similar scene in 'The Fourth Man in the Fire' (1.8), in which vampire Eric takes a soothing bath at Bill's house, surrounded by white candles and listening to Old Swedish folk music. The scene deliberately plays with viewers' expectations: Bill comes home and is startled by the sound of music coming from upstairs. Suspicious, he sneaks up the stairs and to his (and the audience's) surprise, instead

Figure 3.10 Damon performing for the female gaze (3.1). *The Vampire Diaries* © Warner Bros. Entertainment Inc. 2009–17. All rights reserved.

of an attacker, he finds Eric in his bathtub, naked, eyes closed and fully relaxed (see Figure 3.11). Eric, the former Viking warrior, is further portrayed as camp in 'Keep This Party Going' (2.2), when he spends parts of the episode walking around with aluminium foil in his chin-long hair while in the process of dyeing it platinum blonde. The episode expands the campy physical comedy when Eric, after brutally killing and dismembering a man, is worried that blood spilled onto his hair because this would not only ruin the dyeing process but would also force him to have to apologize to Pam (Kristin Bauer), his second in command and, apparently, his hairdresser.

In conclusion, based on the camp features of humour, irony, theatricality and timing, *The Vampire Diaries* manages to playfully destabilize gendered behaviour and gaze paradigms. The frequent overtly ironic positioning of Damon as object of the gaze suggests the showrunners' awareness of tropes and traditions of gender-specific representation, which they intentionally play with. As we have seen, the previously described parody of stereotypically 'female' practices in 'The Birthday' (3.1) is part of Damon's camp role in the series in general. Because it draws attention to the constructedness of gender

Figure 3.11 Eric relaxing in the bath (1.8). *True Blood* © Home Box Office Inc. 2008–14. All rights reserved.

roles by juxtaposing 'male' and 'female' stereotypes, Damon's camp performance for the straight female gaze can be read as a subversive strategy undermining the gender order.

Vampires and the ambiguities of the female gaze in postfeminist culture

This chapter has provided a detailed analysis of the ways in which the *Twilight* Saga, *The Vampire Diaries* and *True Blood* enact a gaze reflecting a specifically female (heterosexual, white) perspective. In doing so, the texts offer pleasurable opportunities for identification with the young female protagonists Bella, Elena and Sookie. Actively gazing upon their vampire lovers, the heroines are the subjects whose desires propel the action and whose experiences are relayed to audiences. Included in their experience is also the feeling of being gazed at – Soloway's 'gazed gaze' (2016). As this chapter has demonstrated, besides providing enjoyable moments of sexual subjectivity and pleasure, the female gaze in the examined vampire series also acts as 'a cultural critic' (ibid.) by offering critical commentary on the contemporary postfeminist culture in which women and girls continue to be pressured and constrained by the constant presence of a male/patriarchal gaze. In foregrounding the perspective of the female protagonists as they become romantically and sexually involved with male vampires – socially excluded creatures – the narratives place emphasis on the experiences of (white, cis, heterosexual, able-bodied) women as they attempt to navigate the complicated sexual mores of a society that is influenced by feminism, yet still patriarchally structured. The vampire, a figure whose Otherness has traditionally linked it with 'femininity' and the transgression of (gendered) boundaries, is well suited to take up a position that is usually reserved for female characters in film and TV, namely becoming the sexualized object of the gaze. The vampire's fluctuation between 'masculine' and 'feminine' positions also opens it up to bring into operation the potentially subversive approach of camp. Thus, through the strategic use of the vampire figure, these paranormal romances offer resistant spaces in which gendered power relations are destabilized and in which heterosexual female desire is validated and rewarded.

The straight female gaze characterizing these vampire romances can be situated in the context of a more sex-positive/sexualized postfeminist climate in which '[s]exuality/femininity . . . undergoes a process of resignification whereby it comes to be associated with feminist ideas of female emancipation and self-determination rather than its previous connotations of patriarchal oppression and subjugation' (Genz and Brabon 2009: 93). Thus, contemporary postfeminism, which stands in the tradition of 1970s pro-sex feminist strands (ibid.: 91), frames heterosexuality and sex as a positive realm, inviting the celebration of 'the pleasures of feminine adornment and sexuality' (ibid.: 93). The postfeminist sex-positive stance has been explored under a variety of terms. For instance, in their study on postfeminism, Genz and Brabon address raunch culture and 'do-me feminism – . . . "bimbo feminism" and "porno chic"' (ibid.: 91). Crucially, the emergence of this type of feminism is embedded in the context of a contemporary culture that is increasingly sexualized (ibid.: 100). The mainstreaming of pornographic aesthetics is part of this trend, and so is an increasing amount of sexual explicitness in advertising, film and television alike (ibid.: 101).

When it comes to this pervasively sexualized and/or sexually open culture, both positive and negative aspects can be identified. On the one hand, Roach argues that 'the category of what's culturally acceptable in love and romance has in many quarters grown much bigger. The slow but ongoing success of the LGBTQ movements . . . is part of . . . this . . . as is increasing social acceptance for difference and diversity in gender expression and sexual orientation based on a notion of informed consent' (2016: 79). In the wake of the sexual revolution, which challenged a variety of traditional sexual norms, sex before and outside of marriage or any other long-term monogamous commitment has become increasingly accepted and common; contraception, abortion and sex education have become normalized; and the discussion of one's sexuality is not nearly as taboo as it used to be. More sexual freedoms are available today, perhaps especially to young women (ibid.: 78–9). On the other hand, Gill denounces the 'uneven gender effects' (2007: 38) of this increasingly sexualized culture and particularly the mainstreaming of pornography, pointing out that it is women's bodies in particular that are subject to sexualization and commodification. As she argues, '[c]ontemporary femininity is constructed as a *bodily characteristic*' (ibid.: 91; emphasis in original), which means that in current media culture, 'femininity' is 'defined . . . as the possession of a young, able-bodied, heterosexual, "sexy" body' (ibid.). Meanwhile, this focus on the sexualized body cannot be found in contemporary constructions of 'masculinity', although men's bodies – as this chapter has demonstrated – are also increasingly objectified and coded as sexually desirable.

Clearly, contemporary sex-positive/sexualized culture and shifting sexual norms come with both new freedoms and constraints. As Rhonda Nicol argues, '[i]f there are more possibilities available to young women than ever before, there are equally more opportunities for failure, and unwise choices carry penalties' (2011: 120). New societal notions concerning sexuality in general and women's sexuality in particular may point towards an overturning of outdated sexual mores, but women and girls continue to be confronted with contradictory demands concerning their performance of sexuality and 'femininity'. While they are expected to perform successfully sexually once they are with the 'right' partner, which suggests that a certain amount of sexual knowledge and experience is demanded, they must acquire this experience in a context in which 'the pernicious and enduring double standard that a woman is nasty and vulgar if she revels in sex' (Roach 2016: 88) persists. To meet society's expectations in terms of sexuality is, at best, a delicate balancing act or, at worst, entirely impossible for women (Nicol 2011: 119–20). If, decades ago, young women were expected to adhere to the ideal of the virgin, with the idea of the 'whore' being invoked as a foil, women today 'are supposed to look sexy but not seek out sex, to be both whore and virgin at the same time' (Roach 2016: 100).

It is in this context of an increasingly sex-positive/sexualized postfeminist culture, with both its pitfalls and possibilities, that the *Twilight* Saga, *The Vampire Diaries* and *True Blood* must be understood. Through their representation of an active (heterosexual) female gaze, the texts connect with postfeminist discourses surrounding female (sexual) subjectivity and sexual empowerment. Essentially, they embody the postfeminist 'shift from the portrayal of women as *sex objects* to the portrayal of women as *active and desiring sexual subjects*' (Gill 2007: 89; emphases in original). In doing so, these texts are both a reflection of changing cultural attitudes towards what is acceptable sexually and a major contributing factor in the circulation of positive images of (straight) female desire and sexuality in the face of enduring constraints and denials of the latter in the larger culture. Considering that '[s]ociety's dread of women who own their desire, and use it in ways that confound expectations of proper female sexuality, persists' (Penley et al. 2013: 14), the portrayal of Bella, Elena and Sookie pursuing desires that can be described as transgressive – after all, their lovers are non-human creatures and therefore essentially Other – opens up a space of resistance to the patriarchal culture. As Crawford asserts, Bella's 'desires are mad, illogical, amoral, impossible, anti-social, wildly excessive – and yet, by some dream-logic, by the end . . . every single one of them has been fulfilled. For many readers[/viewers], anxious about what and when and to what extent they may be permitted to desire at all, this has clearly been exhilarating stuff' (2014: 172).

Because the gaze is primarily available to the white, cis, heterosexual, young and able-bodied female protagonists of the *Twilight* Saga, *The Vampire Diaries* and *True Blood*, it is more accurate to speak of a white straight female gaze here. While the representation of white, heterosexual women's active gazes in popular culture is potentially a step forward from the previously claimed 'unrepresentability of woman as subject of desire' (Smelik 2007: 496), the portrayal of Jacob's character in the *Twilight* Saga shows that the representation of Native Americans in American popular culture is still guided by centuries-old tropes like the 'Noble Savage'. Although it could be argued that the presentation of Jacob's body does not have the sadistic undertone that often accompanies fetishistic scopophilia in traditional Hollywood film because his body is never presented in fragmented close-ups, his casual sexual objectification through a white cinematic gaze remains highly problematic. Another critical aspect regarding the *Twilight* Saga is the fact that heterosexual desire is presented as the unquestioned norm in the texts. Through the strictly heterosexual conception of desire in the Saga, any alternative figurations of desire or sexual identity are completely erased. A similar situation can be found in *The Vampire Diaries*, where nonheterosexual models of desire are kept to a minimum[6] and where female characters of colour, such as Bonnie Bennet, are not afforded the same subject position as the white female lead.[7] In *True Blood*, Tara Thornton suffers a similarly grim fate as Bonnie regarding her (sexual) agency;[8] however, this series offers more conceptions of gay and/or queer sexualities than the other two texts. As Jess Butler has convincingly argued, 'rather than simply an exclusion of racial and sexual others, postfeminism primarily represents an *affirmation* of a white heterosexual subject' (2013: 49; emphasis in original), and this aspect emerges here as well. Some scholars have pointed out that the attainment of sexual subjecthood is linked to even more restrictive conditions in postfeminist culture. For instance, Gill writes that 'it is important to note that only *some* women (beautiful, slim, young) are attributed sexual subjecthood' (2007: 91; emphasis in original), so that for example women who are considered obese, ugly, hairy or wrinkled tend to be excluded from the empowerment narrative, even if they may be white, cis and heterosexual. Not surprisingly, Bella, Elena and Sookie all fall into the restricted category of women whose sexual subjecthood is commonly represented in popular media. Even more clearly than Bella and Elena, Sookie seems to epitomize the postfeminist ideal of the white, straight, cis, young woman endowed with a sexy body and a particularly 'feminine' appearance. As was alluded to in my analysis, Sookie undoubtedly represents the postfeminist phenomenon of the 'do-me feminist' (Genz and Brabon 2009: 92).

As defined by Genz and Brabon, the do-me feminist 'consciously employs her physical appearance and sexuality in order to . . . gain control over her life'. By adopting a sexual/'feminine' agency, she is 'both feminine and feminist at the same time, merging notions of personal empowerment with the visual display of sexuality' (ibid.). In the case of Sookie, this idea is mirrored in the scenes in which she draws power from appealing to the male gaze. As my analysis has shown, Sookie repeatedly uses her sexy body as well as her seduction techniques to gain advantages for herself, be it in her professional or her personal life. In the process, she allows her body to become sexualized by the gaze of male characters and the camera. However, Sookie is represented here not as a 'passive, objectified sex object, but a woman who [is] knowingly playing with her sexual power' (Gill 2007: 89). Importantly, in the postfeminist logic, this is 'power feminism' (Wolf [1993] 1994: 147) in which self-objectification is not indicative of women's subordinate position in society but 'in fact a strategy of "empowerment"' (Gill 2007: 92). In this respect, it is striking that in each of the examined scenes, the narrative and/or dialogue underline that Sookie is acting from a position of 'feminist' strength, struggling to seize power in a sexist conflict, when she actively chooses to cater to the male gaze. Meanwhile, one cannot deny that Sookie does embody the conventional features of the straight male fantasy, which works as a prerequisite for being endowed with agency in the postfeminist cultural logic (ibid.: 258). It is here that the dissemination of pornographic aesthetics into mainstream culture plays a central role.

Many critics dismiss the empowering potential of the equation of sex and power. In fact, some argue that do-me feminism and raunch culture actually exacerbate the sexual objectification of women's bodies while tricking women into thinking that they are sexual subjects (Genz and Brabon 2009: 103). For instance, Gill finds that the self-chosen objectification 'represents a shift from an external judging male gaze to a self-policing narcissistic gaze' (2007: 90). In this view, a pornographic aesthetics is adopted by women as their own, a process through which they actively participate in the repetition of sexist stereotypes. While such criticisms rightfully emphasize the dangers with which sex-positive/sexualized culture is fraught, they fall short with regard to 'the potential for resignification that is lodged within the re-articulations of sexuality' (Genz and Brabon 2009: 104). Thus, in accordance with postfeminism's central feature of contradictoriness, female sexual subjecthood in the contemporary age encompasses both empowerment and subordination. In this paradoxical construction, women become both subject and object at the same time, highlighting 'the complex identity positions that women take up in contemporary society, as both a conscious and unconscious "choice"' (ibid.: 105). As Genz and Brabon write with reference to Ang's *Living Room Wars* (1996), many women in the postfeminist era 'can be said to reside in a strangely unsettled in-between space . . . What makes this contemporary critical site so thought-provoking and contentious is precisely the varying degrees of "freedom" and "boundedness", with critics vigorously debating as to where this precarious balance lies' (ibid.). Thus, the degrees of empowerment and subordination are debatable and may vary from case to case.

When it comes to *True Blood*, the first couple of seasons offer scenes that are more clearly readable as examples of Sookie's empowered (sexual) subjecthood. Placed alongside instances in which Sookie's active gaze and perspective are privileged, a scene like her dream sequence, in which she confidently demands that Bill and Eric accept her conditions for the continuation of their mutual sexual relationship, can be interpreted as demonstrating 'one of the central tenets of postfeminist ideology: that sexual attractiveness is a source of power over patriarchy rather than subjection to it' (Roberts 2007: 233). While the camera work does objectify Sookie's body, she presents herself as a sexual subject in charge of her own fantasy. In later seasons, especially in season six, Sookie's self-chosen objectification becomes less and less plausible and more often a pretext for the showrunners to sexualize Sookie's body in classic male gaze fashion. Furthermore, such scenes appear in a context in which Sookie's subjective gaze is no longer represented, and in which for female characters overall, the objectification of their own bodies seems to become the only option of acquiring agency. Here, 'the promise of power by becoming [the] object ... of desire' (Gill 2007: 90) rings rather hollow and restrictive, and it is doubtful whether a resignification of 'femininity'/sexuality was ever the goal of this kind of representation.

As such, then, proponents of sex-positive/sexualized postfeminist culture operate 'in the controversial gap between sexual objectification and liberation' (Genz and Brabon 2009: 97). Seeing as they rely on practices of re-assigning meanings – fittingly, Sookie attempts to reclaim the word 'whore', as discussed earlier – their objective is the reclamation and re-articulation of 'femininity' and sexuality as active and pleasurable. Characteristic for these postfeminist strands is 'not only a sexy kind of feminism but also an implicit acceptance of the fact that this sexualised feminist stance is necessarily embedded in popular culture' (ibid.: 96). As touched upon in Chapter 1, a media-friendly angle is typical of postfeminism's approach; feminist discourses are now firmly anchored in the contemporary media landscape. While operating from an 'insider position within popular culture' (ibid.:

70) may be beneficial in terms of the ways in which (post)feminist notions can be distributed and normalized in the larger culture, a common criticism has been that, by becoming mainstream, feminism might be rendered less radical (ibid.: 25). For instance, Andi Zeisler has argued in *We Were Feminists Once: From Riot Grrrl to CoverGirl®, the Buying and Selling of a Political Movement* (2016) that by focusing on being 'sellable' (xii), feminism has become 'decontextualized. It's depoliticized' (xiii). Considering popular culture a site that is inherently compromised by the interests of advertisers and the market, Zeisler maintains that instead of continuing to push a collective feminist agenda to challenge the societal status quo, what she terms 'marketplace feminism' (2016: xiii) exclusively addresses women as individuals. In the meantime, 'the actual issues crucial to feminism's forward movement, are as threatened as ever' (ibid.: xiii–xiv) but are brushed off by a feminism that does not take into account structurally and institutionally based inequalities.

It is in this area of conflict that the *Twilight* Saga, *The Vampire Diaries* and *True Blood* exist. On the one hand, the commercial nature of these highly popular texts cannot be dismissed. The privileging of a female gaze may be driven in part by girls' and women's desires, but it may also be understood as a marketing strategy to draw in (straight, white) female viewers. As a result, there is a danger that the supposed (sexual) empowerment proffered by the narratives is actually a façade constructed to lure in viewers, and that indeed, 'feminism's entry into the popular is . . . a damaging attempt to manage and contain the revolutionary potential of the feminist enterprise' (Genz and Brabon 2009: 19). Ariel Levy warns that '[r]aunch culture isn't about opening our minds to the possibilities and mysteries of sexuality. It's about endlessly reiterating one particular – and particularly commercial – shorthand for sexiness' ([2005] 2006: 29–30). With regard to the examined vampire romances, especially *True Blood* runs the risk of simply 'repeat[ing] and giv[ing] flesh to old sexist stereotypes' (Roach 2016: 81) in later seasons, since the series represents Sookie in increasingly sexualized ways; at the same time, no convincing element of empowerment is offered by her depiction as a do-me feminist. On the other hand, it is too 'convenient to conclude that sexual subjecthood is a commercial media ploy' (Genz and Brabon 2009: 104). Instead of conceiving postfeminism's intricate involvement with the popular as an indication of its depoliticization, I suggest that the *Twilight* Saga, *The Vampire Diaries* and *True Blood* do important and sustainable cultural work. Notions of straight female (sexual) agency, pleasure and subjecthood may be particularly media-friendly and 'sellable' topics (Zeisler 2016: xv), but this does not mean that they are without substance. On the contrary, the preceding systematic, in-depth analysis has shown that these paranormal romance texts address and challenge conventional structures of looking in Hollywood film and mainstream television. Here, viewers may not only be drawn in by the representation and validation of active heterosexual female desire but also by the acknowledgement and negotiation of how it feels to become the object of the male/patriarchal gaze from a female perspective.

In this respect, it is interesting that '[a]dvocates of th[e] late twentieth-century sexualised feminist culture call for a vision of the future that is a continuation of the freedoms of the sexual revolution coupled with an awareness of sexual oppression activated by the feminist movement' (Genz and Brabon 2009: 96). As was brought out by my analysis, both *Twilight* and *True Blood* not only explore how male entitlement and structural power materialize in the form of gazes and attempts to control women's bodies in public as well as private spaces. They also shed light on 'how the continuum of men's intrusive practices plays a key . . . role in women's experience of their embodiment as contradictory and ambiguous' (Vera-Gray 2017: 164). Faced with different challenges and/or opportunities at different times, Bella and Sookie find different ways and strategies to deal with, avoid, circumvent, ignore, address, fight, accept, play with or reframe the situations in which they find themselves. In this way, the two series not only illustrate 'the multifaceted and complex ways in which structural oppression impacts, conflicts, points to and limits choice and action' (ibid.: 4), but they also highlight '[t]he complex, multiple and uneasy ways in which women individually . . . live our agency in the current gender order' (ibid.: 48). Part of this complexity is that women, in more than one way, are simultaneously rendered subject and object, which these vampire series illustrate so poignantly. Considering the cultural work that the *Twilight* Saga, *The Vampire Diaries* and *True Blood* do in combining the 'gazed gaze' with an active desiring gaze, it makes sense to conceive, with Soloway, the 'privileging of a female point-of-view . . . as a political tool to generate empathy and, ultimately, demand sociopolitical justice' (2016). Thus, far from being depoliticized, the *Twilight* Saga, *The Vampire Diaries* and *True Blood* are postfeminist texts whose representations of a (straight, white) female gaze offer resistance to heteronormative definitions of desire and agency.

4

Vampire transformation as makeover
The making of ideal postfeminist subjects

The body is a central and recurring topic in contemporary Gothic narratives. In fact, in his description of recent developments within the genre, Xavier Aldana Reyes refers to 'the body and its transformation as the ultimate site of Gothic inscription' (2014: 389). Texts featuring body horror typically display an obsession with metamorphosis and the limits of the body (ibid.: 397) and are rooted in a 'public anxiety about gender, mortality, and control' (Badley 1996: 6). The fascination with physical as well as identity changes in the *Twilight* Saga, *The Vampire Diaries* and, to a degree, *True Blood* can be ascribed to the teen genre, in which the figure of the vampire is used to negotiate issues connected with adolescence, coming of age and the ensuing corporeal changes as well as shifting social relationships and power dynamics (Wilson Overstreet 2006: 15). What is narrated in these texts is a young girl's gradual entrance into adulthood. Thus, while these series may be famous for their male vampires – Edward Cullen, the Salvatore brothers, Bill Compton and Eric Northman being the most prominent ones – when it comes to the powerful *transition* from human to vampire, the emphasis is clearly on female characters undergoing the transformation on screen. As I argue in this chapter, the vampiric transformation, which is framed as a narrative of personal growth, discipline and control for the female protagonists, is rooted in the context of contemporary postfeminist culture. I thus contend that Bella Swan from the *Twilight* Saga, Caroline Forbes from *The Vampire Diaries* and Jessica Hamby from *True Blood* all epitomize the paradox of the active/passive female postfeminist subject, individually empowered and simultaneously ruled by social norms.

One way in which the postfeminist subject is frequently established is the painful process of a makeover, which has become ubiquitous in contemporary film and television. As Diane Negra points out, '[i]n a postfeminist consumer culture the makeover is a key ritual of female coming into being' (2009: 123). Perhaps less obviously than in reality programmes like *The Swan* (Fox, 2004) or teen movies like *She's All That* (1999) and *The Princess Diaries* (2001), I suggest that makeovers play a central role in the *Twilight* Saga, *The Vampire Diaries* and *True Blood*. Corresponding to broader postfeminist discourses, Bella's, Caroline's and Jessica's postfeminist vampiric makeovers can be understood as acts of personal empowerment permitting these characters a new sense of agency, while also demonstrating an aspect of consumer culture that endorses the constant disciplinary shaping of the self by way of working on the body. Heike Steinhoff and Maria Verena Siebert have previously addressed the makeover trope in Stephenie Meyer's *Twilight* novels; I will transfer their findings to the film adaptations and will further explore the ways in which the other two texts make use of this trope. By relating these paranormal romances to postfeminist/neoliberal media culture, this chapter will investigate how discourses surrounding self-surveillance, body work and subjectivation are incorporated and negotiated in the *Twilight* Saga, *The Vampire Diaries* and *True Blood*.

Neoliberalism, postfeminism and the female body

Postfeminism's fundamental entanglement with neoliberalism has already been addressed in Chapter 1. However, the conglomerate of neoliberal and postfeminist discourses deserves a closer look for the purposes of this chapter. Rosalind Gill and Christina Scharff define neoliberalism as 'a mode of political and economic rationality characterized by privatization, deregulation and a rolling back and withdrawal of the state from many areas of social provision that rose to prominence in the 1980s under the Reagan administration in the US and Thatcher's premiership in the UK' (2011a: 5). Most relevant for this study, a crucial aspect of neoliberalism is the transferral of a range of 'quasi-market mechanisms' (ibid.: 6) to other spheres of life. Thus, individual responsibility is internalized by neoliberal subjects with regard to all kinds of areas, such as work, health or social life (ibid.). As 'subjects who are constituted as self-managing, autonomous and enterprising' (ibid.: 5), individuals living in a neoliberal culture are encouraged to forge their self-identity on the basis of a series of lifestyle choices (Genz and Brabon 2009: 166). In other words, by continuously shaping their lives, individuals come to be seen as 'entrepreneurs' or 'enterprises of the self' (ibid.: 170). The shift towards the neoliberalist ideas of autonomous and 'entrepreneurial subjectivity' (Gill and Scharff 2011a: 6) has taken place in an era characterized not only by a loss of faith in the authority of science and other universalist 'grand narratives' (Pilcher and Whelehan [2004] 2011: 110) but also by the decline of other traditions. Life stories are less and less socially prescribed, work biographies no longer carved in stone and lifestyle options have become increasingly divergent (Genz and Brabon 2009: 170). As a result, 'identities in general have become more diverse and malleable and, today more than ever, individuals can construct a narrative of the self' (ibid.: 169–70). The latter is what Anthony Giddens refers to as 'the reflexive project of the self' (1991: 180). Crucially, the construction of an individualized self-identity must be understood as 'an ongoing project that demands the active participation of the subject' (Genz and Brabon 2009: 170).

Individualization is one of the central aspects through which neoliberalism and postfeminism are connected. Thus, Gill and Scharff argue that individualism is at the core of both phenomena in the sense that notions of collectivism or 'any idea of individuals as subject to pressures, constraints or influence from outside themselves' (2011a: 7) are discarded. Postfeminism is not interested in looking at the systemic structures shaping the lives of individuals. Rather, postfeminist discourses suggest that, in the aftermath of the tremendous successes of second wave feminism, women now act as autonomous agents in a world in which gendered power imbalances have been eradicated (Gill 2007: 260). In this understanding, women are free to steer their life into any direction they wish, as long as they work hard enough to get there. As Gill and Scharff point out, 'the autonomous, calculating, self-regulating subject of neoliberalism bears a strong resemblance to the active, freely choosing, self-inventing subject of postfeminism' (2011a: 7). In fact, postfeminism, which 'naturalizes a model of feminine identity and female power inseparable from consumption' (Roberts 2007: 232), is deeply intertwined with neoliberal consumerism. Within the frame of the latter, a new relationship between body and self has developed (Featherstone 1991: 187): Mike Featherstone underlines the 'significance of appearance and bodily preservation within late capitalist society' (1991: 170). Advertising in this society keeps reminding the individual that self-improvement is possible and necessary in all aspects of life (ibid.: 172), and so does the cornucopia of beauty apps and self-help guides available online (Gill 2017: 617; 618). This has resulted in 'ascribed bodily qualities to become regarded as plastic – with effort and "body work" individuals are persuaded that they can achieve a certain desired appearance' (Featherstone 1991: 187). Consequently, individuals assume self-responsibility for the way they look and the body is perceived as a 'mirror' of the self. In the same way that 'fitness and slimness become associated not only with energy, drive and vitality but worthiness as a person' (ibid.: 183), bodily neglect can be taken as 'an indication of laziness, low self-esteem and even moral failure' (ibid.: 186). In this way, someone whose body does not correspond to conventional beauty standards may become less acceptable as a person.

On the one hand, body work is seen as a way of pleasurable self-expression and self-actualization for individuals. The more a body resembles an ideal young, healthy, fit and beautiful body, the more value it seems to be awarded in the culture (Fraser and Greco 2005a: 28), so the achievement of such a body becomes a way to actively increase one's value. Furthermore, postfeminist/neoliberal logic opens up a space for the expression of politicized agency for women based on their bodies (Genz and Brabon 2009: 171). Patricia Mann has proposed a theory of individual agency, which she refers to as 'gendered micro-politics' (1994: 1). Taking into account the different identity positions available to individuals, she argues that '[w]e are micro-political agents insofar as we manage to operate within various institutional discourses without ever being fully inscribed within any of the familial, military, economic, or other corporate frames of reference that engage us' (ibid.: 31). Micro-politics can be engaged in through individual and daily gender-based interactions and practices (Gamble [1998] 2009a: 172). Genz and Brabon discuss the example of sexual micro-politics in particular: in a climate of increasing sexualization of contemporary culture and the sexualized portrayal of women as knowing sexual subjects (see Chapter 3), the scholars see everyday fashion practices as containing 'the seeds of a sexual micro-politics whereby women/girls use their bodies as political tools to gain empowerment within the parameters of a capitalist economy' (2009: 175). On the other hand, Mariam Fraser and Monica Greco describe the process of optimizing the body as 'a disciplining force, placing even greater burdens on individuals' (2005a: 28). Gill, too, is convinced that the shift towards entrepreneurial subjectivity 'represents a higher or deeper form of exploitation' because in this new 'disciplinary regime', 'power is not imposed from above or from the outside, but constructs our very subjectivity' (2007: 258). As she maintains, agency is afforded to the individual only upon condition that he or she becomes a particular kind of individual – one whose body is in line with sexist, racist, classist, ageist, ableist standards (ibid.). Concurringly, McRobbie calls out 'the regulative dimensions of the popular discourses of personal choice and self improvement' in which the 'individual is compelled to be the kind of subject who can make the right choices' (2007: 36).

Over the past fifteen to twenty years, the notion that individuals need to constantly monitor themselves and their bodies has been exacerbated, especially due to the spread of social media and online cultures (Gill 2017: 617). Looking at this time frame, which coincides with the original releases of the *Twilight* Saga, *The Vampire Diaries* and *True Blood*, the occurrence of both shifts and continuities in neoliberal postfeminist discourses can be identified. One major catalyst for these shifts was the 2008 financial crisis, which entailed a marked general decline in national economies globally. Because of the global recession, financial agency and success have become harder to attain even for the most privileged individuals. Consequently, while celebratory, optimistic neoliberal postfeminist discourses were dominating early twenty-first-century culture, post-2008, empowerment no longer lies in acts of material consumption. Rather, the focus is placed even more on the body, which has taken 'centre stage in [the] production of authenticity' (Genz 2017: 26) and in 'constituting the self' (Dejmanee 2016: 127). While the idea of pleasing oneself was highly dependent on one's purchasing power and financial independence prior to the economic crisis, now 'more attention is paid to the body as a source of personal pleasure' (ibid.: 130) via acts of physical consumption and 'aesthetic labour' (Elias, Gill and Scharff 2017a: 37). Thus, surveilling one's body and (increasingly) one's psychic disposition has become even more significant in today's postfeminist culture (Gill 2017: 616–19).

Women are the main addressees of the now ubiquitous demand to monitor and optimize oneself (Featherstone 1991: 179; Gill and Scharff 2011a: 7; McRobbie 2015: 4; Gill 2017: 617). This is doubtlessly reflected in the social expectation for women to resort to an intense regime of personal grooming, like waxing, tanning, manicures and pedicures (Negra 2009: 119), or to consider even more permanent forms of body enhancement like cosmetic surgery. This 'heightened form of self-regulation', to which women are called upon to aspire, has been referred to by McRobbie as 'the perfect' (2015: 9). A striking feature of 'the perfect' is the ability to make its emphasis on individualization and competitiveness compatible with feminism by urging women to exhibit 'an inner drive, a determination to meet a set of self-directed goals' (ibid.: 12). More precisely, the promise of 'the perfect' lies in the achievement of female success, including 'an illusion of control, . . . sexual pleasure, . . . longevity to those who undertake the required amount of personal maintenance' (ibid.: 7). Women are persuaded to choose between different personal grooming and lifestyle options in order to outwardly 'perform' success. Curiously, this performance is also considered to induce 'inner' pleasure: notions of 'being self-determined' and 'pleasing yourself', for instance by 'using beauty' to make oneself feel good and sexy, are central to postfeminist logic (Gill 2007: 259). Thus, the postfeminist emphasis on self-improvement is intimately related to its stress upon personal choice (ibid.: 261). In this context, the body is 'presented simultaneously as women's source of power *and* as always already unruly and requiring constant monitoring, surveillance, discipline and remodelling' (ibid.: 255; emphasis in original). The fact that women in particular are urged to manage and optimize their bodies and selves is suggestive of the strong connection between neoliberalism and postfeminism, according to Gill and Scharff (2011a: 7). In any case, the 'powerful resonance between postfeminism and neoliberalism' (ibid.) becomes palpable in the postfeminist trope of the makeover, which is taken up by the *Twilight* Saga, *The Vampire Diaries* and *True Blood*, as this chapter will demonstrate.

'Born to be a vampire': Bella Swan's vampire makeover

Steinhoff and Siebert have read the *Twilight* series as a makeover narrative, in the frame of which the transformation works 'both as a disciplinary mechanism that functions to transform female bodies in line with patriarchal heteronormative norms of gender and sexuality *and* an experience of female empowerment where the body becomes a project of absolute makeability, a means of self-realization for the female agent' (2011: 2; emphasis in original). This oscillation between two contradictory points is an essential aspect of the makeover trope and indicates its embeddedness in postfeminist discourse. As will become clear throughout this chapter, it is a common thread in the *Twilight* Saga, *The Vampire Diaries* and *True Blood*. While the texts may differ considerably in some respects, they share a focus on external and internal changes requiring the active involvement of the subject and signalling the achievement of a successful self. In the *Twilight Saga*, Bella represents a portrayal of female vampiric transition which, on the one hand, is very different from Caroline (*The Vampire Diaries*) and Jessica (*True Blood*), as vampirism in Bella's case implies not the transgression, but actually a clear reinforcement of the traditional female gender role. On the other hand, Bella's transformation narrative follows a similar logic as Caroline's and Jessica's: it is one of personal growth and empowerment on the basis of self-control.

As a human, Bella is primarily characterized by her physical vulnerability and lack of control. Thus, she starts out from a position in which she holds little power. Not only is Bella portrayed as having trouble with daily physical activities but she is also considerably weaker than most of her vampire and shapeshifter friends due to her human nature. Since she is defenceless in the face of all ordinary and particularly supernatural threats, Bella repeatedly depends on being rescued by Edward, Jacob and other male characters. She recognizes that the only way to reverse Edward's and her role is to become a vampire, too: 'I could protect you if you change me' (*New Moon* 2009). Bella's lack of power is also reflected in the fact that she has little agency when it comes to steering the course of her life, as Edward and/or Jacob tend to pull the strings. In *Eclipse*, the two young men discuss which life script would be the best option for Bella. Jacob argues: 'You have to consider that I might be better for her than you are', while Edward relents: 'I have considered that. I know you can protect her. . . . you can give her . . . a human life, that's all I want for her.' Between them, Bella is lying fast asleep, unable to weigh in on the conversation and decide her own fate.[1]

In essence, Bella's powerlessness is implied through the portrayal of her body, which is presented as specifically human as well as specifically 'feminine', that is: inherently flawed. In *Twilight*, Bella constantly slips, stumbles and trips over things. She refers to herself as 'uncoordinated', and Edward is annoyed by her extreme clumsiness: 'Can you at least watch where you walk?' (*Twilight* 2008). Bella's body, then, is portrayed as 'unruly': 'soft, potentially dangerous to everyone around, and a source of humiliation for the subject' – in short: 'abject' (Steinhoff and Siebert 2011: 5). Julia Kristeva has theorized that the abject must be 'radically excluded' ([1980] 1982: 2) from the place of the living subject, 'propelled away from the body and deposited on the other side of an imaginary border which separates the self from that which threatens the self' (Creed [1993] 2007: 9). Thus, central to the conception of the abject is the idea of a border: that which crosses or threatens to disturb the border of 'identity, system, order' (Kristeva [1980] 1982: 4) is abject. The female body crosses a number of such borders that stabilize the paternal regime. By undercutting the symbolic order and thereby highlighting its fragility, 'femininity' becomes monstrous. In defining Bella's body as inherently lacking and in need of discipline, the *Twilight* Saga is consistent with such cultural notions that construct 'femininity' not only as close to nature and the body but also as monstrous (Steinhoff and Siebert 2011: 9). Barbara Creed has argued that 'when woman is represented as monstrous it is almost always in relation to her mothering and reproductive functions' ([1993] 2007: 7), or the monstrousness is linked directly to questions of sexual desire. A representation of what Creed calls the 'monstrous-feminine' (ibid.: 1) can be found in Bella's 'monstrous' pregnancy in the *Twilight* Saga. Here, the female body's supposed inclination to be excessive and out of control is showcased right before the normalizing makeover is performed on Bella (Steinhoff and Siebert 2011: 9): immediately after the horrific birth of her daughter, Bella is turned into a vampire by Edward to save her life.

The conception of Bella's and Edward's child is unplanned and unexpected. Assuming that Edward's vampire body cannot father any children, the couple was engaging in unprotected sex. This assumption, however, turns out to be inaccurate. While female vampires in the *Twilight* universe are infertile, the male vampire body continues to be able to reproduce, which 'upholds men's natural role as the spreader of the seed' (McGeough 2010: 95). The events leading to Bella's realization that she is pregnant set the tone for the grotesque nature of the scenes that follow. It is during her honeymoon that Bella wakes up in the morning and eats peanut butter from the jar, yoghurt and fried poultry for breakfast; after the incongruous meal, she must leap to the bathroom because she is sick. Upon grabbing her toiletries, she spots an unused pack of tampons in her bag. This 'reference to menstruation and Bella's binge-eating at the beginning of the pregnancy plot signal that the horrific threat of the female body out of control that had before only been implicit will now become explicit' (Steinhoff and Siebert 2011: 8). To Bella's and the audience's surprise, not only is a little baby bump already discernible on her body but she can also feel the foetus moving inside her. As it turns out, the human–vampire hybrid foetus grows at accelerated speed, a fact that Bella's human body is not equipped to deal with. The exaggerated growth of the child, which results in its mother's body being mangled from the inside, is reminiscent of unnatural pregnancies depicted in horror and science fiction movies (Creed [1993] 2007: 44).[2]

Throughout the process of the pregnancy, Bella's body becomes increasingly sick, pale and fragile, emaciated despite the huge belly because she cannot hold any food in. Carlisle (Peter Facinelli) explains to Bella: 'The foetus isn't compatible with your body. It's too strong. It won't allow you to get the nutrition you need. It's starving you by the hour. I can't stop it, and I can't slow it down. At this rate, your heart will give up before you can deliver' (*Breaking Dawn – Part 1* 2011). In order to feed the vampire–human halfling inside of her, Bella must drink human blood, which visibly disgusts Jacob. Thus, a recurring theme within the depiction of Bella's pregnancy is the involvement of bodily wastes, such as blood and vomit – another genre convention of the modern horror film. Moreover, the text underlines continuously that the creature that Bella will give birth to violates the border of inside and outside. Although this bizarre way of nourishing herself makes her feel better temporarily, the problem remains that Bella's body suffers from the consequences of the foetus's unnaturally speedy growth: 'It's breaking her bones now. It's crushing you from the inside out' (ibid.). The awful sound of Bella's bones being crushed accompanies the scene that finally triggers the delivery of her baby: caused by a rash gesture in which she bends forward to catch a cup of blood that is falling to the ground, Bella's spine breaks. Paralleling the paper cup, which falls and results in blood being splashed across the carpet, Bella's body contorts in a grotesque way, and her knees crash to the ground. At the moment of the delivery, her body is at the height of being out of control: 'Although Bella firmly made the decision to give birth, she has little control over the experience of giving birth and ultimately must rely on the help of others to survive' (McGeough 2010: 96).

A striking circumstance is that Bella's advanced pregnancy is (initially) portrayed not from Bella's but from Jacob's perspective; this change in focal character is adopted from the book version of the series, in which Jacob narrates the complete story of Bella's pregnancy. This shift in point of view allows for the action to be portrayed from a distanced, male perspective. By this means, the threat of the monstrous–feminine to the paternal symbolic order is emphasized. Bella's pregnancy is also evaluated by the (almost exclusively) male wolf pack, whose verdict is much the same as Jacob's: 'It's growing fast. It's unnatural. Dangerous. A monstrosity. An abomination. On our land. We can't allow it. We can't allow it' (*Breaking Dawn – Part 1* 2011). Edward, Jacob and the werewolf pack consider the termination of the monstrous pregnancy the only option. Without consulting with Bella at all, Edward shuts her out of the conversation when he learns that she is pregnant. Conferring with Carlisle on the phone, he deliberately withholds what his vampire father is saying at the other end and tells Bella: 'I'm not going to let it hurt you. Carlisle will get that thing out' (ibid.). Similarly, upon learning what is happening to Bella, Jacob immediately turns to the Cullens instead of enquiring what Bella might want: 'Why haven't you done anything? Take it out of her' (ibid.). Meanwhile, Bella has already decided that she will carry the pregnancy to term, no matter the consequences. With the help of Rosalie (Nikki Reed), Edward's vampire sister, she manages to prevail against the opinions of all others who try to deny her the right to do what she wants with her own body. Thus, considering that she is voiceless in so many respects, it is all the more striking that Bella is able to make and abide by a number of important decisions in the course of the *Twilight* Saga. These choices include her entering into a love relationship with Edward (someone who, by nature, threatens Bella's life), her getting married to Edward at an early age and her carrying her unintended pregnancy full term. Moreover, Bella makes the conscious choice to become a vampire, which distinguishes her from Caroline and Jessica.

Significantly, Bella's choices are in line with conservative ideas about romantic relationships, family values and reproductive politics. For instance, Rosalie's and Bella's insistence that everyone refer to the foetus as 'baby' is essentially anti-choice rhetoric which professes to advocate for the unborn. It is in this respect that the postfeminist emphasis on individual choice and empowerment and its disregard for broader structures come into play. The text frames Bella's choices as individual ones but it ignores the gender system they may be a part of. It thus refuses to take into account the larger context in which these choices are made. Here, the *Twilight* Saga can be associated with new traditionalist strands of postfeminism. As Rosalind Gill and Elena Herdieckerhoff contend, while postfeminist agents value the freedom to make individual choices, it is telling that 'they frequently use their empowered postfeminist position to make choices that would be regarded by many second wave feminists as problematic, located as they are in normative notions of femininity' (2006: 499). A similar dynamic can be observed in the final episode of *True Blood*, in which Adele Stackhouse (Lois Smith) holds a fiery (post) feminist speech to convince the adolescent Sookie, who is worried that her disadvantageous supernatural power will impede the fulfilment of her innermost desires, that she can achieve anything she wants in life – in this case an existence as a wife and a mother: 'Stop it! I don't want to hear you talking like that. You can have any kind of life you want. You can persevere. Anything you want, Sookie, you are entitled to it. There are no limits on you if you don't put them on yourself' ('Thank You', 7.10).

After an emergency C-section, Edward turns Bella into a vampire. Steinhoff and Siebert observe that *Breaking Dawn – Part 1* remains faithful to the structure of makeover shows like *The Swan* in the sense that a man carries out the cosmetic surgery while the female patient is unconscious; the surgery is essentially 'a transforming procedure . . . that results in an improved, a revamped body' (2011: 10). This vampire transformation is entirely medicalized: instead of a passionate bite of the neck, we get a large syringe with which Edward inserts his venom into Bella's heart while she is lying on an operating table. The female makeover show candidate then has to endure intense pain, master the physical recovery and work through emotional setbacks, all the while reinventing herself in accordance with her 'new body'. Thus, in makeover shows, '[p]lastic surgery is not depicted as a process passively endured by the candidate', but the unwritten rules of plastic surgery reality TV suggest that 'it is . . . the most devoted, hard-working and radically transformed woman who wins' (ibid.). Correspondingly, Bella's working through excruciating pain is emphasized throughout the transformation process. While she seems dead on the outside, with Edward and Jacob desperately trying to administer first aid, viewers witness the ordeal she is undergoing on the inside. Her organs are literally being burned by Edward's corrosive venom and she is internally screaming in pain; the latter is 'her sacrifice in order to attain that ideal hard body of a vampire' (ibid.). Considering that throughout the film series, Bella has insisted that she wants to be made a vampire despite Edward's and everyone else's reservations, her transformation can be read as an act of triumph and female empowerment. Indeed, Edward acknowledges Bella's accomplishments in the last film: 'I've had a bad habit of underestimating you. Every obstacle you've faced, I'd think you couldn't overcome it. And you just did' (*Breaking Dawn – Part 2* 2012). At the same time, Bella is dependent on Edward to perform the 'operation' on her body; like a contestant on *The Swan*, she cannot carry out the procedure herself but must rely on the skills of a (male) expert (Steinhoff and Siebert 2011: 10).

After the transformation, Bella's new self is revealed to her when she steps in front of a mirror to finally look at herself – a revelatory gesture that is a staple in makeover reality programmes (see Figure 4.1). As a

Figure 4.1 Bella's 'mirror moment'. *Breaking Dawn – Part 2*, directed by Bill Condon © Summit Entertainment 2012. All rights reserved.

newborn vampire, Bella achieves subjectivity and agency: not only is she exceptionally beautiful but she also surpasses Edward in terms of physical strength, which he acknowledges right after Bella's transition: 'It's your turn not to break me' (*Breaking Dawn – Part 2* 2012). Her new unbreakable, untiring body enables Bella to freely enjoy her sexuality with Edward. Contrary to Jessica, who experiments with non-monogamy as a vampire, Bella finally finds fulfilment in her exclusive relationship with her husband. If her relationship had previously been threatened by the mutual attraction between Bella and Jacob, this tension is now resolved. Bella no longer sexually desires her werewolf friend who, as her sensitive vampire nose registers, gives off what Alice (Ashley Greene) has termed a 'God awful wet dog smell' (*New Moon* 2009). Vampires and werewolves/shapeshifters are 'natural enemies' (*Eclipse* 2010) in the *Twilight* universe – a famous and widely used trope in vampire/werewolf fiction. Not only does Bella 'naturally' slide into her role as a loving vampire mother but she also discovers that she has a supernatural ability that provides her with more security in dangerous situations. She is a shield, which is 'a defensive talent, . . . a very powerful gift' (*Breaking Dawn – Part 2* 2012) helping her to protect her loved ones in the family's final battle against the vampire lawmakers, the Volturi. While Caroline and Jessica make use of their vampire strength to actively fight, it is interesting that Bella's vampiric talent is a fundamentally passive one. Physically strong as she may be, she is still not as equally active and aggressive a fighter as Edward. Furthermore, her supernatural shielding ability seems to be an extension of her caring, motherly attitude; Anna Silver draws attention to Bella's shield being 'womb-like' (2010: 134), connecting the character with motherhood.

While vampirism in the *Twilight* Saga apparently works as a way of reaffirming traditional gender roles, which distinguishes *Twilight* from *The Vampire Diaries* and *True Blood*, it is crucial to note that Bella's empowerment is based on the same kind of self-discipline that Caroline and Jessica work on in their vampire lives. Contrary to everyone's expectations, Bella exhibits an unprecedented amount of self-control after her transformation. Experience shows that newborn vampires are 'at [their] most uncontrollable, vicious, insane with thirst' (*Eclipse* 2010), which is why the Cullens anticipate Bella having difficulties in dealing with her infant daughter, a vampire–human hybrid. However, during her first hunt, Bella manages to suppress her thirst for human blood and redirect it towards an animal without needing any help from Edward. When she also successfully refrains from biting her human father, Jasper (Jackson Rathbone) is impressed: 'Well done, Bella. Never seen a newborn show that kind of restraint' (*Breaking Dawn – Part 2* 2012), and Emmett (Kellan Lutz) jokes: 'Not sure she *is* a newborn. She's so tame' (ibid.; emphasis in original). In fact, before discovering her shielding ability, Bella assumes that her supernatural gift is 'super self-control' (ibid.). Having inhabited an inherently insufficient body as a human, 'Bella claims ownership and control over her body as a vampire, and it is through her transformation that she finally becomes Edward's equal' (McGeough 2010: 99). In disciplining herself, Bella adopts the Cullens' way of life, which entails abstaining from drinking human blood. As Edward explains to Bella in *Twilight*: 'My family, we think of ourselves as vegetarians . . . because we only survive on the blood of animals.' Because the Cullens do not attack humans in the area in which they have taken up residence, they are able to maintain their cover. By working on their individual character and adjusting to the values of human society, they gain their place within the community of

Forks. Throughout the Saga, then, the disciplining of the vampire body is portrayed as a marker of character strength and strong morals.

Strikingly, Bella's new vampire body is coded as specifically 'masculine', in stark contrast to her human, feminized body analysed earlier (Steinhoff and Siebert 2011: 12). This 'masculine' body is weirdly at odds with her 'feminine' social role as a mother and (house)wife. In the *Twilight* Saga, the vampire body functions as the ideal body: it is 'a smooth, closed, hard surface, a static body' (ibid.) that keeps intact the border of inside and outside. Importantly, this is the body that Bella desires. As a cultural sign, a hard body indicates 'that one "cares" about oneself and how one appears to others, suggesting willpower, energy, control over infantile impulse, the ability to "shape your life"' (Bordo 2003: 195). Indeed, the Cullens control their vampire bodies through the power of their minds. Particularly Edward and his father Carlisle embody tremendous self-restraint and strength of mind, both of which are highly valued within the text. As Danielle Dick McGeough argues, Edward's 'capacity to assert reason and resolve over emotional, bodily desires reifies the mind/body dichotomy and privileges logic. . . . Because rationality and self-control function as the ideal, Edward is granted power in their relationship' (2010: 100). Of course, intellect and the mind have long been associated with 'masculinity'; the other side of the binary contains the supposedly 'feminine' body and imagination (Creeber 2006b: 52). Another aspect is that Bella's new body can no longer conceive and carry a child. Since the latter is a static body that never changes, it has neither monthly cycles nor reproductive capabilities. In this way, Bella's body's supposed connection to 'nature' is symbolically removed. Thus, although Bella assumes a traditionally 'feminine' role after her transformation, her body is, strangely, rendered more 'masculine'. It seems as if 'the perfected form of the female body is an unchanging, non-menstruating, and none-reproductive one' (McGeough 2010: 95). Curiously, however, as a vampire, Bella feels like herself for once. The fact that she finally feels at home in her made-over vampire body is in line with makeover narratives, in which 'self-transformation fuses the external and the internal. It unites physical crossings, such as passages through space or location or alterations of dress and appearance, with interior rites of passage and psychic changes through the medium of the body' (Ferriss 2008: 42).

'You're just gonna have to work that much harder': Caroline Forbes, entrepreneur of the self

The character of Caroline Forbes in *The Vampire Diaries* shows many parallels to Bella: in the course of the second season, Caroline is turned into a vampire and subsequently experiences the consequences of this makeover, which – similar to Bella's – entails elements of empowerment as well as subordination. At the beginning of the series, Caroline is still human. Contrary to Bella, she is one of the popular girls at school, the captain of the cheerleading squad, honour student and organizer of various parties and campaigns in and around the town. In season one, Caroline wins the title of 'Miss Mystic Falls', which not only testifies to her conventional physical attractiveness but also suggests that she comes from a (white) family of a higher social class. Being composed of members of the same white families since the founding of the town, the local beauty pageant openly showcases the 'most outstanding community leaders in the making' ('My Brother's Keeper', 4.7). Despite the confidence and determination she usually displays, underneath it all Caroline is insecure and always anxious not to belong. She worries about being too socially awkward to find a boyfriend and feels inferior to her best friend Elena. To a large degree, Caroline's energy and dedication are rooted in her insecurity. She regards her relationship with Elena as a competition and is frequently characterized by her friends as neurotic and an 'over-achiever' ('Our Town', 3.11). Giving up is said to be untypical or 'un-Caroline' ('Handle with Care', 5.6) of her, and Elena names 'her control-freakiness [and] her delusional positivity' ('Promised Land', 5.21) as characteristic of Caroline. Her appearance is something in which Caroline puts much effort, as is manifested more than once in her eagerness to find the perfect dress for high school parties and dances. Besides, not only is she a grade-A student in high school but she also shows the same level of ambition when she enrols in college. From the beginning, Caroline's most distinguishing traits are her zealousness and her willingness to work exceedingly hard, whether in professional or personal terms. As I argue, this predisposition makes her the ideal candidate to become a self-surveilling postfeminist subject later in the narrative. 'She likes projects', is how Matt describes her ('She's Come Undone', 4.21), and while Caroline's projects do include the organization of events like 'Senior Prank Night' and the Homecoming Dance, I argue that her predilection for projects extends to the management of the enterprise of her self.

Similar to Bella, Caroline's position before her makeover is characterized by a lack of power and agency. The first season shows the human Caroline being victimized by Damon Salvatore, who abuses her for his personal amusement and instrumentalizes her for his own ends. Among other things, he uses her to obtain information about her friends; he is also granted access to society through her, as he temporarily poses as her boyfriend. Here, Caroline resembles Lucy Westenra in Bram Stoker's *Dracula* (1897), the archetype of the female vampire victim, who is used as a tool by the Count to acquire other victims in his scheme to take over the city of London. While Lucy's vampiric transformation and her ensuing transgression of the female gender role are constructed as worth punishing in *Dracula*, Caroline's story takes a very different and decidedly positive turn after her transformation. At the beginning of season two, Caroline is turned into a vampire: after suffering severe injuries in a car accident, Damon feeds her his blood in order to heal her. With the vampire blood in her system, she is then killed by another vampire, Katherine, which leads to her transition from human to vampire. Being made into a vampire is not Caroline's choice and it is clear that in this moment she is a pawn in the hands of Katherine, who plans to use Caroline to her own advantage by forcing her to do her bidding in the subsequent episodes. The transformation itself is accompanied by a number of 'body horrors', which are evident from Caroline's cries of pain and disgust with her new physical urges. As mentioned earlier, this portrayal matches notions about makeovers requiring the active investment of pain, sweat and tears in order to be successful (Strick 2008: 296). In retrospect, Caroline describes her transition as traumatizing: 'I was alone when I turned. I had no control over my body or my urges, and I killed somebody' ('The Sacrifice', 2.10). However, after draining a man of blood in the wake of her transformation, she does not kill anyone in several months, thus showing an impressive amount of self-control for a newly turned vampire. Caroline quickly learns to adjust to her new vampire body by restraining her desire to attack humans for their blood: instead of actively murdering people, she retrieves banked human blood from hospitals. Caroline recognizes: 'I want to [kill]. It's my basic nature now. But on a healthy diet, I can control it. I'm getting better at it' ('Plan B', 2.6). A decisive factor in her restraint is her predilection for disciplining herself, her mind and her body. As Stefan comments: 'Neat, organized Caroline. Staying within lines. Good at control' ('A Bird in a Gilded Cage', 6.17).

Vampiric bloodthirst in *The Vampire Diaries* is framed as a conflict between mind and body. Here, too, is the disciplining of the body depicted as indicative of a vampire's decent character. Caroline's suppression of her thirst is celebrated as a success within the narrative. In the *Twilight* Saga, the Cullen family's docile, good-natured disposition finds expression in the colour of their eyes: while evil vampires in *Twilight* are characterized by red eyes, which points to their thirst for human blood, the Cullens, who only hunt animals, have golden eyes after having fed. In this way, their inner disposition is literally 'written on' their bodies and can be read for example by Bella. In a similar manner, Caroline's kind nature and sense of justice become explicit in her disciplined body. Her successful enterprise of the self stands out particularly in comparison to Elena, who becomes a vampire a little later in the series. After her transformation, Elena goes completely off the rails and depends on the Salvatore brothers to stop her from endangering herself and others, as she is not at all in control of her vampire urges. In contrast to Caroline, Elena is not allowed to make her own choices because of her lack of discipline, and her transition from human to vampire does not give her access to more agency in the narrative – rather, her lack of restraint means a loss of subjectivity for her. As Elena confides in her diary: 'I lost control. . . . The worst feeling is the moment that you realize you've lost yourself' ('The Killer', 4.5).

Contrary to all other vampires in the series, Caroline manages to control her thirst even when her humanity is switched off. In the *Vampire Diaries* universe, vampires have the benefit of being able to control their emotions by shutting them off. As Damon explains: 'It's like a button you can press. . . . as a vampire, your instinct is not to feel. . . . No guilt, no shame. No regret' ('Isobel', 1.21). When Elena warns Caroline about the potentially deadly consequences of giving up one's humanity, Caroline reminds Elena: 'That is your experience, okay? I have more control over my vampire self than you ever did. My experience will be different' ('Let Her Go', 6.15). Indeed, although '[t]he point of flipping your humanity switch is that you don't care how you leave things' ('A Bird in a Gilded Cage', 6.17), Caroline – after flipping her switch – refrains from actively murdering people for pragmatic reasons. As she argues, killing humans on her college campus 'would be inconvenient. Elena, I shut off my humanity. I didn't turn into an idiot' ('The Downward Spiral', 6.16). Goal-oriented as she is, Caroline has turned off her humanity strategically to escape the grief over the death of her mother, rather than to revel in hedonism and bloodshed. In a conversation with her friends, she pleads her case: 'In return for my good behaviour, I want a year where I don't have to feel pain, or grief, or remorse' (ibid.). Caroline, while intending to reap the benefits of her vampire body, understands that she will only be allowed to exist peacefully within her community if she curbs her appetite: 'I go to school here. . . . I want to keep going to school here. The second that I draw any suspicions – break-ins, broken property, dead bodies – people will try to interrupt my routine' ('A Bird in a Gilded Cage', 6.17). As a consequence, she makes sure to divert her 'instinctual impulse into a socially acceptable activity' ('Because', 6.19).[3]

Contrary to Elena, for Caroline, vampirism turns out to be the admission ticket to an autonomous, self-determined and ultimately happier existence. Becoming a vampire restores the memories of what Damon had conveniently compelled her to forget (in the series, compulsion is a vampiric ability to control the mind of another person simply through eye contact). The recovered knowledge puts Caroline in a position to confront Damon about his actions as well as eventually overcome her victimization. In 'Brave New World' (2.2), she faces Damon in the deserted school corridor and flings him to the ground (see Figure 4.2) – a scene Rikke Schubart has described as 'a spectacle of postfeminist independence' (2018: 138). In the course of the following seasons, Caroline becomes fully accepted and respected in her circle of friends. If she was constrained to the role of 'damsel in distress' ('The Turning Point', 1.10) prior to her change, she is now able to defend herself and the people she loves, and often plays an active part in the protagonists' supernatural missions. Thanks to her superhuman strength, speed and hearing, she is able to rescue her parents as well as her friends in more than one situation. Slowly, she also overcomes her insecurities and develops a mature, complex personality. Her mother

Figure 4.2 Caroline standing up to Damon (2.2). *The Vampire Diaries* © Warner Bros. Entertainment Inc. 2009–17. All rights reserved.

recognizes: 'You've become this strong, this confident person' ('Plan B', 2.6). Here, 'the makeover as personal empowerment trope' (Negra 2009: 123) becomes tangible. Given the option of taking a cure for vampirism in season four, Caroline refuses. As Klaus (Joseph Morgan) interprets her decision: 'You prefer who you are now to the girl you once were. You like being strong, ageless, fearless' ('Down the Rabbit Hole', 4.14).

In postfeminist discourse, 'those engaging in . . . forms of technological self-transformation . . . experience this not as the creation of a new self but the discovery of a more authentic "true self" and therefore as a project of self-realization, of becoming who they "really are"', as Martin Roberts writes (2007: 237). This 'new' self, which was there all along, is understood to have been liberated through the makeover. Interestingly, *The Vampire Diaries*' vampire lore implies that once a person becomes a vampire, their most prominent characteristics are heightened, so in a way people are more themselves. What this means for Caroline is certain; she concludes sarcastically: 'Now I'm basically an insecure, neurotic control freak on crack' ('Bad Moon Rising', 2.3). It should be added that prior to her transformation, a criticism that Caroline received over and over is that she is inauthentic, 'fake' ('A Few Good Men', 1.15), a 'stupid thing . . . and shallow and useless' ('162 Candles', 1.8). Her vampiric makeover finally assures Caroline the acknowledgement of her peers and family that she is a fully fledged, authentic person (not a thing): 'You grew into yourself when you became a vampire. You changed' ('The Rager', 4.3). In Davis's opinion, a makeover functions as a break with the old self, which facilitates the construction of a different self through 'biographical work' (2003: 82) – work on one's own biography that is re-enacted on a physical level. While Caroline's transformation is certainly the actual moment of her makeover, she receives a symbolic funeral in season three on occasion of her eighteenth birthday in order to bury her old self and embrace the new vampiric one. The obituary reads: 'Here lies Caroline Forbes. Cheerleader, Miss Mystic Falls, third grade hopscotch champion, friend, daughter, over-achiever, mean girl . . . She was 17, and she had a really good life. So rest in peace, so that she can move forward' ('Our Town', 3.11).

After successfully completing her vampiric makeover, Caroline's work, however, is not done: when becoming a vampire, she receives a body she must constantly discipline. Paula-Irene Villa points out that in makeover shows like *The Swan*, the focus is not actually on the result of the respective makeover but rather on the continual excruciating work on the body and thereby the self (2008a: 264). This continual nature of the work, which requires an exceptional amount of willpower, reveals the fact that idealized norms or subject positions can never be fully embodied (ibid.: 265). The consequence is an eternal process of approximating the contemporary ideal, which is perfectly captured in Caroline's constant and never-ending work to discipline her vampire body. Thus, along the way, she does slip up a number of times. For instance, she attacks her human boyfriend Matt when becoming overwhelmed by her bloodlust while the two are being intimate. As Stefan explains to her in this situation, living with a vampire body will always require self-discipline, as this body requires constant self-management: 'It's not gonna get any easier. You're just gonna have to work that much harder' ('Bad Moon Rising', 2.3). Caroline acknowledges the continual work that her body/self requires as integral to her new vampire life: 'being good comes so easy to me? Well, . . . it doesn't. I am a vampire, I have . . . impulses. . . . So I'm allowed to make some mistakes along the way' ('Gone Girl', 5.15). Failures are bound to occur, which is what emphasizes the need for perpetual work on the body/self.

'This hunger in me, it's never going away': Jessica Hamby's continual body work

Jessica Hamby's storyline in *True Blood*, again, is different from Caroline's and Bella's but works in a similar way when it comes to the topic of discipline and control. She, too, experiences her vampiric transition as a process of empowerment and a subversion of regulative rules, while simultaneously finding that she is subject to a number of new restrictions as a vampire. Jessica is introduced to the series towards the end of season one, when she is made vampire by Bill Compton. As we learn, she comes from a devout Christian middle-class family with extremely strict rules. Home-schooled by her mother and physically abused by her father as punishment for missteps, she has been suffering under the restrictive regime of her parents and their ideology. The few scenes in which we experience her as a human show Jessica in a state of utter powerlessness: kidnapped by the henchmen of the Vampire Authority – a semi-religious council that exercises ultimate authority over all vampires across the globe – she has been dragged into an arena of bloodthirsty vampires who lust for Bill to transform her. The latter has been sentenced by the Authority to turn a random human victim as retribution for killing another vampire, which underlines Jessica's status as an object caught in the power struggles of the patriarchal vampire system. Following an initial phase of terror and confusion after her transformation, Jessica quickly embraces her vampirism as a way out of her previous living conditions: 'I don't obey anybody! Those days are over!' ('To Love Is to Bury', 1.11). Contradicting Bill's as well as viewers' expectations, Jessica does not show desperation or sorrow when she learns that she is a vampire. Instead, she rejoices upon realizing what this entails for her: 'No more belts. No more clarinets. No more home school. No more rules. I'm a vampire! Whoo!' (ibid.). Here, Jessica resembles Caroline, who breaks generic expectations after Damon has posited that 'Caroline of all people will not make it as a vampire. . . . we all know how this story ends. Let's just flip to the last chapter' ('Brave New World', 2.2). Jessica's vampire transformation is celebrated as a source of empowerment for her, especially as a means of escaping her domineering father and his domestic violence as well as her religiously restrictive upbringing. The 'makeover as personal empowerment trope' (Negra 2009: 123) thereby comes to the fore in *True Blood* as well.

What follows swiftly, however, is the revelation that Jessica is now subject to a new vampiric social order with new authorities, which compromises her agency considerably (Jäckel 2012: 70). She is also the owner of a vampire body requiring constant discipline. Right after her change, Jessica has a conversation with Bill about the implications of her vampire existence. To her, being a vampire means that 'I don't have to sit like a lady and I can kill anybody I want. And there's an awful lot of people I'd like to kill.' However, Bill immediately puts a damper on this: 'You absolutely cannot kill anybody you want. . . . With your new powers come new responsibilities. You are going to mainstream like I do' ('To Love Is to Bury', 1.11). Mirroring the Cullen family's way of life, mainstreaming in *True Blood* involves the peaceful integration of vampires into human society, including their consumption of synthetic 'Tru Blood'. As an advocate of this social movement, Bill expects Jessica to live according to the ideas of the American Vampire League as he does; in the series, the latter is the organization responsible for the public relations of the vampire community and the promotion of vampire rights in the United States. Thus, as Julia Jäckel points out, the law of the father that Jessica must adhere to is not entirely removed but rather shifted from her biological human father to her vampire father (2012: 70) – at least in the beginning of Jessica's vampire life. Fittingly, in her monograph *Bewitched Again. Supernaturally Powerful Women on Television, 1996–2011* (2013), Julie O'Reilly finds that '[t]he surveillance of superpowered women illustrates one way in which these characters are subject to the judicial authorities in their lives. Within television series featuring superpowered women, such authorities . . . are predominantly male, whether representations of traditional systems of law and order or supernatural ones' (191). The way in which the surveillance by Jessica's human father is essentially replaced by that of her vampire father becomes particularly clear when Jessica returns to her childhood home. She threatens to take revenge on her human father by strangling him with the belt he used to beat her with. Jessica manages to reverse their power hierarchy thanks to her vampire strength and confidence, and triumphs: 'Now I get to home-school you in what it's like to be scared.' At the last moment, however, Bill swoops in and stops her. Part of the relationship between maker and progeny in *True Blood* is that vampire parents can force their 'children' to do whatever they want. A verbal expression of a maker's order cannot be defied by the progeny, so Jessica has no choice when Bill orders her to 'let him go! . . . As your maker, I command you' ('Keep This Party Going', 2.2).

As a newborn teen vampire, Jessica also depends on her maker to explain the whole vampire world to her, including her new bodily functions. For instance, she is blindsided by the fact that she now cries blood instead of tears, which Bill had neglected to tell her. Paralleling this circumstance, in *The Vampire Diaries*, it is Stefan who introduces Caroline to the vampire world after her transformation, for example by teaching her how to hunt rabbits. Similarly, Edward shows Bella the ropes of hunting animals in *Breaking Dawn – Part 2*. While maker–progeny relationships vary among vampires in *True Blood*, Bill's relationship to Jessica is clearly that of a father to his daughter. Since her vampiric transformation means the disruption of any ties to her human life, Jessica moves in with Bill and must subsequently get used to the rules around his home: 'Your bed time will be at 4 a.m. and not a minute later. And whilst you're under my roof, hunting is completely forbidden. . . . We also recycle in this house' ('Nothing but the Blood', 2.1). Upon Bill's insistence, Jessica tries different flavours of 'Tru Blood' and arrives at her personal mixture of blood types on which she is supposed to subsist from now on. Biting humans is off-limits according to Bill: 'I would no more allow you to feed on that young man than to watch pornography on television' ('Never Let Me Go', 2.5). Here, it is evident that in *True Blood*, much like in the *Twilight* Saga, vampiric bloodthirst and sexual desire have extensive overlaps and sometimes work as stand-ins for each other. In this respect, *True Blood* is strongly indebted to traditional vampire narratives, which have long been known for their 'overt sexual symbolism' (Antoni 2008). In fact, it is striking that in the first four seasons, Jessica almost exclusively manages these two desires: her storyline involves the struggle for control over her vampire impulses, and her sexual and romantic relationship with Hoyt Fortenberry (Jim Parrack), a young human man. As long as she is not willing or able to discipline and restrain herself, vampire father Bill steps in to exercise control – similar to the Salvatore brothers whose responsibility it becomes to govern Elena's newborn vampire thirst.

Considering the equation of vampiric and sexual desire, to an extent, Bill not only monitors Jessica's bloodlust but also polices her awakening sexuality. For instance, when she invites Hoyt over after meeting him at the local bar, Bill aggressively interrupts the couple's intimacy and sends Hoyt away because of Jessica's supposed 'instability'. His power over her sexuality is further demonstrated when he again disturbs Jessica's and Hoyt's first consensual sexual encounter. Bill justifies his control over Jessica's body and sexuality by emphasizing her alleged unpredictability and dangerousness: 'She is a loaded gun' ('Scratches', 2.3).

Jessica's struggle with disciplining her powerful vampire body positions her, alongside Bella and Caroline, as 'a brave new postfeminist self requiring continual self-monitoring' (Roberts 2007: 237). As pointed out already, her attempts to handle her physical impulses are a distinct focus throughout several seasons. Along these lines, her vampire fangs, which protrude whenever she is upset, hungry or aroused, become almost a running gag in the second and third season (see Figure 4.3). Deeply ashamed, Jessica tells Hoyt: 'I have fangs and they come out and I can't control them' ('Scratches', 2.3). Her attempt to take revenge on her father is later reframed as a loss of control by

Figure 4.3 Jessica, startled by her vampire body's impulses (3.6). *True Blood* © Home Box Office Inc. 2008–14. All rights reserved.

Jessica: 'I swear it was like it wasn't even me doing it. It must be all those new vampire impulse control issues' ('Keep This Party Going', 2.2). Her impulse control issues not only restrict Jessica's agency in the first place but they also lead to a number of social consequences. Here, it becomes clear that she must actively modify her behaviour in order to be socially accepted. For instance, Jessica's lack of self-control results in the temporary breakup of her relationship with Hoyt after she attacks his mother in response to the latter's disdainful attitude towards vampires in general and Jessica as her son's girlfriend in particular. The warning that Jessica issues towards Maxine Fortenberry (Dale Raoul), 'Lady, you have no idea how little control I have over my actions!' ('New World in My View', 2.10), is not only telling in this specific scene but also paradigmatic in terms of most of Jessica's early vampire life.

After feeding on a trucker and killing him accidentally in the process, Jessica finally starts getting a grip on her physical impulses. She recognizes that '[b]iting people, getting so mad that I do bad things by accident, that's in my nature' ('Beautifully Broken', 3.2), and then decides to fight her urges systematically. For this project, she depends on the advice of Pam, one of the only vampires she knows besides Bill, as she cannot count on the latter's help. From Pam, Jessica learns how to feed without killing her human prey, which requires a specific ability to control in order to 'take [someone] to the precipice of death and hold [them] there' ('We'll Meet Again', 5.4). Finding the balance between draining a person and keeping their heart beating at the same time is a skill Jessica soon masters. Mid-season three, she successfully feeds on and glamours a customer at Merlotte's Bar, where she has started working as a waitress. Vampiric glamouring entails controlling a person's mind and/or erasing their memory in *True Blood*; this vampiric ability is similar to what is referred to as 'compulsion' in *The Vampire Diaries*. Finally able to exercise control over herself, Jessica not only is more socially involved through her job at the Bar and Grill but also manages to resume her relationship with Hoyt. By now, Bill's strict educational methods have become obsolete and his attitude towards Jessica is more generous: 'It's your home, too. You can take care of yourself' (ibid.). Interestingly, after going through the process of opting for and learning self-control, Jessica is granted some room for transgression within the narrative, both in terms of her vampiric desires and her sexuality – something that does not apply to Caroline, who is not granted the transgression of flipping her humanity switch in season six, and who is immediately shamed by various characters for her 'misstep' of having a one-night stand in season five. Jessica's space for transgression could be attributed to the series' positioning as more sexually explicit and polarizing than other popular teen vampire TV. When Jessica gets back together with Hoyt, she comes clean about her previous involuntary crime and presents him with the fact that she cannot and will not subsist only on 'Tru Blood' any longer. The couple agrees on a monogamous sexual relationship, which is synonymous with a 'monogamous feeding relationship' in which Jessica exclusively feeds on Hoyt to satisfy her desire for human blood.

Later, this 'permitted transgression' taking place within the confines of monogamy turns out to be insufficient for Jessica in the long term. She feels constrained by her exclusive relationship with Hoyt and wants to act out her vampiric desire to feed on more than one person, which is why she ends up 'cheating on' him by biting a stranger at a nightclub. Once again, the interplay of sexual lust and bloodlust in *True Blood* becomes apparent. Eventually, Jessica's and Hoyt's traditional relationship fails, as Jessica declares: 'I'm not made for this. I have a hunger in the very centre of me, and this, you and me, I can't. It's not enough' ('Spellbound', 4.8). In accepting her inherent vampire urges and the need to satisfy them while continually working on them, Jessica is finally fully 'liberated'. The acknowledgement of her physical impulses enables her to indulge in her vampiric as well as her sexual desires – under the crucial condition that she restrains her appetite insofar as she does not lose control and kill anyone. Towards a fellow female vampire, Jessica expresses all the benefits of her vampire existence: 'It's not just the feeding and the sex and the power but I mean, we're going to live forever, we're going to be young forever. The world, . . . it's wide open to us' ('Let's Boot and Rally', 5.5). Jessica also distances her new vampiric self from her old human self by underlining that she prefers her vampire life to her dull, powerless human life. Just like Caroline, she would never trade in one for the other:

> Jason: 'If you could go back to being the way you were before, would you?'
> Jessica: 'No. Don't get me wrong, it ain't easy. I never see the sun and I'm always hungry. I have all these feelings and these urges and I don't even understand them half the time. But it is exciting. I am fast and I am strong and nobody can hurt me. And I smell and I taste things in a way that I never thought was possible. It's kind of hard to explain but my old world was about that big, and now . . . it's endless'. ('I Wish I Was the Moon', 4.6)

In the course of season four, Jessica feeds on strangers regularly, enjoying her sexual attractiveness and entering into an open relationship with Jason Stackhouse on her own terms. With the latter, she agrees not to be exclusive because she wants no restrictions on her exploration of different sides of herself. As she says to Jason: 'I'm just barely getting to know myself' ('And When I Die', 4.12). This taking into account of the fact that she still needs to learn more about her physical urges and desires points to the continual nature of her body work. In season six, Jessica loses her self-control in the face of five faerie girls, whose blood smells especially appealing to vampires in the *True Blood* universe: she drains four of them of their intoxicating blood and thereby kills them. Later on, realizing what she did, Jessica is horrified and spends the following episodes coming to terms with her deeds. She stops feeding at all for months and slowly degenerates physically as well as emotionally because she does not trust herself to bite without losing herself once again. In line with consumer cultural notions of the body functioning as a reflection of the self, Jessica in turn also questions her own morality and blames herself for actually 'serving the devil': 'Don't get close to me, I can't help myself, I'll rape you or something, and I just need to be put someplace where I won't be tempted' ('Fuck the Pain Away', 6.5). Thus, having lost control over her body, Jessica gives up her agency and freedom at the same time. The fact that her postfeminist vampire body requires perpetual management and disciplining is demonstrated in her recognition that her hunger for human and/or faerie blood will remain ever-present: 'This hunger in me, it's never going away, is it?' (ibid.).

Female vampires and their postfeminist projects of the self

When it comes to the portrayal of the female vampire characters discussed in this chapter, the preceding analyses have unearthed a number of common features. However, I have also uncovered significant differences between the *Twilight* Saga, *The Vampire Diaries* and *True Blood*. What the narratives share is a focus on the characters' transition from human to vampire; for the female vampires, this transition facilitates an increase in agency and their becoming subjects – since subjectivation is tantamount to having agency (Menke 2003: 286). While Caroline and Jessica break prescribed gender roles by becoming more active and aggressive, and by expressing sexual desire, Bella tends to adhere to normative notions of femininity after her vampiric transformation. Thus, Caroline and Jessica cross gender boundaries by displaying not only conventionally 'feminine' characteristics and looks but also incorporating active, 'masculine' qualities. Their transition from human to vampire is celebrated as a welcome challenge to the gender order. Bella may not be crossing boundaries in terms of her gender performance as a vampire, but her transformation is equally framed as a narrative of personal growth and empowerment. The fact that these female characters' transformations are framed in different ways within their respective narratives demonstrates the historically contingent nature of the category of gender. Bella, Jessica and Caroline offer different models of femininity, which attests to the fact that 'femininity is diversifying in popular culture, providing girls with a wider range of identities' (Milestone and Meyer 2012: 89).

Bella embodies what Milestone and Meyer would refer to as a more 'conventional femininity' (ibid.: 89), while Jessica and Caroline can be said to exemplify the 'shift towards a "new femininity" which is more socially and sexually assertive, confident, aspirational and fun-seeking' (ibid.: 88).

Despite their discrepancies, the *Twilight* Saga, *The Vampire Diaries* and *True Blood* share a focus on discourses of self-control and body maintenance, which I trace back to postfeminism/neoliberalism. In particular, what becomes palpable here is the neoliberal logic of the entrepreneur of the self, which has obvious parallels with postfeminist notions of individualism and consumer ideology. Bella, Jessica and Caroline each achieve subjectivity through their vampiric makeovers. In line with typical renditions of this trope, 'the makeover process ... facilitates and charts the development of a new, ideal feminine and feminist subjectivity' (Gwynne and Muller 2013a: 4). In *True Blood*, the disciplining of the body and self is framed as a success as well as a requisite for Jessica's becoming an empowered postfeminist subject. Similarly, in *The Vampire Diaries* and the *Twilight* Saga, Caroline's and Bella's self-control is referred to as unprecedented in the course of the respective series and held up as an example for other vampires to aspire to. For instance, Stefan admires Caroline: 'You're so good at it. At being a vampire' ('The Rager', 4.3), and Bella tells us in a post-makeover voice-over: 'I was born to be a vampire' (*Breaking Dawn – Part 2* 2012). What both descriptions seem to imply is that being a (good, socially accepted) vampire is tantamount to maintaining self-control, and that this is what the respective characters excel in.

The figure of the vampire has proven to be an exceedingly flexible metaphor for different cultural, social as well as political issues in different contexts (Gordon and Hollinger 1997b: 2) – in the *Twilight* Saga, *The Vampire Diaries* and *True Blood*, it functions as a projection surface for postfeminist/neoliberal discourses of the management of body and self. Already in 2003, Sally Miller pointed out that '[o]ne of the most striking features of contemporary vampire fiction is the vampire's reluctance to feed' (53). The recent trend of vampires refusing to subsist on human blood and struggling for self-restraint, which is observable in all three paranormal romances examined in this book, can be placed within a more general evolution of the motif towards a reluctant/sympathetic vampire that differs greatly from the classic Dracula figure in Bram Stoker's novel. As discussed briefly in Chapter 2, this 'new' vampire type is conspicuous for its 'civilized' and humanized nature. About this type, Milly Williamson writes that it 'is a creature troubled by its ontology; it is a being at odds with its vampiric body and the urges that this body generates' (2007: par. 2). Strikingly enough, it is precisely the vampire's struggle with its own body that resonates so strongly with audiences and that accounts for the vampire's popularity (ibid.: par. 29). Indeed, particularly Caroline is a great favourite with fans, and viewers have certainly made a special connection with Jessica through reading about her experiences in her online blog 'Baby vamp Jessica', which is part of *True Blood*'s clever multi-platform marketing campaign (see also Chapter 2). Besides, the fact that the male vampire heroes of these series abstain from drinking human blood forms one of their most appealing characteristics; this observation will be discussed at greater length in the subsequent chapter.

If vampires in the *Twilight* Saga, *The Vampire Diaries* and *True Blood* work as vehicles for postfeminist discourses of self-optimization and body maintenance, what is characteristic of these discourses is their contradictory nature. As Negra points out, 'in the postfeminist era it seems the body is relentlessly owned, claimed and managed but it is simultaneously as fragmented and ruled by social norms as it has ever been' (2009: 117). On the one hand, Bella's, Caroline's and Jessica's personal empowerment is facilitated by their change from human to vampire; on the other hand, they become successful and socially accepted subjects only upon the condition that they discipline and restrain themselves via their vampire bodies. In Jessica's case, the contradictoriness is particularly striking, considering that her freedom to transgress and her socially required subordination to self-control are not only intimately related but in fact mutually dependent. Butler has pointed out that the term 'subjectivation' implies a paradox in itself, as it 'denotes both the becoming of the subject and the process of subjection – one inhabits the figure of autonomy only by becoming subjected to a power, a subjection which implies a radical dependency' (1997: 83). In this sense, subjectivation means submitting to normative ideals while simultaneously gaining subjectivity and agency (Villa 2008a: 264). As Butler writes, the injunction – in this case the prohibition of vampiric feeding on humans – 'sets the stage for the subject's self-crafting, which always takes place in relation to an imposed set of norms.... If there is an operation of agency or, indeed, freedom in this struggle, it takes place in the context of an enabling and limiting field of constraint' (2005: 18–9). In *Twilight*, Bella is empowered and domesticated at the same time (Steinhoff and Siebert 2011: 15). Dissimilar as the three characters may be concerning other aspects, Caroline's and Jessica's transformations can be aligned with Bella's. Particularly Caroline's tendency to work hard on herself demonstrates that she is a successful 'self-surveilling postfeminist subject' (Negra 2009: 119). Meanwhile, especially Jessica's story hints at the fact that the maintenance of the (vampire) body must continuously be carried out, since the conflict between body and mind is never solvable. As Miller argues, 'the vampire can never be entirely free of its hunger and the conflicts surrounding it; ... what is found in these [texts] is a [*sic*] merely a domestication, and not an eradication of appetite' (2003: 53). Thus, the vampire emerges as a figure in which postfeminist/neoliberal discourses promoting the continual necessity for body work and monitoring materialize.

Interestingly, these female characters' new vampire selves also comply with the 'cult of youth' (Tasker and Negra 2007b: 11) that postfeminism is invested in. As Negra argues, '[p]ostfeminism suggests that symbolic forms of time mastery (particularly management of the ageing process) will provide the key to the reclamation of self' (2009: 53) for women. With regard to the *Twilight* Saga, *The Vampire Diaries* and *True Blood*, it is striking that the vampire makeover, with its ensuing subjectivation process, indeed comes with the eradication of aging. The vampire body remains static; due to its immortality, it embodies eternal youth, beauty and health – attributes that bestow a high social and cultural capital on the individual in postfeminist consumer culture. Since vampires do not age, Bella, Caroline and Jessica will be frozen in their highly valued bodies forever. Not only are the represented successful female postfeminist subjects all young, slim, beautiful, healthy and able-bodied but they are also all white. Although postfeminism '*includes* (albeit in specific and limited ways) nonwhite and nonheterosexual subjects' (Butler 2013: 49; emphasis in original), these texts present heterosexuality and whiteness as universal by foregrounding the successful journeys of their white female characters.

While the lack of representation of non-white female characters achieving the level of agency that white female characters acquire through a makeover suggests that non-white women and girls face greater impediments when attaining a subject position in postfeminist media culture, the situation of white female characters also remains ambivalent. It is Bella's narrative that seems to best encapsulate the tensions at the heart of postfeminist makeover culture. Although Bella embraces the conventionally 'female' role of mother and homemaker, which is represented as a triumph for her since she made the 'individual' choice to do so, my earlier analysis has shown that in the process of her vampire makeover, Bella trades her vulnerable, soft, undisciplined, female-coded human body for a powerful, firm, disciplined, male-coded vampire body. As Steinhoff and Siebert argue, this paradoxical situation

> hints at the tug-of-war that the female body and female identity is trapped in: on the one hand, contemporary women are confronted with beauty ideals that prescribe a youthful, unchanging body, a body that does not grow big with child, that does not carry stretch marks or any other traces of a pregnancy, whilst on the other hand, being able to give birth is still often represented as one of the main differences between men and women in a culture that is suffused with notions of natural sexual difference. (2011: 12–3)

The tensions inherent in this hegemonic conception of contemporary (white) female identity also become apparent in the character of Rosalie Cullen, Edward's vampire sister. Having been turned by Carlisle when she was gravely injured and unable to give full consent to her transformation, Rosalie says she would not have chosen a vampire life for herself. As she tells Bella in *Eclipse*, she deeply regrets that she will never have biological children: 'We'll always be this. Frozen. Never moving forward. That's what I miss the most. Possibilities. Sitting on a front porch somewhere. Emmett, grey-haired, by my side, surrounded by our grandchildren. Their laughter.' Admitting that she envies Bella for her ability to choose, Rosalie urges her not to give up her reproductive ability so carelessly by continuing to insist on her transformation into a vampire. The fact that Rosalie mourns her ability to become pregnant 'maintain[s] the idea that women should *want* to have children' (McGeough 2010: 95; emphasis in original); in the novels, Rosalie's and Edward's vampire mother Esme (Elizabeth Reaser) also has a difficult time accepting her infertility. Rosalie's above-cited vision suggests that her wish to reproduce is firmly located within heteronormative, idealized notions of marriage and family. While her story is represented as a tragic one, Bella manages to 'have it all': not only does she give birth to a perfectly gifted child who rarely needs to be taken care of, she also receives the idealized vampire body she has desired for as long as the film series has followed her.

Essentially, the vampiric makeover can be read as a solution to the conflicting demands that contemporary culture makes of women today. As Simone Broders observes, women in the early twenty-first-century US-American 'cultural context appear to be trapped between different life-concepts and thus diverging roles in society ... Integrating all cultural and social expectations into one life plan seems to require superhuman strength – ironically, being a vampire fulfills all requirements' (2011). Bella goes through pregnancy and birth but her body ultimately does not bear the consequences of that considerable physical burden. Due to her unusual story, she is able to both fulfil the traditional role of the mother, which grants her a particular status, and retain a body that will be forever young, slim, physically able and beautiful, which is equally highly valued within the culture. At the same time, Bella's choices may be interpreted as a submission to patriarchal values, with the specificities of the female body implicitly being devalued. As Steinhoff and Siebert put it,

> Bella's makeover is both playing into the hands of patriarchy and at the same time constitutes a moment of female empowerment – sought out, accomplished and enjoyed by the female subject herself. . . . Bella is both empowered and 'tamed'. The latter is particularly expressed by the removal of the most threatening feature of her unruly female boy – its power to give birth. That the ideal female body presented in the text is a body that cannot conceive stands in sharp contrast to the saga's focus on family values and its celebration of motherhood and sheds light on the contradictory hegemonic demands women are faced with in contemporary western culture. (2011: 15)

In other words, the double movement that characterizes postfeminist discourses manifests again here. Not only do the *Twilight* Saga, *The Vampire Diaries* and *True Blood* illustrate the paradoxical expectations that women are meant to meet today, but they also provide fictionalized solutions to these expectations. The result is a model of 'femininity' that caters to contradictory notions about what it means to be a young woman today, a 'postfeminist Gothic Cinderella [who] is . . . subject and object in one' (Genz 2007: 75). This conclusion echoes the findings of Chapter 3, which equally indicated the complex subject/object positions of women and girls in postfeminist culture.

5

Fantasy solutions to postfeminist culture
Vampire heroes and postfeminist masculinity

While the previous analyses have focused on the main female characters of the *Twilight* Saga, *The Vampire Diaries* and *True Blood*, this chapter aims to shed light on what kinds of masculinities can be found in these texts. Since 'discourses of masculinity . . . are crucial to the hegemonic common sense of post-feminist culture and thereby crucial objects for feminist analysis' (Levine 2009: 143), this chapter will investigate the representation of the male vampires Edward Cullen, Stefan Salvatore and Bill Compton as exemplars of postfeminist masculinity. As mentioned in Chapter 2, a central conclusion of both Modleski's and Radway's 1980s seminal romance studies is that the genre presents fantasy solutions to existing issues in women's lives within a patriarchally structured society (1982: 14; [1984] 1991: 213). That is, one of the primary appeals of romance according to these scholars is that it presents male protagonists taking over some of the responsibilities and/ or characteristics usually ascribed to women, such as the performance of emotional labour. Such scenarios are welcomed by the largely female consumers who, as wives and mothers, are expected to constantly put their own needs on hold on behalf of the family (Radway [1984] 1991: 211). Considering that twenty-first-century paranormal romance emerges under different historical and cultural circumstances from the romances that Modleski and Radway examined almost four decades ago, the question arises whether the *Twilight* Saga, *The Vampire Diaries* and *True Blood* still address similar gender-related issues or if they have other and/or additional functions.

Crucially, the time frame in which these three cultural products crop up is 'a turbulent and highly unsettled economic and social moment' (Negra 2009: 15). In pointing to 'terrorist, environmental, and other threats and a conservative political climate' (2009: 51), Negra names a number of prominent spheres of anxiety that provided the backdrop of these series' releases. Along with the long-term effects of 9/11, the consequences of the Great Recession between 2007 and 2012 and an increasingly tight labour market, Americans were also faced with 'social, cultural and demographic changes that include high rates of divorce, the growth of new family forms and broader transformations of intimacy' (Gill 2007: 225). With traditional structures of security increasingly breaking away and rapidly shifting gender roles being widely accompanied by unease, romance is 'offering a secure meta-narrative in unsettling times' (ibid.: 226). It is paranormal romance in particular, with its ability to represent psychological and social realities in allegorical form and thereby negotiate issues that are otherwise difficult to address, that speaks to contemporary audiences' insecurities concerning fluctuating gender roles and relations. As Eric Murphy Selinger has noted, popular culture of the noughties reveals a prevalent 'nostalgia for or a fascination with the idea of a radical difference between the sexes. . . . [P]aranormal takes that model and shows it to us in a way where differences between the genders can be . . . asserted as fundamental ontological differences, even sometimes differences between species' (2013). The resurgence of conventional binary gender roles is an aspect that is visible in the *Twilight* Saga in particular, but also in *The Vampire Diaries* and *True Blood*. Aiming at and being marketed to predominantly heterosexual female audiences,[1] these paranormal romances present male vampires as romantic leads who 'offer the security and stability of old-fashioned gentlemen that some readers [and viewers] may now crave without being able to clearly articulate that craving' (Mukherjea 2011a: 3). However, these vampire romance heroes are not simply a resurrection of conservative gender roles. As idealized men with supernatural capacities, Edward, Stefan and Bill can both satisfy a longing for supposedly simpler traditional gender roles and offer a new version of masculinity which accepts feminism's ideals. As I argue, these male vampires capture the defining features of the 'postfeminist man', whom Genz and Brabon describe as 'the epitome of "bricolage masculinity"' (2009: 137). This chapter, then, explores the ways in which postfeminist masculinity is presented as the most successful and popular version of maleness in this selection of paranormal romances.

The evolution of the postfeminist man

The postfeminist man is a hybrid formation, 'a melting pot of masculinities, blending a variety of contested subject positions, as well as a chameleon figure still negotiating the ongoing impact of feminism on his identity' (Genz and Brabon 2009: 143). Emerging in the early 2000s, this contradictory form of masculinity is often conceived as a product of the so-called 'crisis in masculinity', which was widely discussed in the academic as well as the popular realm in the United States and Britain around the turn of the century. Scholars and critics describing this crisis delineate the ways in which social and economic shifts on a domestic as well as global level have increasingly resulted in the loss of power and independence for men in general, and for white, hegemonic masculinities in particular. In more conservative accounts, feminism is made responsible for these shifts (Robinson 2007: 90). However, Brian Baker locates the 'crisis in masculinity' in the context of 'the dominance of neoliberal economics in the global North, crises of legitimacy in "democratic" political processes, the experience of war and the effects of terrorism, as well as emergent social and cultural formations produced by digital networks and globalized travel' (2015: 1).

The destabilization of 'masculinity' has been understood to take place both actually and symbolically, in the sense that men have actually had to give up certain privileges, and that the traditional concept of masculinity has waned in popularity in American culture (Robinson 2007: 90). While most scholars seem to agree that shifts in gender roles have recently been – and are currently – occurring, some have exposed the idea 'that American masculinity was stable and fulfilling prior to feminism' as a 'myth' (Abele 2016: xvii). Rather than claiming that the 'crisis in masculinity' is a new phenomenon, these scholars argue that there was never a time when masculinity was 'stable and well-defined' (ibid.: xv). Instead, it would be more accurate to speak of a 'continual crisis' (ibid.) since masculine gender identity is persistently shifting. Kenneth MacKinnon argues that what informs the contemporary 'crisis' is a shift to an understanding of masculinity not as a 'natural', biologically given set of attributes, but as performative (2003: 14). If masculinity 'once was taken for granted as transparent, normal, too natural to require explanation, it has become something of an enigma. A masculinity which takes up so much energy and demands so much attention is self-evidently unconfident about its nature and attributes' (ibid.: 21). In this sense, feminism may indeed have played a part in masculinity's 'crisis': as Elizabeth Abele suggests, 'feminism's process of revealing and questioning the artificial limitations placed on women by society . . . cannot help but reveal the social construction of men as well' (2016: xiii). Thus, the relatively recent perception of masculinity as a social and cultural construct is accompanied by an awareness that men are performing certain roles, which may then be questioned and put up for discussion. Furthermore, the theory that masculinity, like femininity, is dependent on a continual reproduction of specific ways of 'doing gender' highlights the fragility of the concept – hence its being 'in crisis' (MacKinnon 2003: 21).

As hybrid models of masculinity that are located at the intersection of different economic and social tensions, postfeminist masculinities 'hold continuities with hegemonic, and even archaic, depictions of masculinity alongside "new" emergent masculine images, emphases and values' (Thompson 2013: 150–1). Thus, while postfeminist masculinity continues to incorporate features that are traditionally understood as 'masculine', such as aggression and (professional) ambition, it also 'increasingly redefine[s] itself in terms of its sensitivity, emotional expressiveness and nurturing qualities, and also in terms of its openness to improving interpersonal relations and to taking a lead part in child-rearing' (MacKinnon 2003: 73). As a consequence of being characterized by contradiction and ambiguity, postfeminist masculinities are both 'haunted by the threat of "backlash"' and by the opportunity of subversion, as 'invocations of older forms of masculinity are re-signified by pro-feminist interventions' (Brabon 2013: 117).

Postfeminist masculinity's contradictory nature is a result of its incorporation of different constitutive elements. It combines features of three earlier discourses of masculinity: the 'new man', the 'metrosexual' and the 'new lad' (Genz and Brabon 2009: 137). Most clearly, postfeminist masculinity can be described as 'a reimagined and reconstructed version of the 1980s "new man" archetype' (Burns 2013: 134), which developed under the influences of feminism, individualism and consumer society (Milestone and Meyer 2012: 117). The historical context in which the 'new man' originates has moulded his character; he has been described as 'pro-feminist' (Genz and Brabon 2009: 137) and '"feminized"' (Milestone and Meyer 2012: 117), but also as 'self-absorbed' (Genz and Brabon 2009: 137). Two strands of the 'new man' type can thus be distinguished: 'the "nurturer" (men as sensitive, emotionally expressive and domesticated) and the "narcissist" (men as ambitious fashion- and body-conscious consumers)' (Burns 2013: 134). The postfeminist man is indebted to both. From the 'nurturer' version of the new man, he inherits emotional and caretaker skills as well as a liberal and feminist political outlook. Like his predecessor, the postfeminist man is comfortable with traditionally female-coded activities, like performing household duties and child-rearing (Milestone and Meyer 2012: 116–17). At the other end of the spectrum, the 'new man' as narcissist 'is well groomed and looks sexy. He possesses a fit and muscular body, achieved through regular exercise and diet regimes, wears expensive and stylish clothes . . . and uses beautification products' (ibid.: 116). This version of the 'new man' is a result of the increasing 'commercialisation of masculinity witnessed from the 1980s to the present day' (Genz and Brabon 2009: 136). Indeed, the possession of a sexy body and an aestheticized appearance are requirements for successful postfeminist masculinity in contemporary culture (Thompson 2013: 151).

The increased focus on consumer cultural values is further amplified in the figure of the 'metrosexual', who is commonly associated with the 1990s. Although he is usually characterized as heterosexual, the 'metrosexual' man displays behaviours that were then rather associated with gay men or 'femininity': he intentionally puts his body on display and is interested in grooming and fashion trends (Milestone and Meyer 2012: 117). As a result, the 'metrosexual' has been defined as '[s]exually ambivalent' (Genz and Brabon 2009: 139), blurring the lines between heterosexual and homosexual masculinities. Like the 'new man', the 'metrosexual' is usually middle class with a certain amount of money on his hands, which is a prerequisite of him being able to fully embrace the prevailing culture of late capitalism. This type of masculinity is closely dependent on lifestyle choices, which, as Genz and Brabon point out, 'are limited and limiting', as they are only accessible to individuals who are rich in resources. Foreshadowing the contradictory make-up of the postfeminist man, the 'metrosexual' 'illustrates the precariousness of masculinity in the twentieth century, as "new" and "old", homosexual and heterosexual masculinities compound and evolve in increasingly "hybrid" forms' (ibid.: 140).

The third figure that the postfeminist man draws upon is the 'new lad', a masculinity discourse that is largely associated with British working-class culture of the 1990s (Milestone and Meyer 2012: 118). 'New laddism' is generally understood as 'a backlash against feminism, which it associates with political correctness, and against male responsibilities linked with traditional breadwinning roles' (Pattman 2007: 358). Thus, the 'new lad' has been linked with retro-sexism, homophobia and the demonstrative objectification of women. A key characteristic of this figure is laddish humour, which aims to uphold gendered hierarchies through the use of irony (ibid.). Ultimately, the postfeminist man is very much a hybrid of the 'new man', the 'metrosexual' and the 'new lad'. Through the hybridization of different versions of masculinity, postfeminist masculinity mixes 'old and new elements' (Milestone and Meyer 2012: 119) in a way that allows both progressive and regressive readings.

Humanized vampires as postfeminist romance heroes

Hybridizing the prototypes of the 'new man', the 'metrosexual' and the 'new lad', the postfeminist man is a combination of different and even conflicting masculinities. As I argue, these contradictory qualities of postfeminist masculinity become manifest in the humanized vampire romance heroes featured in the *Twilight* Saga, *The Vampire Diaries* and *True Blood*. As creatures straddling the border between a range of oppositional categories, vampires are ideally suited to embody the postfeminist man's incongruous features. Functioning as preferred partners for the human heroines and, by proxy, the narratives' audiences, these vampire heroes are modelled in many ways after the typical hero of the romance genre. However, they also deviate from the latter's characteristics in some crucial aspects, which signals their embeddedness in a postfeminist culture in which 'feminist gains, attitudes, and achievements are woven into our cultural fabric' (Douglas 2010: 9). The typical romance hero, too, is an inherently contradictory character blending different features – some of which are traditionally gendered 'masculine', some 'feminine'. As Radway maintains, although the hero of the romantic fantasy is 'characterized by spectacular masculinity' ([1984] 1991: 128), he also displays a 'capacity for tenderness and attentive concern' (ibid.: 14), which complicates his otherwise extremely 'masculine' demeanour. The hero's supposedly feminine features are key to the transformation of the hero into a viable romantic partner, which is achieved through the efforts of the heroine; this is the process through which she brings him 'to his knees' (Modleski 1982: 45). Like the romance hero, the vampire becomes eligible as a romantic partner through its domestication/ humanization.

The gradual domestication and/or humanization of the vampire figure in popular culture is a development that has been widely examined in vampire academia.[2] This shift in the vampire genre forms the basis for the contemporary vampire's particular suitability for incorporating and mirroring discourses surrounding postfeminist masculinity. As heroes of paranormal romances, vampires integrate a number of antithetical properties, each of which may be desirable to their audiences. For instance, while the vampire hero has usually been turned into a vampire decades, possibly even centuries, ago, he takes on the appearance of a young man or – as in the *Twilight* Saga and *The Vampire Diaries* – a teenage boy. As Mukherjea argues, the vampire boyfriend's 'beloved can benefit from the intensity of his desire for her but not suffer from his inability to control it or to express it elegantly.... this is the physical glory of youth combined with adult accomplishments and restraint' (2011a: 7). According to Abbott, while vampires are usually 'seen as stretching back into far reaches of the past' (2007: 2), those in twentieth- and twenty-first-century film and television are 'intrinsically linked to the modern world' (ibid.: 5) and firmly anchored in their contemporary setting, usually the urban realm (ibid.: 3). Thus, because of his immortal nature, the vampire hero typically stems from an era associated with traditional gender roles and moral values. At the same time, he is fully assimilated into contemporary culture and can act as an advocate of modern, including feminist ideas. Essentially being 'simultaneously very much of the past and of the future' (Mukherjea 2011a: 4), then, the vampire hero neatly incorporates both traditional, retrogressive ideas about masculinity and more recent, potentially progressive ones. The vampire thereby functions as a personification of postfeminist masculinity, which may both carry retro-sexist ideas about gender roles and offer new images of manhood emerging under the influence of feminism.

In the humanization process, the vampire has largely lost its folkloristic features, which entails its becoming less Other (Zanger 1997: 19); this concerns both its characterization and its visual portrayal. Not only does the modern vampire look more human, it is also depicted as more conventionally attractive and even attains common beauty standards (Clements 2011: 36). As Recht argues, the transformation of the male vampire body towards established notions of attractiveness can be considered a humanization strategy that goes hand in hand with the construction of the sympathetic vampire (2011: 251). The representation of male vampire characters as eroticized objects of the gaze in the *Twilight* Saga, *The Vampire Diaries* and *True Blood* was examined in detail in Chapter 3. In this chapter, I want to focus on the sexualized depiction of our humanized vampire heroes as taking up discourses of narcissistic, commercialized postfeminist masculinity. Strikingly, since the emergence of the 'new man' in the 1980s, men's bodies have started 'to become objects to be displayed and looked at by spectators' (Milestone and Meyer 2012: 119). In this context, Milestone and Meyer argue (with reference to Sean Nixon) that the 'new man' is characterized by 'a contradictory "hard-soft" look. [He] is sensual yet tough, masculine in both an old and a new way' (2012: 120). This combination of hard/'masculine' and soft/'feminine' features is retained by the idealized postfeminist man: while he resorts to trending beauty practices, the portrayal of his body also typically focuses on 'his toned arms and torso' (Burns 2013: 136), emphasizing 'the importance of a highly muscular physique' (Milestone and Meyer 2012: 120) for men in contemporary culture. According to Amy Burns, the postfeminist hero 'can be found readily on "display" . . . as he is presented to both female characters within the text and the female audience as an "object for consumption"' (2013: 134). The figure of the humanized male vampire is particularly well equipped to capture this self-displaying, self-grooming quality of the postfeminist man. As figures of fantasy, vampires are able to meet and maintain otherwise impossible beauty standards via their idealized bodies. In contemporary paranormal romance, the supernatural creatures often 'possess nearly perfect physical forms, immense physical prowess, and some manner of prolonged youth or immortality. In addition to being powerful, . . . the men are handsome with bodies that range from chiseled to muscular' (Willms 2014: 139). Furthermore, vampirism is often associated with affluence and (white) privilege, as immortality and supernatural skills offer access to high amounts of time and resources, which facilitate the accumulation of money as well as knowledge in the form of education. This principle is most clearly embodied by Edward Cullen, whose superior styling, fashion and grooming choices cannot be separated from his social class and white privilege.

A further result of the increasing humanization of the vampire figure is that contemporary sympathetic/reluctant vampires are no longer portrayed as monsters but as equipped with free will and a conscience (Zanger 1997: 22). We see this for example in *New Moon*, when Bella tells Jacob with regard to the question of what makes one a monster: 'It's not what you *are*, it's what you *do*.' What defines the vampire hero, then, is that he makes an individual choice to deploy his power for the sake of the heroine and her loved ones. On the one hand, vampirism functions as an extension of the romance hero's 'masculine' characteristics, 'like violence, passion, sexual desire and the rest of the standard "Alphaman" traits' (Crawford 2014: 106). The physical dominance and propensity for violence, which is inherent in the figure of the vampire despite its substantial domestication, is part of the allure of the vampire romance hero. On the other hand, his overpowering dominance is made safe by the vampire hero's willingness to restrain his monstrous power with the support of the heroine. Here, it is crucial to bear in mind that the vampire lover's attractiveness is based on 'the generic guarantee . . . that the violence of the hero is only ever an index of his virility, power and passion, and never of the actual likelihood of him inflicting physical harm upon the heroine' (ibid.: 167–8). While he is welcomed as a protector for the heroine in a setting containing many supernatural and other, more mundane threats, he is also depicted as kind and caring, demonstrating high levels of emotional intelligence and being eager to talk about his feelings. In paranormal romance, the vampirism of the hero can thus function as a welcome 'fantasy thrill', while the relationship 'is essentially absolutely safe' (Clements 2011: 116) for the heroine. In short, with the humanized vampire hero, the heroine wins someone who can be both 'her passionate first love but also the adult figure who protects her from the possible excesses of that relationship' (Mukherjea 2011a: 9). The vampire boyfriend's combination of differently gendered features can be read as an expression of postfeminist masculinity, as the latter is simultaneously indebted to more traditional ideas of 'masculinity' and demonstrating 'feminine' emotional as well as domestic skills.

In this context, an interesting argument put forward by Williamson and Recht is that the sympathetic/reluctant vampire hero is intimately connected with the 'feminine' realm of emotion and melodrama (2007: par. 6; 2011: 88). Taking Barnabas Collins from *Dark Shadows* as an example, Williamson draws a number of parallels between the reluctant vampire and the character of the heroine in the Gothic melodrama. Like the heroine, the vampire is 'depicted as one who is caught in circumstances beyond his control' (ibid.). While the heroine's pathos is grounded in her relocation from the safety of her own home to her new husband's or employer's house, the vampire's victimization typically stems from the fact that he was transformed into a supernatural creature against his will. Discovering his thirst for human blood, he is faced with the horrors of his abject vampire body that he fails to come to grips with (ibid.: par. 12). Importantly, then, the reluctant vampire's 'pathos is performed through the body' (ibid.: par. 15). Corresponding to the melodramatic genre, the reluctant vampire's melodramatic identity 'involve[s] excess (of expression, emotion, and gesture)' (ibid.: par. 19), which may seem at odds with the vampire's stereotypically masculine features discussed earlier. However, the reluctant vampire's pathos is a fundamental part of his appeal, as it serves to engage (female) audiences in compelling ways. Indeed, television viewers have interpreted vampire Barnabas Collins as sympathetic because they were 'identifying with his plight' (ibid.: par. 21).[3] As Williamson argues, Barnabas's struggle against society's misrecognition of his innocence and his own tragic internalization of society's misjudgement of the meanings of his body mirror female viewers' experiences with 'socially unacknowledged dilemmas and injustices' (ibid.: par. 23) in a patriarchally structured world. In a sense, 'Barnabas as a vampire ... acts out our ... inability to articulate our own experiences of the injustices that we cannot fully name' (ibid.: par. 29). The parallels between the heroine – who works as a stand-in for the female viewer – and the monster are a well-known observation in studies of the horror genre. For instance, Linda Williams has argued that in the classic horror film, the monster functions as a 'double' (1996: 20) for the woman because both have a 'similar status within patriarchal structures of seeing' (ibid.: 18). From the perspective of the male, both the monster's and the woman's bodies are endowed with 'the feared power and potency of a different kind of sexuality' (ibid.: 20). As Williams suggests, the woman 'recognizes the sense in which [the monster's] freakishness is similar to her own difference. For she too has been constituted as an exhibitionist-object by the desiring look of the male' (ibid.: 21). Here, too, the body is at the core of the affinity between heroine and monster.

Williamson's analysis of the similarities between the reluctant vampire and the melodramatic Gothic heroine ties in nicely with an argument put forward by Brabon in his article 'The Spectral Phallus: Re-Membering the Postfeminist Man' (2007), in which he examines postfeminist masculinity in the context of postfeminist Gothic texts. As Brabon contends, a striking shift in the Gothic genre has been that by the late twentieth and twenty-first centuries, 'an inversion has taken place, as the female Gothic heroine cedes her position and role to the postfeminist man. . . . the postfeminist man's new status of victim is defined and delineated by his masculinity – he is trapped between the loss of his essentialist quality of masculinity and his attempt to reassert a strong masculine identity' (60). Although Brabon is not referring to the figure of the vampire in his essay, his argument may be transferred to the paranormal romance texts investigated within the frame of this book. Thus, as I suggest, the postfeminist vampire hero's 'troubled reluctance at [his] vampiric urges' (Williamson 2007: par. 2) can be interpreted as a metaphor for his discomfort with his 'masculine' identity, which – as discussed earlier in this chapter – is 'in crisis'. Torn between his 'natural' bloodlust and the expectation that he must restrain his appetite, the reluctant vampire bundles postfeminist discourses surrounding a self-aware masculinity that is in the process of interrogating itself and its privileges as well as responsibilities. Confronted with 'old' and 'new' expectations and duties, the postfeminist man has a complicated relationship with traditional forms of hegemonic masculinity, which for him exist 'in a latent, at times nostalgic but always unattainable, form' (Brabon 2013: 122). He may enjoy the privileges he is afforded due to his hegemonic status in the patriarchal culture, but given that his perception of his own masculinity has, among other things, 'been altered by second-wave feminism' (ibid.), he may also be aware of and attempt to work against retaining these privileges. Thus, the postfeminist man 'now must engage with his own masculinity' (Brabon 2007: 60) – a process which takes place 'at the physical level of the body' (ibid.: 61) in postfeminist Gothic texts. In the case of the vampire romance hero, this engagement with one's own masculine identity is mapped onto the vampire body with its propensity for predatory violence and thirst for human blood. In the *Twilight* Saga, *The Vampire Diaries* and *True Blood*, storylines tend to revolve around the vampire romance heroes' willingness to engage in critical self-reflection and their efforts in directing their (physical) dominance into 'appropriate' or benevolent channels. As I contend, this self-reflexive and self-critical postfeminist masculinity, with which the vampire heroes in these vampire romances are endowed, holds high appeal for audiences and therefore enjoys the hegemonic status as the accepted version of ideal masculinity in the texts.[4]

Both 'overbearing' and 'emo-metrosexual': Edward Cullen

In academic discussions of the *Twilight* franchise, the character of Edward Cullen has widely been understood as a re-inscription of deeply conservative, traditional masculinity.[5] While such analyses have a point in signposting the regressive aspects of Edward's characterization, which are indeed troubling, this vampire hero also displays traits that deviate from traditional conceptions of masculinity. As Wilson points out, Edward is 'representative of the neither too macho nor too feminine male characters that the saga depicts. While Edward is traditionally masculine in many regards, he is also an emo-metrosexual' (2011: 86). An interesting point is Wilson's reference to the figure of the 'metrosexual'. As my analysis will demonstrate, in the *Twilight* film series, Edward functions as an embodiment of hybrid postfeminist masculinity, which – as discussed – incorporates aspects of the 'metrosexual' as well as other forms of masculinity.

According to Milestone and Meyer, 'traditional masculinity is very much tied to an age of clear gender roles and family structures' (2012: 115). Born in 1901, Edward Cullen represents such an age in which gender roles were supposedly clear-cut, stable and satisfying for all genders. An outsider at contemporary Forks High School due to his antiquated speech and demeanour, Edward 'indulge[s] a craving for an old-fashioned, generally wealthy, and socially dominant gentleman' (Mukherjea 2011a: 1). The decades in which Edward was raised and educated have shaped his understanding of romance, courtship, sexuality and family. *New Moon* and *Eclipse*, for instance, chronicle Edward's attempts to convince Bella to marry him. When he proposes to her with a romantic gesture, he locates the motivation for his proposal in a more desirable traditional past: 'I know it's not a modern notion.... I'm from a different era. Things were a lot less complicated. And if I had met you back then, I would have courted you. We'd have taken chaperoned strolls or had iced tea on the porch. I may have stolen a kiss or two. But only after asking your father's permission' (*Eclipse* 2010). In his speech, Edward presents a highly romanticized version of the early twentieth century, in which gendered expectations were supposedly clearly regulated and simple to live up to. As Milestone and Meyer contend, 'traditional masculinity, more than any other type of masculinity, directly juxtaposes men and women' (2012: 114). This juxtaposition of men's and women's 'typical' characteristics also becomes visible in Edward's ideas about the part he ought to play in his relationship with Bella. In *New Moon*, he articulates what viewers have already been able to infer from his actions: Edward's self-understood role is to guard Bella from harm. In response to her wish to be turned into a vampire and thereby become his equal in terms of power, he insists: 'But it's my job to protect you.' Edward not only sees his role in protecting Bella's life and safety; he is also adamant in protecting her 'virtue' (*Eclipse* 2010). Contradicting Bella's openly expressed desire for sexual intimacy, he insists that they should be married before any sexual interaction. Appealingly, Edward, 'with his "old-school" ideas about love and sex... and his certainty about exactly what is entailed in his "job description" as a husband, has a strikingly clear... vision about exactly what constitutes correct, masculine behaviour' (Mukherjea 2011b: 80).

Besides representing an old-fashioned approach to sexuality and relationships, Edward also symbolizes ideas about the desirability of the traditional nuclear family. Bella herself is a child of divorce and her parents no longer play a big part in each other's lives. Renée (Sara Clarke), Bella's mother, prioritizes her new husband's career as a minor league baseball player over her relationship with her daughter. Throughout the Saga, she is portrayed as eccentric, childish and insufficient in her mothering capabilities. In contrast, Edward's mother Esme 'defines herself primarily as a mother' (Silver 2010: 127) and thereby takes her 'appropriate' place in the traditional family hierarchy. Contrary to Bella's biological family, the Cullen family is depicted as harmonious and functional, with every family member fulfilling a particular gendered role (ibid.: 126). Essentially, the traditional family structure with its gendered division of labour is what Edward offers to Bella when proposing to her. At the same time, he also advocates for Bella going to college instead of becoming a homemaker – something she herself is rather reluctant to do – and thereby represents a more contemporary approach to gender roles within the family.

Other characteristics associated with traditional masculinity are physical strength, competitiveness, social power, authority, cognitive skills and rationality (Milestone and Meyer 2012: 114–5), which Edward naturally displays. For instance, his superhuman strength becomes palpable in *Twilight* when he saves Bella's life by stopping a van from crushing Bella with his bare hand. Edward's competitiveness is depicted most prominently in relation to Jacob, who is also courting Bella. Due to his appearance as a teenage boy, Edward is neither involved in the workplace nor is he in a position to 'make important decisions in the public realm and directly shape society' (ibid.: 114), as a traditional man would be. However, being the son of the chief doctor at Forks Hospital, Edward benefits from his father's social status. Carlisle, who used to be closely associated with the patriarchal royal family of the vampire world, the Volturi, is held in high esteem by the locals because of his professional skills and service to the community. Furthermore, Carlisle's job affords the Cullen family the opportunity to live in a spacious and modern mansion as well as lead an expensive lifestyle. The Cullens' wealth makes Edward perfectly able to provide financial support to Bella and – later in the narrative – his daughter Reneesme (Mackenzie Foy). As Bella learns upon arriving at Forks High School, Edward is admired by most of the school's female populace and has a high social standing among his peers. Although he usually keeps to himself, he is shown to be socially competent and often assumes an assertive role in his interactions with the public world. Thanks to his immortality, Edward has not only completed the school cycle many times but also attended several colleges and universities. His rationality comes to the fore in *New Moon*, when he makes the thoroughly rational decision to leave Bella for her own good. Apparently able to distance himself from his feelings if it is the reasonable thing to do, he breaks up with Bella despite still wanting to be with her, telling her: 'You're just not good for me.' In this instance, Edward exerts authority over his and Bella's relationship without revealing the real reasons behind his decision to part with her, namely his fear of physically hurting her.

The manipulative and potentially abusive quality of Edward's actions, which has become infamous in both academic and media discourse about the *Twilight* Saga,[6] plays a role in all five films. *Eclipse* in particular details the ways in which Edward sets himself up as the sole decision maker in his relationship with Bella. By assuming the role as an authority figure, he follows the generic tradition of the romance hero who 'protects the heroine from the consequences of immature behavior and teaches her how to behave in an appropriate manner as his wife' (Mussell 1984: 117). In various instances in *Eclipse*, Edward disciplines Bella and puts her under surveillance. He also deliberately withholds information from her, arguing in his defence: 'I was trying to protect you.' Importantly, however, the Saga makes it a point to demonstrate Bella's refusal to put up with this type of dominating behaviour. In response to Edward's defence, Bella identifies his action as lying and makes it clear that conduct like this is unacceptable to her. Instead, she insists that: 'We're going to talk about this. . . . Edward, you have to trust me' (*Eclipse* 2010). Thus, the movie adaptations deliberately highlight or insert scenes conveying Bella's defiance against Edward's attempts to control her. When he tells her to stay in the car while he handles a conflict, she does not listen and joins the conversation. When he imposes conditions in their discussion about their shared future, she negotiates her own conditions. When he ignores her voice in the debate about how to handle her unplanned pregnancy, she secures the support of her sister-in-law and asserts herself. In the course of the Saga, Edward thus learns to adjust his behaviour and act in a less domineering way. For instance, in *Breaking Dawn – Part 1*, he apologizes to Bella for failing to empathize with her experience and decision making regarding the pregnancy: 'I'm sorry I've been so angry. . . . I've left you alone in this.' As I suggest, Edward's capability of reflection and willingness to revise some of his problematic behaviours are a fundamental part of his appeal. As a character, he combines elements of traditional masculinity, which may be read as 'natural' and possibly even desirable by audiences, with elements that reflect the incorporation of feminist principles into contemporary culture.

Likewise, while the films continually portray Edward's and Jacob's competition for Bella's affection as a 'naturally' occurring phenomenon, they also problematize the two boys' possessive behaviour. When Edward and Jacob once again act competitively, measuring their strength against each other in a testosterone-filled verbal battle in *Eclipse*, Bella cuts in: 'Stop! I'm tired of this.' In fact, the boys' performances of protective and competitive masculinity may be read as indicating a fundamental insecurity about their suitability as men and as partners for Bella. Nicole Willms has argued that Edward and Jacob 'are preoccupied in their struggle over [Bella's] affections with their relative attractiveness and masculine worth, as well as with what their respective bodies can or cannot do. They seem, in short, to have a degree of anxiety about their masculinity' (2014: 139). Because their confidence in their identity is fragile, they feel the need to 'engag[e] in many demonstrations of masculine protectiveness toward Bella' (ibid.: 140). As previously discussed, the destabilization of the discourse of manhood forms one key backdrop of postfeminist masculinity. The ways in which the male characters handle this kind of destabilization is a central aspect of their portrayal as postfeminist men. Not only is Edward aware of the constructedness of his own 'masculinity', he also displays a consciousness of his appearance and deliberately invests in his attractiveness, as was already mentioned earlier. Indeed, the character is known for his particular hair and clothing style – Edward obviously grooms himself and has the necessary income to afford expensive fashion and sunglasses. In this regard, he clearly deviates from the script of traditional masculinity, since 'appearance, aside from physical strength, is not key to traditional masculinity: looking good, beautifying yourself and being sexually attractive is the realm of women, not men' (Milestone and Meyer 2012: 114). Edward's interest in fashion and styling trends as well as his propensity to put his body on display for the (female) gaze mark him as a postfeminist man.

Another point in which Edward departs from traditional masculinity is his being comfortable with the display of emotions. As I have discussed earlier in this chapter, 'sensitivity, emotional expressiveness and nurturing qualities' (MacKinnon 2003: 73) are part of the postfeminist man's repertoire. Indeed, Edward openly talks about his feelings for Bella and discusses his fear of harming or losing her. He also displays a penchant for nurturing his girlfriend. As Ann Thurber points out, Edward's empathy and capacity to discern the needs and feelings of others is symbolized by his supernatural ability of telepathy, which she refers to as a '"feminized" attribute . . . Mind reading is associated with "a woman's intuition"' (2011: 39). While a certain sensitivity and readiness to take care of someone vulnerable are crucial elements of the conventional romance hero's appeal (Mussell 1984: 117), the genre normally does not provide that the hero is outspoken about his feelings. Quite the reverse, romance heroes are usually 'incapable of expressing emotions or of admitting dependence' (Radway [1984] 1991: 127). In this respect, Edward differs both from the format of traditional masculinity and that of the ideal romance hero. The function of emotional reticence on the part of the hero is not only to provide suspense in the plot but also to reinforce male authority (Mussell 1984: 126). As Kay Mussell argues, '[t]he man always unbends at the end to show his love and need for her, but he retains the mastery to be firmly in control of himself and the heroine' (ibid.). Curiously, although Edward's emotional expressiveness may be read as a relinquishing of authority over Bella, control plays a key role in Edward's relationship with his own vampire body and, metaphorically, the threatening aspects of his own hegemonic masculinity.

As already pointed out, Edward leads a 'vegetarian' lifestyle, renouncing human blood and instead drawing on animal blood as an alternative food source. His 'special diet', as he calls it, is a result of his trying to come to grips with his vampire nature, which he sees as monstrous and sinful. Deeply uncomfortable with his urge to suck the blood out of humans, Edward tells Bella: 'I don't want to be a monster' (*Twilight* 2008). Especially at the beginning of the narrative, Edward believes the lethality of his body to be an expression of his truly evil self (Bealer 2011: 142). This is the dilemma of the reluctant vampire. Like most of his family members, Edward was turned into a vampire by Carlisle on the brink of death while he was succumbing to Spanish Influenza. In the course of the *Twilight* Saga, he continually self-reflects and works on himself in order to lead an existence in which he does not endanger anyone, especially not Bella. Others are impressed by his extraordinary self-control. For instance, Aro wonders: 'How can you stand to be so close to [Bella]?' 'It's not without difficulty', Edward admits, modestly downplaying the enormous amount of willpower that is necessary for him to avoid exploiting his physical superiority over his human girlfriend (*New Moon* 2009). The situation is made even more difficult for Edward because Bella's personal human scent appeals to him in a special way.

Crucially, Edward's impeccable self-control is twofold: his restraint in terms of vampiric feeding goes hand in hand with his striving for sexual abstinence. Here, the *Twilight* Saga provides an interesting reversal of gendered sexual relations between young adults. Throughout the films, Bella is presented as the desiring subject (an aspect discussed at length in Chapter 3) and Edward as the one refusing sexual gratification. The implications of these role assignments are unusual both for a conventional vampire narrative and a romance text. Historically, the figure of the male vampire has been 'associated with dangerous sexual pleasure' (Wisker 1998: 63) at least since the publication of *Dracula* by Bram Stoker (1897). Indeed, Edward as a vampire is 'most definitely both a sexual menace and a sexual enticement' (Byron 2008: 181) for Bella. However, although the vampire is 'the sexual initiator *par excellence*' (Creed [1993] 2007: 65; emphasis in original) in conventional vampire narratives, in the *Twilight* Saga, it is Bella as the supposed victim of the vampire who is depicted as the sexual aggressor. Meanwhile, Edward repeatedly interrupts Bella's attempts to become intimate, citing both moral and physical concerns as reasons for his preference to delay sexual intimacy. Because Edward's vampiric urge to feed and his sexual arousal are linked, engaging in sex entails a tremendous physical risk for Bella. Corresponding to the successful 'diversion' of his dangerous appetite, Edward also manages his sexual desire.

Edward's and Bella's role distribution also deviates from classic romance scripts, in which 'the heroine's innocence is often contrasted explicitly with the hero's previous promiscuity' (Radway [1984] 1991: 130). Thus, the romance hero typically has a considerable amount of sexual experience, which essentially functions as a sign of his 'virility' (ibid.) and his capacity to introduce the heroine to the realm of sexuality. In other words, romance heroes are usually assigned an active role when it comes to sexuality, being depicted as generally interested in and driven by the urge to have sex. In comparison, romance's heterosexual female protagonists are portrayed as less experienced and not active in the pursuit of their sexual pleasure. Instead, they are often represented as 'enforcers of the traditional code of sexuality that limits sexual expression' (Christian-Smith 1991: 41), meaning that they often halt sexual activity, play coy or withdraw from their always-ready male partners. This allocation of male/active and female/passive roles within the sphere of sexuality is not confined to the classic romance genre but is representative of American cultural norms in general. According to Milestone and Meyer, conventional gender roles provide that '[m]asculine sexuality is characterized by a natural, strong sex drive which needs constant satisfaction' (2012: 20), while '[f]emale sexuality is deeply bound up with emotions, relationships and commitment rather than purely bodily pleasure' (ibid.: 21). If (traditional) men are supposedly 'focused on the sexual conquest of women' (ibid.: 115), women are expected to be 'the sensible gender responsible for curbing men's excesses' (ibid.: 21). In this way, heterosexual women and girls become the sexual gatekeepers, responsible for deciding when it is the 'right' time to have sex and the 'right' time to turn interested men and boys down. Performing their gender role adequately is complicated for women and girls in particular, since there is a range of contradictory cultural norms concerning 'appropriate' female sexual behaviour (Nicol 2011: 119–20; see Chapter 3 for further discussion of this issue). In this cultural climate that defines men as pursuers of sexual activity and women as being in charge of granting or declining sexual requests – saying 'yes' or 'no' – in heterosexual encounters, the *Twilight* Saga provides an interesting complication of these typical roles. Bella emerges as the constant initiator of sex, while Edward is presented as 'the stalwart naysayer to any of the usual teenage fun', as Layla Forrest-White puts it (2009: 28). The Saga thus invites an ambiguous reading of gender roles.

On the one hand, 'the cultural script of male sexual desire remains essentially the same; it is still constructed as predatory and dangerous' (Nicol 2011: 116). In line with prevailing cultural notions which conceive of the male sex drive as an instinctual, 'unstoppable biological force' (Vitellone 2007: 377), Edward's sexuality is built in a way that implies the constant risk of a loss of control, so that it must be contained by force of will. Nicol argues that '[t]he (male) vampire body both makes the dangers of male sexuality overt and obvious and pathologizes the male body rather than the female body; it is the male vampire body that is unruly and must be subject to discipline' (2011: 118). Not leaving any doubt about the dangers of his predatory body, Edward warns Bella repeatedly before becoming involved with her: 'If you're smart, you'll stay away from me.... What if I'm the bad guy?' (*Twilight* 2008). On the other hand, being a postfeminist man/vampire, Edward is well aware that his bloodlust is triggered by his sexual impulses and that he must therefore rigorously police these impulses (Nicol 2011: 118). Indeed, he breaks off the couple's first sexual encounter abruptly, telling Bella that 'I can't ever lose control with you' (*Twilight* 2008). Based on his self-awareness, Edward is predestined to 'bear the primary responsibility for reining in his darker impulses, ironically making him less of a threat than a human male' (Nicol 2011: 119). While human boys may be oblivious to their physical dominance and the ways in which their sexuality is shaped by discourses framing the male body as an aggressive 'instinctual force' (Vitellone 2007: 377), vampire Edward has done the mental labour of recognizing and working on his body's pitfalls and has acquired decades of experience in curbing his sexual and culinary appetites. In this way, this vampire romance hero is – paradoxically – both more dangerous and safer than a non-supernatural partner. As Nicol puts it: 'If your boyfriend is a vampire, then his "otherness" (read maleness) can be qualified and therefore made manageable' (2011: 118). The fantasy of the stable vampire romance hero who 'can simply restrain the overriding vampiric impulse (to penetrate/bite, to consume)' (ibid.: 119) holds great appeal for young female audiences concerned with real 'fears of being damaged (emotionally and/or physically) even should they willingly choose to engage in physical intimacy' (ibid.: 118). Indeed, Mukherjea, who conducted a survey of self-declared fans of the *Twilight* franchise, concludes that safety is a central aspect of Edward's allure in the eyes of audiences (2011b: 80).

A postfeminist vampire romance hero who is an expert at controlling his impulses also functions as an idealized romantic partner because he assumes the role of sexual gatekeeper, relieving the heroine of the responsibility of managing men's sexual desires as well as her own. Because Edward takes over the burden of disciplining his male vampire body, Bella is 'free to explore her sexual desires without fear of degradation' (Nicol 2011: 119). Indeed, as shown in Chapter 3, the *Twilight* Saga radically foregrounds its female protagonist's romantic and sexual desire, allowing audiences to experience Bella's point of view first hand. Bella makes her transgressive desires known and actively pursues them over the course of the film series. It is a paradoxical scenario: while Bella cedes control over the couple's sexual relationship to Edward, as he is the one responsible for setting the boundaries during their sexual encounters, she simultaneously receives sexual agency by being freed from conventional gender role ascriptions. Doreen Thierauf interprets this set-up as liberating viewers for a limited time from the kind of 'rational and political thought-labor' (2016: 617) that normally structures straight women's sex lives – thought-labour that involves not only the consideration of prevailing sexual norms and double standards in contemporary culture but also 'an intricate fine-tuning of social context, emotional disposition, and relationship with the partner' (ibid.: 613). As Thierauf argues, '[r]omance creates a contained space of irrational fantasy in which (mostly female) authors put overbearing men in charge of female sexuality because it allows readers to jettison temporarily an overdetermined "biopsychosocial" realm of desire' (2016: 619). Thus, Edward functions simultaneously as an 'overbearing man' and thereby as a revalidation of traditional masculinity, and a figure facilitating a subversion of conventional gender roles concerning the realm of (hetero-)sexuality. This incorporation of contradictory elements makes him a functional bundling of discourses surrounding postfeminist masculinity. Ultimately, Edward's deviation from the traditional masculine role opens up the possibility of a non-heteronormative portrayal of his sexual relationship with Bella.

A compassionate hero with a penchant for self-criticism: Stefan Salvatore

At first glance, *The Vampire Diaries* – similar to the *Twilight* Saga – may be criticized for providing a fairly retrogressive portrayal of gender roles, especially when it comes to the relationship between the human female protagonist Elena Gilbert and both of her vampire suitors, the Salvatore brothers. Elena is often confined to a passive position based on her human and 'feminine' fragility, driven by emotions rather than reason, and characterized by empathy as well as a proclivity to care for others. Meanwhile, both Stefan and his brother Damon usually take an active role in rescuing or defending Elena, are portrayed as physically and mentally strong, and are routinely 'represented as going to extremes' (Milestone and Meyer 2012: 20). Here, the series follows a typical script of the vampire romance genre. As Chiho Nakagawa argues, by 'coupl[ing] a vulnerable human heroine with a dangerous, physically superior and much older male vampire', vampire romance fosters a troubling 'gender inequality' (2011). This regressive binary split between gender roles is perpetuated in countless situations throughout the *Vampire Diaries* seasons. Similar to Bella, Elena is often kept in the dark about what is going on in conflicts with an enemy. She is frequently assigned a protector – usually someone with supernatural powers who is then officially 'on Elena patrol' ('By the Light of the Moon', 2.11) to make sure that she does not get involved in any dangerous activity. The display of traditional masculinity with its 'natural' features of authority and aggression is clearly validated within the series. Stefan in particular personifies the benevolent characteristics of traditional masculinity, and he is held in high esteem for them by other characters: he is described as 'the guy who always comes to the rescue. Stefan's a hero. It's who he is at his core' ('The Cell', 5.9). The narrative also frequently develops in ways that show that he was right and Elena was not, thereby affirming his rightful authority over her.

At the same time, however, the series also sides with Elena at certain points. In these situations, Elena rebels against her dominating 'protectors', either verbally or by action. In a quintessentially postfeminist manner, *The Vampire Diaries* is trying to have it both ways: while male-gendered dominance is romanticized, displayed as 'natural' and often as desirable, the series simultaneously manages to criticize and counter it by pointing out the problematic aspects of traditional hegemonic masculinity. Typically, then, characters in *The Vampire Diaries* make self-referential comments demonstrating the creators' awareness of the sexist tropes they continually choose to re-employ. For instance, in 'All My Children' (3.15), Rebekah comments on the fact that '[f]or some reason everybody seems to want to bend over backwards to save [Elena's] life. Which is incredibly annoying.' On the one hand, such comments can be understood within the framework of the strategies of irony and knowingness, which are typical of postfeminist discourses and postmodern consumer culture in general (Gill 2007: 110). By relying on sexist tropes and simultaneously ironically distancing itself from them, *The Vampire Diaries* adopts an approach that Gill calls a 'catch-all device' (ibid.) allowing the creators to essentially pre-empt critique (ibid.: 111). In addition, they are 'hailing audiences as knowing and sophisticated consumers, flattering them with their awareness of intertextual references' (ibid.: 266) and their understanding of feminist principles. As is typical of postfeminist discourses, feminism is both paid tribute to and repudiated at the same time (Braithwaite 2004: 25). On the other hand, some of the comments and interventions by Elena and other characters read as more serious attempts to illustrate Elena's struggle for agency in a male-dominated supernatural environment. Similar to Bella, who negotiates her relationship with Edward, Elena, time and again, pursues her own interests, either by seeking autonomy from the vampire brothers or by demanding to be treated as their equal. To provide just one example, in 'Katerina' (2.9), Elena decides to obtain more information about her role as the Petrova doppelgänger and the danger that the vampire Klaus Mikaelson will potentially pose to her, instead of waiting for the Salvatores to take care of the issue – despite Stefan's promise that 'You don't have to worry. I'm not going to let anything happen to you.' Later, Elena strikes a deal with the Salvatores, standing up for her right to be filled in about events at all times, so that she is able to make informed decisions for herself: 'If we're going to do this, you can't keep anything from me anymore. From this moment on, we're doing it my way' ('The Dinner Party', 2.15).

Despite being fiercely protective of his heroine, Stefan breaks with a number of traits of traditional masculinity, which marks him as a postfeminist man/vampire. For one thing, he has a predilection for beautifying and grooming himself. Having access to adequate resources as well as a large wardrobe containing clothes in the style of all decades of the twentieth century, Stefan – like Edward – embodies the fashion-consciousness of the postfeminist man. As discussed in Chapter 3, Stefan's well-trained, muscular body is regularly put on eroticized display for the enjoyment of the audience. In terms of style, Stefan is frequently modelled after 1950s style icons and sex symbols James Dean and Marlon Brando – sometimes explicitly, when Stefan dresses up as James Dean at the Whitmore Historical Ball in season five (see Figure 5.1), sometimes implicitly by visual reference. These visual historical references exemplify postfeminism's 'tendency . . . to locate and idealize masculinities in and of the past' (Hamad 2013: 110) and to blend them with modern images of idealized 'masculinity'. As Carol Dyhouse writes, in contemporary culture, 'historical performances of masculinity – as well as femininity – are endlessly reshuffled, judged, and reassessed. . . . the past is continually raided to enrich and to inform the imagination of the present' (2017: 191). This combination of 'old and 'new', regressive and progressive features constitutes the key characteristic of postfeminist masculinity.

For another thing, Stefan frequently relinquishes authority over Elena for the sake of her autonomy. Over the course of the seasons, it becomes

Figure 5.1 Stefan as James Dean (5.5). *The Vampire Diaries* © Warner Bros. Entertainment Inc. 2009–17. All rights reserved.

a recognizable pattern that Stefan is willing to listen and be mindful of Elena's opinion, while Damon disregards Elena's choices and often comments sarcastically on her supposed inability to make sensible and rational decisions: 'It's a little hard to keep track of all your choices lately, Elena' ('Growing Pains', 4.1). Sometimes Damon even goes explicitly against what Elena wants for herself and her life. Towards the end of season two, Elena has made a plan to ensure her survival of the ritual to break the Hybrid Curse, which will be performed by Klaus. While Damon dislikes Elena's plan, Stefan respects her decision to work with Elijah, Klaus' brother, in this matter, and instructs Damon: 'You need to back off. . . . Look, I don't like this any more than you do, but we need to trust her. We've got to just let her do her thing' ('Klaus', 2.19). Seeing that Elena's plan entails a risk that she will not come out of the ritual alive, Damon then forces her to drink his blood, thus making sure that she will return as a vampire, should she die during the ritualistic procedure. In doing so, he disregards not only Elena's authority to make plans for her own safety and that of her loved ones but also her explicitly stated wish that she does not ever want to become a vampire. Set up in contrast to Damon, Stefan puts Elena's needs before his own in this matter:

Stefan: 'Look. If it were *my* choice, I'd want to be with you forever.'
Elena: 'Why have you never brought it up?'
Stefan: 'Because I knew if it was an option, *you* would have. It would be selfish for me to ask you.' ('The Last Day', 2.20; emphases in original)

While Damon acts selfishly, belittles Elena and deliberately ignores her choices, Stefan is depicted as the brother who respects Elena and her decisions, no matter the consequences. Therefore, although Stefan displays some central features of traditional masculinity, he also represents modern ideas about the equality of the sexes. The text itself emphasizes Stefan's advocacy for the recognition of Elena's personhood as one of his most appealing traits. Thus, in later seasons, Elena looks back on her relationship with Stefan and remembers: 'When we were together, you used to let me make my own decisions. You trusted me' ('Dangerous Liaisons', 3.14). According to Elena, Stefan's willingness to acknowledge her autonomy makes him 'the perfect boyfriend. You valued what I wanted, even if it wasn't what you agreed with' ('For Whom the Bell Tolls', 5.4). Here, *The Vampire Diaries* explicitly states where Stefan's allure lies: while he is valued for his capacity to provide safeguard via his 'masculinity', he also lives up to values that could be described as based on feminism.

Crucially, Stefan's respectful attitude towards Elena's decisions and his ability to empathize with her experience are grounded in his identity as a reluctant vampire. Despite the fact that he is always in danger of reverting back to his bloody 'ripper' ways, which he does for example in season three, Stefan can be paralleled with Edward when it comes to his chosen eating behaviour: he draws on a diet of animal blood, with bunnies being his preferred prey.[7] Stefan's disturbing past, in which he made a name for himself as 'the Ripper of Monterey' ('1912', 3.16), involved a loss of control as well as a loss of self for Stefan. The experience of not being able to steer his own life has shaped his understanding of autonomy and agency as a fundamental need. Stefan knows what it feels like to be at the mercy of outside forces, which is why he is able to empathize with Elena's experience of occupying a subordinated position in the context of largely male-dominated (supernatural) power structures. Thus, based on his identity as a reluctant vampire, Stefan radically supports Elena's claim to have a mind of her own:

> Matt: 'So, you're just going to let her call the shots?'
> Stefan: 'I'm letting her make her own decisions.'
> Matt: 'Even if they're wrong?'
> Stefan: 'Nothing wrong with free will, Matt. Trust me, you don't realize that till you lose it.' ('The Departed', 3.22)

Following Williamson's argument in 'Television, Vampires and the Body', I argue, then, that Stefan's experience as a reluctant vampire determined by his bodily urges parallels Elena's struggle against a patriarchally structured environment that regularly restricts her agency. At the same time, Stefan himself functions as an active contributor to this same environment. Thus, on the one hand, Stefan benefits from the prevailing hierarchically constructed social system and is himself a part of it. On the other hand, he reflects on the consequences of his actions within that system and uses his privilege to take a stand for Elena, for example by confronting his own brother. Here, *The Vampire Diaries* mobilizes the generic convention of the affinity between heroine and monster in a way that is based on Stefan's identity as a postfeminist man/vampire. Similar to Edward, Stefan is very much in conformity with Williamson's definition of the reluctant vampire as a 'pathos-ridden creature' (2007: par. 6): 'A monster, a predator, that's who I am, Elena. . . . The blood brings out what's inside of me' ('Miss Mystic Falls', 1.19). Despite his propensity for violence, Stefan continually works on rehabilitating himself, believing that '[w]e choose our own path. Our values and our actions, they define who we are' ('Haunted', 1.7).

Although the position of the two brothers switches in the course of the seasons, with Damon temporarily taking over Stefan's role as the sensible, responsible one, while his brother is roaming through the country as a 'ripper', generally speaking, Stefan conforms to the characteristics of the type of romance hero whom Mussell describes as 'the more conventional, sensitive, mature and competent husband-lover' (1984: 119). As in Edward's case, however, Stefan's character goes beyond the typical attributes of the traditional romance hero. Like Edward, Stefan is adept at expressing emotions and talking about his feelings for Elena. As mentioned previously, the crux in *The Vampire Diaries* is that '[w]hen someone becomes a vampire, all of their natural behaviours get sort of amplified.' For Stefan, this means that 'as a human, I cared deeply for people, how they felt. If they were hurting, I felt their pain, and I felt guilty if I was the one who caused it. And as a vampire, all of that got magnified' ('Bad Moon Rising', 2.3). Thus, empathy and self-criticism are Stefan's core personality traits; Elena at one point describes him as 'the most compassionate person' ('For Whom the Bell Tolls', 5.4) she has ever met. Stefan's ability to discern the needs and feelings of others as well as his own marks Stefan as a postfeminist man. As he explains to Elena, being a (newborn) vampire involves being overwhelmed by a range of emotions: 'The thing is, . . . especially when you're new, it's difficult to separate your feelings. Love, lust, anger, desire, it can all blur into one urge, hunger' ('Haunted', 1.7). Because of years of exercise, Stefan has acquired the ability to recognize, distinguish and manage his emotions to achieve his goal of becoming a 'good' vampire, which demonstrates his high emotional intelligence.

While Stefan's tendency to self-flagellate is referred to as his 'curse' ('Blood Brothers', 1.20) within the series, for Elena and for audiences of the series, it is precisely the factor that makes Stefan attractive. The fact that his vampire body is continuously at risk of spiralling out of control creates a constant state of awareness for Stefan, and he is continually interrogating himself and his body's aggressive (read: 'masculine') impulses. This engagement with one's own 'masculinity', which is a fundamental feature of the postfeminist man, is represented by Stefan's 'brooding and existing in [his] own head' ('162 Candles', 1.8). Interestingly, the series points out that Stefan's choice to self-reflect and reign in his vampire urges has resulted in a loss of supernatural abilities for him: because he subsists on animal blood instead of human blood, Stefan is not as physically strong as Damon, and he cannot compel (i.e. hypnotize) humans properly. Damon ridicules Stefan for his inability – and/or his unwillingness – to fight back 'appropriately' when attacked: 'Your choice of lifestyle has made you weak' ('The Night of the Comet', 1.2). As a result of his 'lifestyle', then, Stefan is at risk of failing to protect Elena and is apparently less capable of exerting control over other people's actions. In other words, a consequence of Stefan's self-critical engagement with his own 'masculinity' is his loss of some of his 'masculine' power and privileges. By combining Stefan's traditional 'masculine' features, which are employed in favour of the romance heroine, and his self-critical reflection with regard to these features, *The Vampire Diaries* constructs a postfeminist man who holds high appeal for heterosexual female audiences.

An old-fashioned gentleman willing to look forward: Bill Compton

True Blood's Bill Compton is certainly related to Edward and Stefan, while also differing from them, potentially due to the varying target audiences of the texts. In comparison, *True Blood* adopts a darker tone and is decidedly more graphic in terms of sex, violence and gore. The following reading of the character of Bill mainly focuses on the first two seasons of the series, in which Bill functions as an appealing postfeminist vampire romance hero. The subsequent seasons introduce some fundamental revisions to the character. As a matter of fact, the show ends up retrospectively re-writing the events of the first season: in the season three finale, Sookie learns that the circumstances of her getting acquainted with Bill and falling in love with him were actually staged. That Bill is turned from an attractive romance hero into a questionable manipulator is in tune with the fact that the series employs fewer and fewer romance conventions overall. Crawford has interpreted *True Blood*'s dark overturning of established romantic certainties as 'an implicit critique of the genre from which it arose' (2014: 261). The series finally ends with Bill sacrificing himself for the sake of Sookie, who then finds fulfilment in a 'traditional' role as mother and wife to a human partner. *True Blood*'s conventional ending curiously mirrors the *Vampire Diaries* finale, which sees Stefan sacrificing himself so that Elena may lead a happy life with a human-turned Damon, ultimately securing her in her 'proper' place, removed from the space of supernatural transgression. Here, too, are paranormal romance ideals taken and then 'vastly complicate[d] and subvert[ed]' (ibid.: 269) over the course of the seasons. Presenting denouements that strongly reaffirm conventional gender roles, both series seem to be indebted to the classic reassuring ending of Gothic/horror narratives, in which the threat to society and the norm is banned and the status quo reinstated (Carroll 1990: 200). Rather than focusing on this ultimate reinstatement of conservative gendered norms, however, I want to turn my attention to preceding moments in which interesting challenges to the traditional gender order do happen. As I contend, such moments are neither erased nor undone by the respective 'happy endings'. On the contrary, the serial nature of these paranormal romances allows for an emphasis on, and revelling in, the early phase of 'disruption' (ibid.) that comes long before the neat resolution of the series finales – a phase in which postfeminist masculinities are granted the spotlight.

Like Edward and Stefan, Bill – via his vampire nature – retains the link to a past associated with traditional, supposedly more clear-cut and satisfying gender roles, while simultaneously being rooted in a contemporary setting and 'embrac[ing] the future' (Abbott 2007: 3). Similar to Edward, Bill's appreciation of traditional gender relations becomes visible in his courtship of Sookie. Being an old-fashioned gentleman, the language he uses to politely ask Sookie out on a date stems from a different era and is therefore initially not understandable to her:

Bill: 'May I call on you sometime?'
Sookie: 'Call on me?'
Bill: 'May I come and visit with you at your home?' ('Strange Love', 1.1)

Unlike most of the human men whom Sookie deals with, Bill acts respectfully towards her, asks for permission before kissing her and follows gendered rules of etiquette. For Sookie, Bill's old-school understanding of romance, courtship and gender are both attractive and deterring. While she appreciates his unusually courteous and considerate attitude, she also voices her disagreement with some of the traditionally 'masculine' behaviours that Bill displays. These include violence and an overly dominant, possessive and patronizing demeanour. In 'Mine' (1.3), Sookie calls Bill out on proclaiming that she belongs to him in front of a group of vampires. After the other vampires have left, she confronts him: 'And what the hell did you mean, "Sookie is mine"?' In 'Nothing but the Blood' (2.1), Sookie finds out that Bill has hidden some important information from her. Bill's apology – 'If I withheld anything, it was only to protect you' – is reminiscent of Edward's response when charged with manipulating Bella. Like Bella and Elena, Sookie demands to be informed about things that might impact her life and exposes Bill's authoritative concept of 'protection' as a lack of confidence in her ability to deal with whatever issue arises. Soon after communicating her disappointment in her vampire lover, she discovers that Bill has murdered her uncle after she had told him that the latter sexually abused her as a child. Horrified by Bill's propensity for violence, Sookie rejects his toxic masculinity:[8] 'I cannot have people dying every time I confide in you. . . . I feel sick.' Bill promises to make amends for his actions: 'Sookie. I cannot and I will not lose you. For all the ways I have dismayed, aggrieved or failed you, I swear I will atone' ('Never Let Me Go', 2.5). Similar to the *Twilight Saga* and *The Vampire Diaries*, *True Blood* both presents images of traditional hegemonic (sometimes toxic) masculinity and contextualizes/problematizes them via its female protagonist's reactions to them. Crucially, these elements of traditional masculinity are complemented by more contemporary conceptions of masculinity that can be identified as defining features of the postfeminist man. One of these aspects associated with postfeminist masculinity involves Bill's willingness to reflect on and revise his toxic behaviour after being called out by Sookie. Nudged into the 'right' direction by the romantic heroine, vampire Bill learns to reconsider his old-school ways and adapt to a present shaped by the influence of feminism.

Besides being open to revise his stance on relationships, Bill is also characterized as a vampire embracing modern ideas based on his being dedicated to the 'mainstreaming' agenda of the American Vampire League. The latter is spearheading a social movement stipulating the integration of vampires into everyday human society by 'moderat[ing]' ('Mine', 1.3) their monstrous behaviour. Having been recruited to the movement by Nan Flanagan (Jessica Tuck) in 1982, when vampire scientists were close to synthesizing human blood, Bill is a vocal supporter of the cause. Although the mainstreaming agenda has since officially been adopted by the Vampire Authority, there are still factions among the vampire community that continue to cling to the traditional ways of predatory feeding and killing humans. Bill is often juxtaposed with these 'traditionalists'. For instance, the Vampire Magister of North America (Željko Ivanek), an opponent of mainstreaming with a superior position in the vampire society, reproaches Bill with diverging from the ancient traditions: 'You have no nest. You prefer to consort with humans. You seem to have lost all sense of our priorities' ('I Don't Wanna Know', 1.10). In setting up the 'mainstreamers' and the 'traditionalists' as antagonists in the series, *True Blood* fits into a pattern which Abbott defines as typical for the contemporary vampire genre. As she argues, the latter frequently features modern vampire protagonists seeking to replace a group of traditionally oriented vampires, often the former ruling class of the vampire world. These forward-looking vampire protagonists, among whom Bill can be counted, 'are modern, not only because of their contempt for the old ways ... but also because the act of destroying the traditional vampire in order to take its place, effectively replacing the old with the new, is one of the distinctive characteristics of modernity' (2007: 4).

Like Edward and Stefan, Bill did not wish to be turned into a vampire and struggles with his body's violent urges. A flashback in 'Sparks Fly Out' (1.5) reveals that it is precisely Bill's moral code and decency that convinced vampire Lorena (Mariana Klaveno) to make him her supernatural companion in 1865. Like Stefan, Bill first engages in a period of hedonism and violence, which he spends with his maker. In 1935, he distances himself from Lorena since he has come to despise himself for the cruelties he has committed. In contrast to his maker, Bill makes the decision to become a 'good' vampire and to 'hang onto some semblance of [his] former humanity' ('Mine', 1.3). Naturally, this means that he must reign in his violent impulses and spare human lives when feeding – and, as soon as it goes on sale, live on 'Tru Blood'. As a reluctant vampire, Bill constantly interrogates himself and his vampire body, which he understands as a sign of evil: 'I have spent my entire life as a vampire apologizing, believing I was inherently wrong somehow. Living in fear. Fear that God had forsaken me, that I was damned' ('Save Yourself', 5.12).

Interestingly, the parallels between Bill and Sookie, *True Blood*'s Gothic heroine, are even more clearly emphasized in this series than in the other two. Thus, the two share a kind of outsider status based on their respective supernatural natures. While Bill is a vampire, Sookie finds out in season three that she is a human/faerie halfling. From early childhood on, she has been able to listen to people's thoughts – a supernatural skill that constrains her more often than is useful to her. In 'Never Let Me Go' (2.5), she reveals that she has struggled with not being 'normal', often feeling 'like I have a disability'. Sookie's Otherness is constructed as a parallel to Bill's Otherness. As Sookie herself points out: 'I used to get so mad when people judged vampires just for being different. It's like they were judging me, too' ('Scratches', 2.3). The correlation between Bill's and Sookie's positions as (supernatural) outsiders is again made explicit by Sookie in 'Night on the Sun' (3.8): 'What I can do in my brain, it's every bit as deadly as Bill's fangs. I know what it's like to be afraid of my own body, to not be sure what it's going to do next. I've killed. I may not have cheated but I wanted to. Me and Bill, we ain't so different.'[9] Thus, Sookie's and Bill's similarity is framed as one based on bodily characteristics, which is in line with horror's tendency to suggest a 'sympathy and affinity . . . between the monster and the girl' (Williams 1996: 21) that is grounded in the fact that each of their bodies is (perceived as) different from the male body.

Sookie's feeling of kinship with Bill is what initially draws her to him, and it is the reason she is committed to making him feel welcome when he first arrives in town. As the first vampire taking up residence in Bon

Temps, Bill has a particularly hard time with the citizens of the small town and is often faced with exclusion, discrimination and violence based on his vampire nature. In *True Blood*, '[v]ampirism serves as a trope for social and legal marginalization and minoritization' (Hudson 2013: 665), with vampires being presented as equivalent to real-world marginalized groups. Obvious examples of this parallelization are the show's invention of the term 'Vampire American' as a counterpart of 'African American' and the background story of the legalization of vampire marriage. As I argue, Bill's struggle with people's biases and discriminatory practices mirrors Sookie's experience of gender-based discrimination, for example in the workplace. As a human and a white woman, Sookie is neither affected by racism – like her friend Tara, a Black woman – nor by institutionalized 'speciesism' (Blayde and Dunn 2010: 43), like Bill. However, she regularly faces sexism in her private as well as professional life; see Chapter 3 for an examination of Sookie's experience of misogyny and sexism in all its facets. Arguably, it is this shared experience of prejudice and discrimination that plays a key role in *True Blood*'s parallelization of the Gothic heroine and the monster. Bill's ability to understand and empathize with structural inequality may then be particularly appealing for (female) viewers who can identify very well with Sookie's experience. As a postfeminist man/vampire, Bill sees through the workings of power and the ways in which marginalized communities are oppressed by groups seeking to bolster and maintain their hegemonic social position. Although Bill himself at times functions as an upholder of sexist gendered hierarchies, his experience-based knowledge of social inequalities and his willingness to critically examine his own practices of (toxic) masculinity render him a compelling romantic hero for postfeminist audiences.

The contradictions of the postfeminist vampire romance hero

In this chapter, I have examined Edward from the *Twilight* Saga, Stefan from *The Vampire Diaries* and Bill from *True Blood*, arguing that these characters work as embodiments of contemporary postfeminist masculinity based on their identity as reluctant vampires. In these paranormal romances, postfeminist masculinity is represented as the idealized and preferred, that is: the hegemonic version of masculinity. This allows viewers to immerse themselves into a fantasy of 'old-school gentleman-vampires' (Mukherjea 2011a: 3) who incorporate all the benevolent characteristics of traditional masculinity without eschewing feminism's ideals. Considering that these series are highly popular and commercial products, the inherently ambivalent vampire romance hero works as a model of masculinity that may speak to a variety of consumers with differing values, from liberals to conservatives. Introducing paradoxical constructions of masculinity, the texts invite both progressive and regressive readings, which will be explored in the following.

A regressive reading of postfeminist masculinity is offered by Sarah Godfrey and Hannah Hamad, who have observed a post-9/11 (popular) 'cultural preoccupation with rescuer masculinity' ([2011] 2014: 166). The crux of this particular version of 'protectorate masculinity' (ibid.: 165) is its blending of the protective, aggressive action hero with the figure of the postfeminist father (ibid.: 157). As such, the focus on male paternity is representative of the tendency in postfeminist culture towards male investment in traditionally 'female' responsibilities, such as child-rearing, domestic duties and taking care of others. However, Godfrey and Hamad find that 'action-oriented machismo has been renegotiated into extant postfeminist masculinities' (ibid.: 170). Thus, the potentially troubling traits of machismo are offset 'through explicatory recourse to fatherhood' (ibid.: 169) in films like *Taken* (2008) and TV shows like *24* (Fox, 2001–10). On the flipside of the male protector, we have women and children, particularly daughters, who are depicted as vulnerable and fearful. Because innocent individuals – and, above all, the macho father's own family – need protection from outside forces, the 'benevolent protective patriarch' (ibid.) is exonerated even from morally dubious and extremely violent actions.

I suggest that the narratives of the *Twilight* Saga, *The Vampire Diaries* and *True Blood* follow a similar logic. As I have elaborated at length in this chapter, Edward, Stefan and Bill are characterized by a combination of patriarchal and progressive elements – a hybridization of traits that indicates their rootedness in postfeminist discourse. Interestingly, besides performing the function of patriarchal protection, these vampire lovers not only display characteristics such as emotional expressiveness, empathy and a willingness to moderate themselves, but they also sometimes perform a kind of paternal role for their beloved romance heroines. Needless to say, because of their vampire nature, they are all substantially older and more experienced than the female protagonists. Edward most clearly works as a father figure for Bella: his position of authority is bolstered by his ability to take care of his human girlfriend's physical and emotional needs at any time. Edward runs with Bella on his back, sometimes carries and cradles her, helps her put on the buckles in the car, composes a lullaby for her, sees to it that she eats enough and encourages her to send out college applications. By characterizing its vampire hero in this way, the *Twilight* Saga conforms to romance formulas determining that the typical romance hero be defined by a 'combination of paternal and erotic qualities' (Mussell 1984: 133). Thus, our vampire romance heroes, especially Edward, could be described as 'paternally signified, and therefore "sensitive", leading men' (Hamad 2013: 105), although they are not literally the heroines' fathers. Within the respective texts, the vampires' assumption of responsibility for the female protagonists' physical and emotional safety is often explained with recourse to how much they love and care for them – perhaps even in a paternal way.

Godfrey and Hamad refer to this legitimizing mechanism as an 'ideological alibi for the revalidated enactment of protectorate masculinities' ([2011] 2014: 162). Crucially, because the texts 'construct a fictional framework allowing heroic masculinity to succeed' – the vulnerable heroine is saved, the town is defended from the season's antagonist(s), the status quo is more or less restored – they 'have a cathartic function in the context of the national trauma of

9/11' (ibid.: 168). Following Godfrey and Hamad, the *Twilight* Saga, *The Vampire Diaries* and *True Blood* 'narrativize cultural anxieties over masculinity' and quell these anxieties by bolstering benevolent rescuer masculinity. In the process, they 'rearticulate and reinvest in female powerlessness' (ibid.: 170). Essentially, Godfrey and Hamad argue, patriarchal masculinity, which had become 'increasingly anachronistic' (ibid.: 159), is able to re-establish itself by using postfeminist masculinity/fatherhood as a validating factor. A similar argument is made by MacKinnon, who questions the validity of the postfeminist redefinition of masculinity in terms of sensitivity and nurturing qualities, suggesting that a 'sizable proportion of gender critics see it as largely a means to hold on to male power' (2003: 73). As he argues, '[t]he most cynical interpretation would be that, in order for masculinity to remain hegemonic, it must admit the feminine at certain historical moments' (ibid.: 15). In this pessimistic view, men have not really changed but have selectively taken on some 'feminine' characteristics for strategic reasons; their ultimate goal is the maintenance of their dominant social position, which they are unwilling to share or give up.

Rather than adopting this cynical, regressive reading, my research aims to emphasize the ambivalence of the examined paranormal romances by pointing to their openness towards not only regressive but also progressive interpretations. Importantly, more progressive readings are also built into these representations of postfeminist masculinity. As my analyses have shown, the protective paternalism performed by Edward, Stefan and Bill does not remain unquestioned by/in the texts. Traditionally 'masculine' behaviours that seem anachronistic in their modern-day context are frequently addressed and problematized by the female protagonists. The *Twilight* Saga, *The Vampire Diaries* and *True Blood* thus set out to stage their heroines' active resistance to some of the regressive gendered expectations that the vampire heroes are – consciously or subconsciously – holding as a result of their socialization in a distant, 'traditional' past. In this way, normative ideas about traditional masculinity are effectively deconstructed. Responding to the heroines' criticism, the male vampire protagonists make conscious efforts to re-evaluate their notions of appropriate and acceptable behaviour. Thus, in contrast to the 1980s romance texts examined by Modleski, in which the heroines' expressions of frustration with their partners were often neutralized and 'turned into a way of pleasing men, of keeping them . . . "entertained"' (1982: 47), today's vampire romances do not neutralize their heroines' anger but seem to represent it as justified and consequential.

Furthermore, as we have seen, Edward, Stefan and Bill exceed both traditional masculinity and the conventional romance hero in their capacity to express, recognize and manage emotions. Displaying the ability to take care of their female lovers' needs and desires, they keep up the established romance formula of the nurturing lover, which apparently continues to be relevant in early twenty-first-century culture. This incorporation of conventionally 'feminine' skills distinguishes them from the benevolent protective patriarchs discussed by Godfrey and Hamad. Thus, the authors describe post-9/11 rescuer masculinity as 'hav[ing] dispelled the emasculatory effects of postfeminist reconstruction, expressing fatherly protection through action, violence, and sacrifice over nurturing sensitivity' ([2011] 2014: 168). This is not true of our vampire romance heroes, whose incorporation of 'feminine' traits is actually central to their gender performance and their appeal for postfeminist (female) audiences. This fact can perhaps be taken as an indication that the postfeminist revision of masculinity is indeed more profound than Godfrey's/Hamad's and MacKinnon's pessimistic reading would suggest.

In this context, MacKinnon points out that a number of 'commentators voice suspicion of the way that masculinity may soften, become more feminine, without addressing patriarchal power or capitalist work relations' (2003: 15). Countering this suspicion, I maintain that our postfeminist male vampires *are* represented as having an awareness about patriarchal power relations and making an effort to rework them. As I have stressed, the *Twilight* Saga, *The Vampire Diaries* and *True Blood* present a vision of postfeminist masculinity that is in the process of interrogating and revising its approach to its own gendered dominance – a process that is projected onto the male vampire body. Based on their experience as reluctant vampires, all three protagonists have acquired a deep understanding of what it means to have one's agency restricted by outside forces, and – in the case of Bill – of how power structures operate in society. This experience-based knowledge, which may parallel many female viewers' struggle with institutionalized gender-based discrimination in a patriarchally structured world, is the reason for the vampire heroes' readiness to question and modify their patriarchal behaviours. The fact that the vampires continually restrain themselves can be read as an indication that power relations are actually challenged here, which would refute MacKinnon's argument. Thus, these vampire romances – despite their problematic aspects – do invite progressive readings.

In fact, both Godfrey/Hamad and MacKinnon do refer to the double movement inherent in representations of postfeminist masculinity. For instance, the former observe the simultaneous occurrence of acknowledgement and rebuttal, 'writing in' and 'writing out' of feminism in the figure of the protective patriarch – a dynamic that is, of course, central to postfeminist discourses. As they conclude, 'these mediations of [paternal rescuer] masculinity are complicit in a discursive undoing of feminism while perpetuating, recuperating, and celebrating the discourses of involved fatherhood granted by postfeminism' ([2011] 2014: 170). This paradox, which is constitutive of postfeminist masculinity, is also commented on by MacKinnon when he writes that '[m]asculinity . . . becomes less hegemonic precisely in order to stay hegemonic' (2003: 73). Following this understanding, postfeminist masculinity has become subordinated and is still hegemonic at the same time, which is a contradiction in itself. Interestingly, Raewyn Connell and James W. Messerschmidt argue that the concept of hegemonic masculinity allows for such a paradoxical construction:

> the conceptualization of hegemonic masculinity should explicitly acknowledge the possibility of democratizing gender relations, of

abolishing power differentials, not just of reproducing hierarchy. A transitional move in this direction requires an attempt to establish as hegemonic among men . . . a version of masculinity open to equality with women. In this sense, it is possible to define a hegemonic masculinity that is thoroughly 'positive'. (2005: 853)

As I suggest, the postfeminist masculinities exemplified by Edward, Stefan and Bill can be considered such 'transitional' forms of masculinity, seeing as they are simultaneously hegemonic and open to critically reflecting and potentially shedding their hegemonic status. Consequently, the *Twilight* Saga, *The Vampire Diaries* and *True Blood* – despite their limitations – can be understood as attempting to reform contemporary gendered hierarchies.

An interesting aspect is Connell's and Messerschmidt's comment on the difficulty of imagining such a positive hegemonic masculinity 'in practice' (ibid.). Indeed, inherent in the concept of hegemonic masculinity is the idea that it expresses 'widespread ideals, fantasies, and desires' (ibid.: 838), which are predominantly shaped by media discourses: exemplars of bearers of hegemonic masculinity are largely 'fantasy figures, such as film characters' (Connell 2005: 77). In the fantasy space of the *Twilight* Saga, *The Vampire Diaries* and *True Blood*, then, postfeminist masculinity functions as a successful, albeit not always a consistent version of manhood. This idealized variant of masculinity is not necessarily preferable in real men; in fact, the 'vampire nature of the characters and the fantasy element in these stories . . . make qualities desirable, which, in actual men in real relationships, might be quite unsettling' (Mukherjea 2011a: 12). In contrast to the often-made assumption that (female) readers and viewers of paranormal romance are influenced by the content they consume to such an extent that they are looking for a vampire lover's qualities in real men, fans of Edward, Stefan and Bill are likely well aware of this. What paranormal romance offers these viewers is instead a productive space in which current gender norms and relations can be explored in complex ways. By representing successful negotiations between human female protagonists and male vampire heroes about the terms of their relationships, these texts reflect – and provide fantasy solutions for – crucial aspects of women's and girls' experiences in navigating heterosexual relationships in contemporary postfeminist culture. The vampire hero's 'convoluted personality' (ibid.: 11) enables viewers to immerse themselves in the fantasy of secure gender relations while also benefiting from decades of feminist activism. In other words, what these postfeminist vampire heroes offer their audiences is the pleasure of submitting to patriarchal masculinity, combined with the satisfaction of resisting and challenging it.

Conclusion
Paradoxical pleasures

In this work, I have understood and examined the *Twilight* Saga, *The Vampire Diaries* and *True Blood* as a locus for the articulation of postfeminist ideologies and a host to prevalent discourses about gender, sexuality, subjectivity, agency and the body. Adopting a Cultural Studies framework, I set out to situate and investigate these tremendously popular paranormal romances in their contemporary American cultural context and determine their cultural politics. Applying key ideas of this field of cultural analysis, my study started from the premise that 'culture is never only a site of consumption or manipulation but also allows for productive, tactical, and even subversive engagements with even the most conservative of texts/ideologies' (Wilson 2011: 7). Conceiving of these popular cultural products as a terrain of ideological struggle or a 'semiotic battlefield in which . . . a conflict [is] fought out between the forces of incorporation and the forces of resistance' (Storey 2011: 217–8), this work sought to bring to light and discuss some of the conflicting meanings that coexist in the texts. To this end, my study has addressed such questions as: Why were the first two decades of the twenty-first century so accommodating to these vampire romance fictions? What specific desires, issues and fears are addressed and negotiated by them? What concerns in women's/girls' (and men's/boys') lives are being played out, explored, alleviated, resolved, concealed, ignored here? In what ways is the figure of the vampire drafted and employed in these narratives, and how does it intersect with the discourses of postfeminism? As my analysis has shown, the *Twilight* Saga, *The Vampire Diaries* and *True Blood* can be seen both as indicators of deep cultural tensions rooted in the contemporary postfeminist age and an imaginary space for the articulation of pleasures and desires, some of which tend(ed) to remain unaddressed in mainstream popular culture overall. In this respect, my book has highlighted the pleasures that these texts offer to (heterosexual, white) female viewers in particular. My findings are thus in line with Spooner's recent identification of 'a counter-narrative of Gothic texts that combine conventional markers of the Gothic with a mood of pleasure, lightness or celebration' (2017: 23), for which she has coined the umbrella term 'post-millennial' (ibid.: 6) or 'happy Gothic' (ibid.: 3). Although the phenomenon is not an entirely new one, happy Gothic texts, which cater particularly to 'the tastes of women, children, teenagers, queer and subcultural communities' (ibid.: 187), have proliferated since the turn of the twenty-first century (ibid.: 23).

Buffy the Vampire Slayer (broadcast between 1997 and 2003), which has repeatedly been cited in this book, can be seen as exemplary for an early generation of happy/postfeminist Gothic narratives. Classified as 'part of a groundswell of popular programming . . . featuring strong female protagonists' (Pender 2016: 30), *Buffy* is often set in stark contrast with the *Twilight* franchise by academic as well as cultural critics.[1] Wisker even goes so far as to declare these texts 'the two extremes of postfeminist Gothic' (2019: 55): one 'positive, politicised, energetic', the other 'vacuous' and offering 'nothing feminist' (ibid.: 56) at all. There are, indeed, differences between the earlier generation of postfeminist Gothics and the slightly later generation explored in this book. For instance, Rebecca Munford and Melanie Waters argue that the physically and mentally powerful models of female heroism exemplified by *Buffy* and the like have since 'been supplanted by those which might be more readily reconciled to the demands of home and family' (2014: 140). Notwithstanding, I suggest that the slightly later generation of postfeminist Gothics is best understood as a continuation of the earlier generation. As my analyses have demonstrated, the *Twilight* Saga, *The Vampire Diaries* and *True Blood* actively enter into a dialogue with *Buffy* at various points throughout the respective series. Among the themes that these texts examine, it is particularly the exploration of ambiguous and/or unhealthy romantic relationships, the portrayal of 'masculinity' as 'in crisis', the instalment of a female gaze and the use of a camp aesthetic that these paranormal romances – often quite self-consciously – adopt from the earlier *Buffy*. These continuities reveal that many of the concerns of turn-of-the-century postfeminism are still relevant in the postfeminist world of the 2010s. The major factors forming the cultural and political backdrop of the slightly later generation of postfeminist Gothics include both the Bush and Obama presidencies (2001–9 and 2009–17, respectively), the long-term effects of the 9/11 terrorist attacks, the 2008 financial crash, the continuing hegemonic spread of neoliberalism, the increasing visibility of feminism in on- and offline spaces, and developments in the cultural industries, such as 'the changing culture of texts for young adults to include more explicit discussions of tragic outcomes including death, as well as greater explorations of sexual desire for young people' (Smith and Moruzi 2020: 610). Taken together, these factors have facilitated and shaped the establishment of postfeminist (teen) paranormal romance as a ubiquitous popular cultural genre.

Echoing my general findings regarding the representation of gender and sexuality in the *Twilight* Saga, *The Vampire Diaries* and *True Blood*, Jowett concludes in her seminal work *Sex and the Slayer* (2005) that despite the dominant or preferred reading of *Buffy* as progressive, the latter 'presents neither a "subversive" nor a "conservative" view of gender but, rather, a contradictory mixture of both' (1). Similarly, Patricia Pender emphasizes that *Buffy* 'delights in deliberately and self-consciously baffling the binaries', thereby producing inherently 'ambivalent gender dynamics' (2016: 9). According to Pender, *Buffy* combines symbolic representations of second wave feminist struggles, such as 'the challenge to balance personal and professional life, [and] the fight against sexual violence' (ibid.: 22), with ideas of third-wave feminism, for example the 'embrace of contradiction and paradox' (ibid.: 51).[2] Pender therefore describes *Buffy* as being 'at the cusp of second- and third-wave feminisms' (ibid.: 35). Looking at the vampire romances explored in the frame of this book, one might argue that this later generation of happy Gothics has since come to fully embrace the deeply contradictory discourses of postfeminism. Nevertheless, here, too, '[f]amiliar feminist issues concerning gender and power... remain but are replayed differently' (Wisker 2019: 53). The fact that these texts are both 'dealing with new and old problems facing women' (ibid.: 58) is unsurprising since postfeminism, in my understanding, does not constitute a complete break with earlier strands of feminism, but also encompasses continuities of thought with the latter.

Postfeminism has been conceived within this research as a hybrid phenomenon emerging in/from a number of contexts and influences, such as feminism, neoliberalism, consumer culture, individualism, postmodernism and mainstream media. My understanding of postfeminism was established in Chapter 1, where I gave a definition of my study's contextualizing approach to the phenomenon. Chapter 1 identified one of the key characteristics of postfeminist discourses, namely the double movement between the threat of backlash and the potential for innovation. Thus, due to its hybridity, 'postfeminism is by definition contradictory, simultaneously feminist, liberating and repressive, productive and obstructive of progressive social change. Whether critics see feminism or antifeminism as more dominant in the end is a matter of interpretation and degree' (Projansky 2007: 68). Rather than adopting an 'either/or' approach in the sense that the selected paranormal romances would be either defined as feminist or anti-feminist texts, this book has shown that the *Twilight* Saga, *The Vampire Diaries* and *True Blood* can really be considered 'both/and' texts. Despite being deeply problematic in some respects, they also offer highly interesting, potentially subversive moments in which gendered power dynamics are challenged. The texts thereby engage in what Siegel has called a 'politics of ambiguity' (2007: 154), which is characteristic of postfeminism. Thus, contrary to some scholars' opinion that 'the transition to a postfeminist culture involves an evident erasure of feminist politics from the popular' (Tasker and Negra 2007b: 5), I have not conceived postfeminism as depoliticized. Rather, my work has started from the premise that postfeminist political practice needs to be understood as revising typical second wave political activism. Thus, postfeminist approaches are marked by attempts to resignify 'femininity' and sexuality, a focus on individual empowerment, an acceptance of 'the paradoxes of postmodern subjectivity' (Brabon 2013: 126) and a straddling of binaries – features that have been identified as central to the *Twilight* Saga, *The Vampire Diaries* and *True Blood* through the analyses performed here.

As elaborated in Chapter 2, Gothic and twentieth-century popular romance, the historical precursors of the contemporary paranormal romance genre, have both been theorized as inherently ambivalent genres torn between conservative generic conventions and feminist subtext. Scholars like Moers and Ferguson Ellis have read Gothic romance's stereotypical portrayal of female victimization by the hands of violent male villains as a subversive commentary on women's experience and oppression in a male-dominated society, particularly their confinement to the domestic sphere. Similarly, a scholarly consensus in romance studies is that romance as a genre is 'structured both by familiar romance formulas as well as an engagement with feminism' (Veldman-Genz 2012: 115). For instance, Modleski and Radway have argued that despite romance's precarious depiction of male violence against the romantic heroine, the genre's function is to represent, protest and find symbolic solutions for problems in women's circumscribed lives under patriarchy. My research has taken its cue from these feminist analyses of these 'women's genres' and has critically looked at the hybrid paranormal romance genre's engagement with (post)feminist issues, such as everyday sexism and violence against women, power relations in heterosexual relationships, sexual autonomy and pleasure, (self-)empowerment and (self-)surveillance. For this purpose, the *Twilight* Saga, *The Vampire Diaries* and *True Blood* employ the figure of the vampire, which turns out to be ideal for the incorporation of postfeminist discourses surrounding gender, sexuality, identity and the body.

Chapter 2 has also investigated the polarizing effect of the paranormal romance genre in general and the incongruous reception history of the *Twilight* franchise in particular. The 'both/and' nature that is fundamental to postfeminist media culture is perhaps what is reflected in many consumers' mixed reactions to the postfeminist vampire romances investigated in the frame of this monograph. As Anne Helen Petersen has found in her ethnographic study of readers of the *Twilight* series, 'the single best way to characterize feminist readers' response to *Twilight* is *ambivalence*. Having voiced immense pleasure in the narrative, these readers were nonetheless deeply troubled by it – incensed and repulsed by several elements of the text that were readily labeled by readers as culturally regressive, non-feminist, and affirmative of patriarchal values' (2012: 61; emphasis in original). Confirming this finding, Sarah Wagenseller Goletz has coined the term 'Giddyshame Paradox' to describe 'the contradictory reactions of many friends – usually women, often self-described feminists' (2012: 147) – to the *Twilight* franchise. This ambivalent reading/viewing experience is referred to by Merri Lisa Johnson as a '"paradox of spectatorship" – [rooted in] the conflicted identity of the feminist fangirl' (2007a: 10). As Johnson observes, a delicate 'balance between appreciation and skepticism' shapes her own viewing experience of contemporary television. Considering that the progressive elements of currently popular TV shows are often 'intercut with moments of containment, flashes of stereotypes, plot crutches, and predictable jokes' (ibid.: 19), Johnson proposes a media theory that takes into account the fact that

> we take what we need from the available culture, sieve out the rest. This 'negotiated reading' is . . . an acknowledgement that incremental shifts in power may be the most we can hope for, and that the kinds of pleasure available to women in the current media culture include the pleasures of oppositional reading as well as the pleasures of seeing feminist concepts dramatized on television. (ibid.: 11)

Committing myself to the notion of polysemic texts as well as adopting Hall's theory that audiences are actively involved in the meaning production of popular cultural products, I – like Johnson – have operated under the assumption that viewers of the *Twilight* Saga, *The Vampire Diaries* and *True Blood* not only actively construct their own interpretations of these narratives, but they also draw a number of meaningful pleasures from the texts. Generally speaking, popular cultural texts offer a number of potential pleasures to consumers. Fiske has theorized that (popular) '[c]ulture is the constant process of producing meanings of and from our social experience, and such meanings necessarily produce a social identity for the people involved.... Within the production and circulation of these meanings lies pleasure' (1989: 1). Thus, the consumption of media texts functions as a process of deliberate identity construction enabling audiences to appropriate or reject elements of respective texts, thereby negotiating cultural ideas and values. Furthermore, identity formation takes place through consumers' active participation in fan communities (Thomas 2012: 212). Relatedly, Pamela H. Demory underlines the particular pleasures provided by the film adaptations of the *Twilight* series in opposition to the novels: 'One of those pleasures is experiencing the story in a community of like-minded people.... Reading is a solitary experience; film-going is (or can be) a group experience. For the target audience – teenage girls – the way that the film fosters a community experience may be part of the attraction' (2010: 206). Drawing on Demory's observation, one might argue that the screen adaptations of the *Twilight* Saga, and perhaps also *The Vampire Diaries* and *True Blood*,[3] offer particularly significant opportunities for audiences to engage in the satisfactory processes of identity formation.

Chapter 2 went on to discuss the pleasure potential contained in the consumption of genre texts. As explained here, genre products combine the pleasures of recognizing familiar structures and being surprised by new combinations of generic elements or even ruptures of these structures. In other words, consumers may enjoy genre texts not only based on the fact that their expectations are being met, but also that the latter are defied. Throughout its chapters, my work has pointed towards instances in which the *Twilight* Saga, *The Vampire Diaries* and *True Blood* conform to or deviate significantly from genre conventions, and has highlighted the ways in which such deviations change the ideological impetus of the narratives. Following Branston and Stafford, the identified shifts in representation provide a range of potential pleasures to audiences familiar with genre conventions, seeing as these shifts offer alternative configurations of gender that run counter to hegemonic norms (2010: 75). For instance, Chapter 3 discussed some of the playful, self-aware approaches adopted by these vampire romances in order to draw attention to, question and/or disrupt sexist genre/media tropes, first and foremost the male gaze but also, for example, the figure of the *femme fatale*. Potential destabilizations of genre conventions and encapsulated gender roles are also achieved through the strategies of camp and parody, which I have detected in *The Vampire Diaries* and *True Blood*. Chapter 4 drew attention to the fact that both Caroline in *The Vampire Diaries* and Jessica in *True Blood* break generic expectations by shifting the conventional story of the female vampire victim exemplified by Lucy Westenra's character development in Bram Stoker's *Dracula*. Instead of suffering under their transformation into vampires and receiving deadly punishments for their transgression of traditional gender roles, these contemporary female vampires experience their conversion into vampires as personally empowering. Chapter 5 elaborated the ways in which the vampire romance heroes Edward, Stefan and Bill deviate from conventional romance genre scripts, which exhibits these characters' embeddedness in contemporary postfeminist culture. This chapter detailed how the *Twilight* Saga in particular reverses the roles of romance hero and heroine with regard to the portrayal of sexuality in the text. Contrary to classic romance tropes, Bella is afforded the active role of the sexually desiring subject and pursuer of sexual intimacy, while Edward is delegated the responsibility of being the gatekeeper of sexual action, assuming the passive role of the pursued.

Importantly, pleasure has emerged as one of the defining keywords or catchphrases of postfeminism. For instance, Gill and Herdieckerhoff acknowledge postfeminism as 'a discourse of freedom, liberation and pleasure-seeking' (2006: 500). As discussed in Chapter 1, postfeminism is discursively constructed as contrary to a supposedly restrictive, serious and extremist 'old' feminism through its focus on the pleasures connected with the realm of sexuality, consumerism and individualism. In the postfeminist logic, empowerment can be drawn from 'individualistic assertions of (consumer) choice and self-rule' (Genz and Brabon 2009: 24) as well as the visual display of one's sexy body (ibid.: 92). As the analyses conducted within this book have shown, part of the *Twilight* Saga's, *The Vampire Diaries*' and *True Blood*'s appeal is their provision of a number of compelling postfeminist pleasures, which are flexible and contradictory in themselves. Thus, while some satisfactions may be derived from resisting the hegemonic culture, others may involve a 'complicity in subordination' (Gill 2007: 16). As Gill points out, implicitly acknowledging the multiple subject positions of individuals today, 'it is perfectly possible to derive significant pleasure from representations that politically one may wish to critique' (ibid.). While mass culture theory suggests that 'the experience of pleasure in mass culture is a false kind of pleasure' (Ang [1982] 1993: 17) that manipulates consumers into buying into the dominant messages conserving the status quo, this research has taken seriously the complicated pleasures that the *Twilight* Saga, *The Vampire Diaries* and *True Blood* offer their predominantly female audiences. Here, I have followed Ang, who argues that '[i]t is certainly not the aim to simply glorify ... pleasures *because* they are popular among women ... but to understand more thoroughly what concerns women today' (ibid.: 132; emphasis in original).

Chapter 3 argued that one of the central postfeminist pleasures offered by all three paranormal romances is their privileging of a heterosexual female gaze. Thus, pleasure may be drawn from the series' feminine address and their potential for feminine identification. Through the systematic representation and foregrounding of a subjective female gaze, girls and women are offered the opportunity to locate themselves as subjects in the texts. This is especially important in light of the dominant patriarchal culture, in which the perspectives and stories of women and girls remain underrepresented. With the help of what Soloway terms 'the being seen gaze [and] the I SEE YOU gaze truth gaze [sic]' (2016; emphasis in original), particularly the

Twilight Saga and *True Blood* grapple with young women's experiences of becoming the object of the gaze in the context of a male-dominated society. The female gaze found in these texts is therefore a critical gaze, which lays bare the constraining, pressuring and potentially violating experiences of women and girls being observed and controlled by men. By addressing women as subjects while also showing how they are treated as objects in the culture, the texts represent 'the ambiguity and contradictions of women's living experience under patriarchy: the experience of the body as both the self and not the self' (Vera-Gray 2017: 158). In all three series, the female protagonists are then allowed to return the gaze. In keeping with postfeminist discourses of female sexual self-determination and empowerment, the *Twilight* Saga, *The Vampire Diaries* and *True Blood* represent their heroines as assertive sexual subjects. Sookie's personal empowerment entails her knowingly playing with her sexual power and exploiting the dynamics of the male gaze for her own benefit in *True Blood* – an ambiguous strategy that raises questions concerning the extent of her agency while catering to a sexist gaze paradigm. In contrast, the *Twilight* Saga and *The Vampire Diaries* illustrate the sexual subjecthood of their female protagonists predominantly through the latter's sexually desiring gazes at their vampire lovers. As I have demonstrated, all three series use the figure of the vampire to invite and legitimize the straight female gaze. A supernatural creature that represents difference in a variety of ways, the vampire occupies the position of the eroticized object here, which is conventionally assigned to women in mainstream screen texts.

Chapter 4 investigated the *Twilight* Saga, *The Vampire Diaries* and *True Blood* in relation to their incorporation of postfeminist/ neoliberal discourses of entrepreneurial subjectivity, self-optimization and individualism, which – as I have argued – are projected onto the female vampire body. As my analyses have shown, Bella's, Caroline's and Jessica's transformations from human to vampire can be read as representations of postfeminist makeovers. Here, it became evident that these female characters exist in a tug of war between active self-realization and the disciplinary forces that determine the limits of their becoming subjects. Through their makeovers, they are individually empowered while simultaneously being subjected to new social norms requiring them to continually monitor, discipline and work on their powerful vampire bodies. On the one hand, the makeovers depicted here portray the female body as a project that facilitates a process of self-realization and self-empowerment for the female agent. All three young women enjoy an increase in agency and (supernatural) power after their vampire transformations, and they experience their vampire natures as their 'true' or 'better selves'. As Suzanne Ferriss suggests, the pleasures of makeover narratives lie in the idea that empowerment is available to each individual woman: 'Ultimately, both makeover television and flicks offer the female viewer reassurance.... they suggest that the means of gaining recognition are easily within her reach, and, in more recent films, increasingly under control' (2008: 56). On the other hand, Bella's, Caroline's and Jessica's agency is compromised by the governing influence of the series' respective vampire social orders, which are often represented by male authorities introducing the female vampires to their new world and its relevant rules. All three vampire women are expected to rein in their bloodthirst and perform socially acceptable 'femininity' by keeping their violent impulses in check.

In the course of their vampire makeovers, then, Bella, Caroline and Jessica gain subjectivity and agency while simultaneously submitting to normative ideals. The paradox at the heart of successful postfeminist femininity, which entails being subject and object in one, mirrors the contradictory status of women as both subject and object of the gaze that emerged in Chapter 3. What comes to light here are the conflicting expectations women and girls are faced with in contemporary postfeminist culture. They are both called upon to be self-determined and seek self-realization by means of body work and more extreme forms of body enhancement like cosmetic surgery, and asked to orient themselves towards cultural beauty norms. Despite the makeover's presentation as a 'choice' and an emancipatory practice, it must be noted that 'the concept of choice is itself enmeshed in social and cultural norms' (Gillespie 1997: 79). Genz and Brabon point out that this is 'one of the contradictions of the rhetoric of choice that the postfeminist woman grapples with: what looks like individual empowerment, agency and self-determination can also signal conformity and docility' (2009: 151). O'Reilly writes that TV shows featuring female characters with supernatural powers seem to offer 'viewers a foot in two worlds: a fantastic one in which women could be the most powerful beings in their universe and a realistic one in which that same universe limits that power. In other words, such series present the fusion of one world that is only imaginable and another that is relatable' (2013: 198) – a combination that may be particularly pleasurable to see represented for many female viewers. The ambiguous portrayals of empowerment found in the examined texts may mirror the experiences of many women in postfeminist culture, which tells them that feminism is no longer needed, while their lives are actually shaped by very real hurdles and restrictions.

Chapter 5 dealt with the pleasures contained in the consumption of images of idealized masculinity in the form of the vampire romance heroes of the *Twilight* Saga, *The Vampire Diaries* and *True Blood*. As I have argued here, these paranormal romances provide a redefinition of hegemonic masculinity through the characterization of their male vampire protagonists as postfeminist men. This redefinition of socially admired masculinity is a highly attractive one for (heterosexual) female audiences in particular, as the postfeminist man offers a configuration of masculinity that is less oppressive and more open towards a reduction of gendered inequalities than for example the 'old man'. The contradictory characteristics of postfeminist masculinity are neatly captured by the figure of the humanized/reluctant vampire, who is simultaneously rooted in a distant past nostalgically associated with traditional gender roles, and located in the contemporary present that has been shaped by the influences of feminism and postmodernism. On the one hand, Edward, Stefan and Bill retain culturally valued markers of 'masculinity', such as physical strength, authority, power and aggression, which are depicted as 'natural' features of the vampire. On the other hand, these heroes also comfortably incorporate traits conventionally designated as typically 'feminine', such as emotionality, empathy and the inclination to take care of others. Included in this adoption of 'feminine' behaviours are the postfeminist man's indulgence in beauty routines and the (sexualized) display of his body. It is perhaps the exaggerated 'masculinity' of the vampire – he is considerably stronger, more powerful and more aggressive than human men because of his supernatural status – that enables him to carry conventionally 'feminine' features without becoming unattractive within the hegemonic system that penalizes extensive transgressions of gender.

A central part of postfeminist masculinity is also an increasing self-awareness and willingness to question and problematize its own privileges as well as responsibilities. As I have shown by means of the case studies in Chapter 5, this readiness to interrogate and challenge one's own gendered dominance is mapped onto the male vampire body in the *Twilight* Saga, *The Vampire Diaries* and *True Blood*. Thus, the texts metaphorically depict the difficult process of negotiating a progressive male identity in a patriarchally structured world influenced by feminist principles. Despite the progressive potential of these versions of 'postfeminist vampire masculinity', they can also be read as regressive representations, considering that the adoption of 'feminine'/feminist traits may function as a strategic move serving to legitimize male protective paternalism, which reinscribes 'femininity' as powerless and in need of rescuing. Because of their oscillation between liberating and containing impulses, I consider the postfeminist masculinities exemplified by Edward, Stefan and Bill 'transitional' (Connell and Messerschmidt 2005: 853) forms of masculinity – still hegemonic but potentially open towards rethinking their own hegemony.

If romance permits (female) audiences to temporarily withdraw from the pressures and challenges of the contemporary world (Radway [1984] 1991: 212), the vampire romance hero 'embodies . . . a desire for *limited* escape: not a wild flight into amoral liberty, just a version of ordinary life which is a bit freer and more exciting than the one most of us actually inhabit' (Crawford 2014: 104; emphasis in original). The configurations of masculinity manifested by Edward, Stefan and Bill are not radically revolutionary ones. Despite the subversive potential contained in these representations, it is important to also acknowledge their limits. In the analysed vampire romances, female subjectivation, the expansion of agency and the achievement of empowerment do not work in uncomplicated ways either. Thus, the conception of '"empowerment" as it is understood within postfeminist discourse' (Gwynne and Muller 2013a: 8) is highly debatable and has indeed been criticized by many feminist scholars because of its exclusionary workings. As Tasker and Negra write with a nod to bell hooks, subjectivation and empowerment are not accessible to everyone in a postfeminist culture that elevates 'consumption as a strategy . . . for the production of the self' (2007b: 2). The fact that the *Twilight* Saga, *The Vampire Diaries* and *True Blood* privilege the experiences, opportunities, gazes and desires of young, heterosexual, cis, able-bodied, white, middle-class[4] women confirms Gill's argument that postfeminist themes 'coexist with stark and continuing inequalities . . . that relate to "race" and ethnicity, class, age, sexuality and disability – as well as gender' (2007: 255). Postfeminism's omissions, its 'cultural erasure of non-mainstream representation' (Gwynne and Muller 2013a: 9) and its concealment of 'underlying power relations that reproduce hegemonic ideas about race, gender, sexuality, and class' (Butler 2013: 50) remain extremely problematic issues. A highly conflict-ridden phenomenon, postfeminism often presents only partially useful solutions to existing inequalities in the 'white supremacist capitalist patriarchy' (hooks 1984: 118) because of its wilful ignorance of systemic and institutionalized power structures.

One way to make sense of the fundamental flaws ingrained in postfeminism is to consider its incorporation into popular/consumer culture. While this work has not considered 'feminism's entry into the popular as necessarily a depoliticisation and dilution' (Genz and Brabon 2009: 25), it should be noted that a popular version of feminism may have to make certain concessions in terms of its radicalism. Thus, postfeminism can only amplify women's/girls' voices and bring more people to feminism if it does not alienate too many media consumers. Postfeminism walks a tightrope between different aspirations, 'seeking to reconcile feminist ideas of female emancipation and equality, consumerist demands of capitalist societies and media-friendly depictions of feminine/masculine empowerment' (ibid.: 41). The 'tension between . . . disruption and containment' (Projansky 2007: 69) is an essential ingredient – and predicament – of postfeminist media texts; sometimes the balance tilts to one side, sometimes to the other. Mostly, however, both elements exist simultaneously. An aspect that surfaced at several points throughout the preceding analyses is that problematic, limiting or retrogressive representations are acknowledged but at the same time reinscribed in the texts. This double movement cannot be considered separately from postfeminism's existence as a 'cultural media phenomenon' (Genz and Brabon 2009: 18). Instead of envisioning a complete turning upside down of patriarchal power structures, postfeminism's 'form of politics accepts the necessity of working within what already exists and forging a future from resources inevitably impure' (ibid.: 40). As Suzanne Ferriss and Mallory Young suggest, postfeminism is 'cognizant that, despite naïve expectations to the contrary, there is no way of living outside of contemporary consumer culture' (2008b: 55). Thus, while Mulvey opted for the complete destruction of the cinematic apparatus and its accompanying scopophilic pleasures because of their entrenchment in the patriarchy, the *Twilight* Saga, *The Vampire Diaries* and *True Blood* manage to offer female visual pleasures in the frame of mainstream screen texts. These visual pleasures are neither straightforward nor without problems (see for example the racist rendering of *Twilight*'s character Jacob Black as a sexualized object of the gaze). What they demonstrate, however, is 'that the contradictions of capitalism and patriarchy allow space for disturbances of dominant meanings to occur in the mainstream, with results that may not be free of contradictions, but which do signify shifts in regimes of representation' (Gamman and Marshment [1988] 1994a: 4).

Postfeminist political practice may also be understood as containing fundamental 'problem areas' (Gwynne and Muller 2013a: 9) because it mirrors the complicated and necessarily flawed everyday practice of feminism in an unequal contemporary society. As already stated, instead of investing in second wave feminist political practices grounded in collectivism and activism (Genz and Brabon 2009: 35), postfeminism proposes a 'reconceptualisation of political and critical practices' (ibid.: 34), for example by reworking notions of individual agency. Crucially, postfeminist politics are a 'politics of contradiction' (ibid.: 36) because they reflect the plurality of people's experiences in a contemporary culture characterized by such developments as constantly shifting gender norms, neoliberalist ideas of consumer capitalism and the unsettling of former economic, environmental and social stabilities. The *Twilight* Saga, *The Vampire Diaries* and *True Blood* engage in this kind of postfeminist politics by raising and examining in a supernatural context situations that illustrate the complex struggles of women and girls in the current society.

Interestingly, Budgeon argues that 'lived contradictions' (2011: 283) expose the instabilities of contemporary conceptions of masculinities and femininities, which opens up a space from which gender roles and relationships may be revised or remodelled. The antithetical nature of postfeminist culture might therefore offer liberating opportunities to all genders. Thus, similar to the paranormal romances' teenaged protagonists, who occupy a state of in-between-ness, postfeminism may be conceptualized as inhabiting a 'transitory space' (de Toro 1999a: 20) that maintains continuities with established paradigms but is also able to foster innovations. This transitory space, which is inherently incomplete, conflicted, undecided and polysemic, works as a site of struggle for meaning and representation – a struggle that might produce new and creative configurations of gender. As this book has demonstrated throughout its extensive and nuanced analyses, in the *Twilight* Saga, *The Vampire Diaries* and *True Blood*, a range of cultural values are actively debated, which shows that definitions of (gender) identities are continually evolving.

Notes

Introduction

1 Some of the more popular vampire romances are Melissa de la Cruz's *Blue Bloods* series (2006–13), Mari Mancusi's *Blood Coven* series (2006–17), Rachel Caine's *The Morganville Vampires* series (2006–14), Cassandra Clare's *The Mortal Instruments* series (2007–14), P.C. and Kristin Cast's *House of Night* and *House of Night: Other World* series (2007–14 and 2017–, respectively), Richelle Mead's *Vampire Academy* series (2007–10), Claudia Gray's *Evernight* series (2008–12) and Deborah Harkness's *All Souls* trilogy (2011–14), a number of which were later adapted to the big or small screen. The resurgence of paranormal romance, particularly narratives featuring vampire love interests, has been observed by a variety of scholars, including Deborah Lutz (2007), Kathleen Miller (2010), Catherine Roach (2010), Brigid Cherry (2012a) and Andreea Şerban (2012). Besides, the existence of vampire romance parodies, such as *Vampires Suck* (2010) and *Breaking Wind* (2012), is indicative of the fact that teen vampire romances were relevant enough to generate their own spoofs and that a number of elements and tropes are clearly associated with this genre. After all, parodies will only be successful if audiences have acquired a certain amount of familiarity with what is being made fun of.
2 Throughout the book, I will be referring to Stephenie Meyer's novel tetralogy as the *Twilight* series, while the film series will be referred to as the *Twilight* Saga. Where both are concerned, I will use the term *Twilight* franchise. I make it a point not to lump together the source texts and the adaptations in the frame of my analysis.
3 Mellins bases her findings on the evaluation of questionnaire surveys and personal interviews with members of the London-based vampire subculture between 2006 and 2012.
4 The literary source of the *Fifty Shades* film series is actually a series of novels by E. L. James (2011–17), which started out as *Twilight* fan fiction (Clayton and Harman 2014a: 1).

5 Some of these differences can be tied back to the fact that one of the texts is a series of films (the *Twilight* Saga), one is a network television series (*The Vampire Diaries*) and one is a premium cable television series (*True Blood*). These are all different media that have different methods of producing content and must comply with different rules, such as FCC regulations (Thurber 2011: 8). While all of the texts appear in the form of series, the differences between cinematic and TV seriality should be noted. Film and television certainly differ in terms of narrative structure and hours of storytelling involved. Nevertheless, both film and television seriality may entail greater narrative complexity and openness, character density and ambiguity (Creeber 2004: 2–3). A common differentiation in TV studies is the one between 'serial' and 'series'. Thus, one of the key differences between the two formats involves 'the series' use of self-contained episodes with relatively autonomous plotlines, [which is set] against the serial's use of continuing storylines' (Turner 2008a: 8). As Graeme Turner argues, '[t]oday, there are elements of the serial in many of what the industry would regard as series' (ibid.). Indeed, *The Vampire Diaries* and *True Blood* can be described as incorporating aspects of both the serial and the series. For the sake of simplicity, both texts are referred to as 'series' within this research.

6 For an overview of common criticisms in the media and academia, see for example: Ames, M. (2010), 'Twilight Follows Tradition. Analyzing "Biting" Critiques of Vampire Narratives for Their Portrayals of Gender and Sexuality', in M. A. Click, J. Stevens Aubrey and E. Behm-Morawitz (eds), *Bitten by Twilight. Youth Culture, Media, & the Vampire Franchise*, 37–53, New York, NY: Peter Lang. For an ethnographic study of readers who view *Twilight* critically, see: Petersen, A. H. (2012), 'That Teenage Feeling', *Feminist Media Studies*, 12 (1): 51–67. doi:10.1080/14680777.2011.558348.

7 See for example: Keller, J. and M. Ryan (2015), 'Call for Papers: Emergent Feminisms and the Challenge to Postfeminist Media Culture', circulated 12 May; Retallack, H., J. Ringrose and E. Lawrence (2016), '"Fuck Your Body Image": Teen Girls' Twitter and Instagram Feminism in and around School', in J. Coffey, S. Budgeon and H. Cahill (eds), *Learning Bodies: The Body in Youth and Childhood Studies*, 85–103, Singapore: Springer.

Chapter 2

1. For instance, paranormal romance 'inherited from paranormal detective fiction . . . a preference for plots which featured action, deception, conspiracy and crime' (Crawford 2014: 73) as well as 'the generic structure of a mystery format' (McLennon 2014).
2. McLennon further suggests that the genre label 'dark fantasy' is a term no longer in use among current fans of urban fantasy/paranormal romance and is therefore neglectable (2014).
3. Although *True Blood* also develops other storylines and is regularly associated with a male audience because of its focus on violence and gore, the centrality of Sookie's relationship drama within the series can be derived for example from the promo posters of seasons two and four, which feature Sookie together with her male love interests relevant to the respective seasons. Besides, Brigid Cherry points out that '*True Blood* maintains a large female fan following and characters such as Bill, Alcide and (especially) Eric are subject to "Team . . ." affiliations (in the same way that Team Edward and Team Jacob dominate *Twilight* fandom)' (2012a: 11).
4. In 'The Night of the Comet' (1.2), Stefan and Elena talk about the Brontë sisters and *Wuthering Heights*; it is implied that Stefan read the novel when it was first published, as he gives Elena his original edition. In *Twilight*, the novel, Bella is also reading *Wuthering Heights* (Meyer 2005: 30); in *Eclipse*, it is described as one of her favourite books (Meyer 2007: 28). The novel version of *Eclipse* also includes several direct quotes from *Wuthering Heights*, and Bella compares her relationships with Edward and Jacob to Catherine's relationships with Heathcliff and Edgar (ibid.: 517). Intertexts of the *Twilight* series, such as *Wuthering Heights*, *Pride and Prejudice* and *Jane Eyre*, have been examined in a great number of essays in *Twilight* academia; articles include: Deffenbacher, K. and M. Zagoria-Moffet (2011), 'Textual Vampirism in The *Twilight Saga*: Drawing Feminist Life from *Jane Eyre* and Teen Fantasy Fiction', in G. L. Anatol (ed.), *Bringing Light to* Twilight: *Perspectives on a Pop Culture Phenomenon*, 31–42, New York, NY: Palgrave Macmillan; Kapurch, K. (2012b), '"Unconditionally and Irrevocably": Theorizing the Melodramatic Impulse in Young Adult Literature through the *Twilight*

Saga and *Jane Eyre*', *Children's Literature Association Quarterly*, 37 (2): 164–87; Morey, A. (2012a), '"Famine for Food, Expectation for Content": *Jane Eyre* as Intertext for the "Twilight" Saga', in A. Morey (ed.), *Genre, Reception, and Adaptation in the "Twilight" Series*, 15–27, Farnham: Ashgate; Wakefield, S. (2011), 'Torn between Two Lovers: Twilight *Tames* Wuthering Heights', in M. Parke and N. Wilson (eds), *Theorizing* Twilight: *Critical Essays on What's at Stake in a Post-Vampire World*, 117–31, Jefferson, NC: McFarland & Company.

5 For instance, the 1930s witnessed the birth of the superhero, with Superman emerging as one of the first superhero characters to use physical force and other superhuman abilities in the fight for good (Crawford 2014: 45).

6 In the *Vampire Diaries* mythology, rippers are extremely feral, savage and predatory vampires who sadistically torture and mutilate their victims. Because they have turned off their humanity, they have no empathy and do not care about their actions.

7 Abbott's and Jowett's argument is developed with explicit reference to the medium of television. However, I would suggest that their reasoning may potentially be extended to include cinematic serial texts like the *Twilight* Saga.

8 This dominant conception frames adolescence as a process of constant and linear growth towards maturity and relies on the binary construction of childhood and adulthood, innocence and experience, asexuality and sexuality, in the middle of which adolescence is located (Waller 2009: 30). Alison Waller points to the rise of the new sciences of sociology and psychology in the early twentieth century, which 'instilled developmentalism as the governing framework for adolescence' (ibid.). One may criticize the developmental approach for its reductive perception of children and adolescents because in some ways, it presents the latter as 'lesser beings' (ibid.: 32) – in other words, for its adultism. Children and teenagers have recently been redefined 'as a marginalised group in its own right' (Davis and Dickinson 2004a: 11) and recognized along with other disenfranchised groups involved in political struggles for empowerment (Waller 2009: 97). Waller also emphasizes that developmentalism as a discursive framework is rooted in a patriarchal context: 'In its concern with linear progression it prioritises a masculine

version of time and any diversion from the correct sequence is considered to be unhealthy (unhealthily feminised, perhaps)' (2009: 35). Considering that the developmental conception of adolescence as a series of stages or tasks that lead towards maturity is based on stages of a male biography (one that is typical for the early twentieth century when these ideas are emerging), this conception can be described as androcentric.

9 TV programmes focused on breaking social and cultural taboos are not likely to be originally envisioned for teenage audiences. Glyn Davis and Kay Dickinson argue that because teen TV is created by adults, it tends to 'raise crucial issues (of *adult* choosing) in a "responsible manner" that is entirely hegemonically negotiated' (2004a: 3; emphasis in original).

10 Kevin Williamson, who developed the *Vampire Diaries* series together with producer and writer Julie Plec, is also the creator of *Dawson's Creek*, the tremendously popular teen show whose trademarks were, among other things, 'a use of language which is too sophisticated for the ages of the characters; [and] frequent intertextual references' (Davis and Dickinson 2004a: 1). Williamson has implemented these elements as central features in *The Vampire Diaries* as well.

11 See for example: Anyiwo, U. M. (2012), 'It's Not Television, It's Transmedia Storytelling: Marketing the "Real" World of *True Blood*', in B. Cherry (ed.), *True Blood: Investigating Vampires and Southern Gothic*, 157–71, London: I. B. Tauris; Utsch, C. (2014), 'True Blood: Scheiternde Rationalität', *POP-Zeitschrift*, 16 June. Available online: http://www.pop-zeitschrift.de/2014/06/16/true-bloodscheiternde-rationalitatvon-carolin-utsch16-6-2014/ (accessed 10 April 2021).

12 See www.fellowshipofthesun.org/, www.keepamericahuman.com/ and www.vamps-kill.com/ (the websites no longer exist at the time of writing).

13 Similarly, a central merchandise product for *Twilight* fans was Bella's engagement ring, replicas of which could be purchased after Edward gave the ring to Bella in the *Eclipse* movie adaptation.

14 In contrast, distinctions within *Twilight* audiences have been drawn and discussed by a variety of authors in the academic context. For analyses of the paradoxical *Twilight* anti-fandom, 'Lolfans', 'Twi-Hards', 'Twi-Haters' and relationships between different audience groups who define themselves against each other (inter-fandom), see for e.g.: Gilbert, A. (2012), 'Between Twi-Hards and Twi-Haters: The Complicated Terrain

of Online "Twilight" Audience Communities', in A. Morey (ed.), *Genre, Reception, and Adaptation in the "Twilight" Series*, 163–79, Farnham: Ashgate; Godwin, V. (2014), '*Twilight* Anti-Fans: "Real" Fans and "Real" Vampires', in C. Bucciferro (ed.), *The Twilight Saga: Exploring the Global Phenomenon*, 93–106, Lanham, MD: The Scarecrow Press; Hills, M. (2012), '"Twilight" Fans Represented in Commercial Paratexts and Inter-Fandoms: Resisting and Repurposing Negative Fan Stereotypes', in A. Morey (ed.), *Genre, Reception, and Adaptation in the "Twilight" Series*, 113–29, Farnham: Ashgate; Sheffield, J. and E. Merlo (2010), 'Biting Back: Twilight Anti-Fandom and the Rhetoric of Superiority', in M. A. Click, J. Stevens Aubrey and E. Behm-Morawitz (eds), *Bitten by Twilight: Youth Culture, Media, & the Vampire Franchise*, 207–22, New York, NY: Peter Lang.

15 In works that followed Moers's feminist analysis of Gothic romance novels, the Female Gothic was distinguished from Male Gothic not only in terms of the gender of the respective authors but also in terms of narrative technique, plot and the predominance of terror versus horror. Thus, a Female Gothic narrative was stereotypically associated with a 'female point of view, happy ending, explained ghosts and an adherence to terror' (Smith and Wallace 2004: 2). Critical debates have focused on the term 'Female Gothic' because of its essentializing nature, and as a result of the consolidation of poststructuralist thinking at universities in the 1990s, the term is now considered obsolete or is at least widely problematized (ibid.: 1). I use the term here in order to summarize Moers's main arguments.

Chapter 3

1 Joey Soloway is most known for creating, writing, executive-producing and directing the Amazon original series *Transparent* (2014–19), which focuses on the transitioning process of transgender parent Maura Pfefferman and the lives of her queer family members. More importantly, Soloway also created the Amazon series *I Love Dick* (2016–17) together with Sarah Gubbins, a show which is notable for its privileging of the female protagonist's subjective gaze. As Soloway said in an interview with

The Guardian: 'if Transparent was about the trans community then Dick is really about the female gaze. This really is a celebration of the feminine.' Soloway has publicly stated that they prefer 'to be referenced with gender-neutral pronouns (they/them/their)' (Freeman 2017), which is why I use these pronouns in reference to Soloway.

2 For instance, Fiona Vera-Gray lists a range of studies attempting 'to measure the frequency with which women and girls experience intrusion from unknown men in public space' (2017: 7); these intrusions include uninvited gazing (ibid.: 7–9).

3 While *Twilight* is replete with subjective shots signifying Bella's investigative/desiring gaze and transmitting her interiority, the subsequent films of the Saga are characterized by a steady decline of Bella's gaze. Interestingly, this is paralleled by a decline in the female protagonist's voice-over. A possible explanation for this phenomenon is given by Katie Kapurch, who points out that Summit, the *Twilight* Saga's film production company, sought to attract 'a broader audience – one beyond the female fans' (2012a: 194) with the subsequent films. Whether this is really the case cannot be determined here. Notwithstanding, as Kapurch writes, the circumstances under which Bella's voice and perspective are eclipsed in the course of the Saga raise 'concerns about the sexist treatment of female youth – whether as characters or as consumers of media' (2012a: 195).

4 The TV Tropes website defines the so-called sexophone as a 'short riff on the saxophone used to indicate the arrival or presence of a sexy woman (or occasionally man)' ('Sexophone').

5 In 'You're No Good' (6.3), before Jessica leaves to recruit/kidnap the science professor who synthesized 'Tru Blood', she is told by Bill to 'wear something inappropriate. Takahashi's got a thing for young women'. In 'At Last' (6.4), Sarah Newlin (Anna Camp) attempts to manipulate her male partner into proposing to her by using sex. In the vampire concentration camp, both Willa (Amelia Rose Blair) and Pam offer sexual favours to guards in exchange for being transferred or to escape (episodes 'Don't You Feel Me' (6.6) and 'In the Evening' (6.7)).

6 Gay characters include Bill Forbes (Caroline's father; Jack Coleman), Luke (Chris Brochu), Mary Louise (Teressa Liane) and Nora (Scarlett Byrne), all of whom are killed after appearing on the show for relatively short periods of time.

7 Bonnie desires several men over the course of the seasons, but she is rarely allowed to gaze at them like Elena gazes at the Salvatore brothers. What is more, none of her romantic and/or sexual entanglements end well: Ben (Sean Faris) turns out to be an evil vampire who is then staked by Stefan; Luka (Bryton James), Carter (B. J. Britt) and Enzo (Michael Malarkey) are killed due to various circumstances; Bonnie's fling with Jamie (Robert Ri'chard) is simply not mentioned again, and Jeremy moves on with his life after his relationship with Bonnie does not work out.

8 In season two, Tara's and her boyfriend Eggs's (Mehcad Brooks) sexuality is controlled by maenad Maryann (Michelle Forbes); Eggs is then accidentally killed by Jason. Later, Tara is kidnapped, abused and raped by sociopathic vampire Franklin (James Frain). After sacrificing her life for her friend Sookie and being turned into a vampire against her will, Tara is killed at the beginning of the final season.

Chapter 4

1 Interestingly, *The Vampire Diaries* and *True Blood* feature similar scenes. In 'Bringing Out the Dead' (3.13) of *The Vampire Diaries*, Klaus Mikaelson engages in a conversation with the Salvatore brothers, presenting his opinion about what Elena (who is absent) should do with her life: 'What she needs right now is to be rid of you lot and to fall in love with a human. Maybe that nice football player, you know, the blonde one. . . . Yeah, why not? They'll marry, live a long and fruitful life and pop out a perfect family.' Similarly, in *True Blood*'s final episode, Bill makes the decision to leave Sookie for good by killing himself despite Sookie's protest. As a reason for his decision, he gives his vision for Sookie's future, which entails marriage, motherhood and a 'normal life': 'I've seen you around children, seen how you light up around them. I would hate for you to never know what that feels like, to have children of your own' ('Thank You', 7.10). What keeps resurfacing here are conservative ideas about 'femininity' and the 'ideal' female life script, which are proffered by male characters in the series.

2 Films featuring monstrous pregnancies and births include: *Rosemary's Baby* (1968), *Demon Seed* (1977), *The Brood* (1979), *Alien* (1979) and *The Unborn* (1991).

3 Despite her impressive display of self-control, Caroline is not granted her year without humanity by her friends or by the series, respectively. In the subsequent episodes, Elena, Bonnie and the Salvatore brothers torture Caroline and force her to switch her humanity back on. Apparently, the potential for unruliness is too great a risk, even in the case of the self-disciplined Caroline.

Chapter 5

1 It is easily conceivable that the representations of masculinity offered here might speak to (heterosexual) male viewers as well – not only but also because these representations are tremendously successful with women. Likewise, gay male viewers may find satisfaction in identifying with the female protagonists of the narratives (Mukherjea 2011a: 17), so the *Twilight* Saga, *The Vampire Diaries* and *True Blood* certainly hold appeal for a variety of different audiences. However, because these three series are predominantly known for the fact that they fairly clearly address the heterosexual interests of women/girls, this chapter will concentrate on the appeal of the texts for this particular audience segment.
2 See for example: Abbott (2007), Abbott (2016b), Carter (1997), Clements (2011), George and Hughes (2013b), Gordon and Hollinger (1997a), Kane (2006), Kungl (2003), Ní Fhlainn (2019), Recht (2011), Senf (1988) and Williamson (2005).
3 In this context, it is important to note that the viewership of *Dark Shadows* consisted largely of 'middle-aged women, usually housewives home raising their children, and teenage boys' (Jowett and Abbott 2013: 46). This fits well with Wheatley's argument that Gothic television primarily addresses a 'domestic, female viewer' (2006: 24).
4 The term 'hegemonic masculinity', which was coined by Raewyn Connell in the 1980s with recourse to Antonio Gramsci, 'embodie[s] the currently most honored way of being a man' (Connell and Messerschmidt 2005: 832). However, hegemonic masculinity is not actually enacted by the majority of men. Connell and Messerschmidt argue that '[t]o sustain a given pattern of hegemony requires the policing of men as well as the exclusion or discrediting of women' (2005: 844). Thus, men are offered the

incentive to practice gender according to the hegemonic system because they otherwise 'run the risk of subordination' (Levy 2007: 254). Crucially, hegemonic masculinities are constantly subject to contestation and 'older forms of masculinity might be displaced by new ones' (Connell and Messerschmidt 2005: 833).

5   See for example: Miller, M. (2011), 'Maybe Edward Is the Most Dangerous Thing Out There: The Role of Patriarchy', in M. Parke and N. Wilson (eds), *Theorizing* Twilight: *Critical Essays on What's at Stake in a Post-Vampire World*, 165–77, Jefferson, NC: McFarland & Company; Donnelly, A. (2011), 'Denial and Salvation: The *Twilight* Saga and Heteronormative Patriarchy', in M. Parke and N. Wilson (eds), *Theorizing* Twilight: *Critical Essays on What's at Stake in a Post-Vampire World*, 178–93, Jefferson, NC: McFarland & Company.

6   See for example: Goodfriend, W. (2011), 'Relationship Violence in "Twilight": How "Twilight" Teaches Teens to Love Abusive Relationships', *Psychology Today*, 9 November. Available online: www.psychologytoday.com/us/blog/psychologist-the-movies/201111/relationship-violence-in-twilight (accessed 10 April 2021); Merskin, D. (2011), 'A Boyfriend to Die for: Edward Cullen as Compensated Psychopath in Stephanie [*sic*] Meyer's *Twilight*', *Journal of Communication Inquiry*, 35 (2): 157–78. doi:10.1177/0196859911402992; Miller, M. (2011), 'Maybe Edward Is the Most Dangerous Thing Out There. The Role of Patriarchy', in M. Parke and N. Wilson (eds), *Theorizing* Twilight. *Critical Essays on What's at Stake in a Post-Vampire World*, 165–77, Jefferson, NC: McFarland.

7   Contrary to the *Twilight* Saga, *The Vampire Diaries* does not combine Stefan's self-restraint in terms of biting humans with sexual abstinence. One exception is a scene in 'Under Control' (1.18), in which Stefan interrupts one of his sexual encounters with Elena because he is suddenly overcome by bloodlust. This scene remains the only explicit reference to the fact that there might be a connection between Stefan's vampiric and sexual impulses. The series does not provide any revolutionary representation of sexuality: sex is primarily depicted as taking place within monogamous heterosexual relationships. However, it is worth noting that the show provides a surprisingly uncomplicated depiction of teenage sexuality. Unlike in the *Twilight* Saga, Stefan's vampirism in *The Vampire Diaries* does not constitute an obstacle to him maintaining a healthy sexual relationship with Elena.

8 The concept of toxic masculinity, which has become a standard term in academic and media discussions of harmful variants of masculinity, is defined by Terry A. Kupers as incorporating 'extreme competition and greed, insensitivity to or lack of consideration of the experiences and feelings of others, a strong need to dominate and control others, an incapacity to nurture, a dread of dependency, a readiness to resort to violence, and the stigmatization and subjugation of women, gays, and men who exhibit feminine characteristics' (2005: 717).

9 In this particular instance, the equation of Sookie's Otherness with Bill's is rather problematic, as it serves to excuse Bill's horrific domestic violence towards Sookie. After being tortured and starved by Lorena, Bill has attacked Sookie and almost killed her by sucking her blood. Sookie's friend Tara criticizes Sookie for relativizing Bill's violence: 'You know what you sound like? One of those sad country songs about dumb bitches who let their man cheat and beat on them, all for the sake of true love' ('Night on the Sun', 3.8).

Conclusion

1 See for example: Jenson, J. and A. Sarkeesian (2011), 'Buffy vs. Bella: The Re-Emergence of the Archetypal Feminine in Vampire Stories', in G. Schott and K. Moffat (eds), *Fanpires: Audience Consumption of the Modern Vampire*, 55–72, Washington, DC: New Academia Publishing; McIntosh, J. (2009), 'Buffy vs Edward: Twilight Remixed – [original version]', *YouTube*, 20 June. Available online: https://www.youtube.com/watch?v=RZwM3GvaTRM (accessed 10 April 2021).

2 Since the 1990s, the term 'third wave feminism' has been used in opposition to postfeminism by some feminist activists and scholars, with third-wave pioneers trying to 'establish an ideological and political split between the two' (Genz and Brabon 2009: 160). This rhetoric of antagonism ignores the significant overlaps between both terms and is mainly based on the assumption that postfeminism is depoliticized, while third-wave feminism 'defines itself as a budding political movement' (ibid.: 156). In contrast to many third-wave feminist positions, my research offers a politicized reading of postfeminist media texts. Thus, I align

myself with Braithwaite as well as Genz and Brabon, who emphasize the commonalities of third-wave feminism and postfeminism (Braithwaite 2002: 337; Genz and Brabon 2009: 162).
3 Although film-going is assumably done in groups more frequently than television-watching is, both media can facilitate community experiences. The same is hard to achieve with the consumption of literary texts.
4 An exception is Sookie Stackhouse, who has a working-class background; her father was a mechanic, her mother a waitress/homemaker.

References

Print and online sources

Abbott, P., C. Wallace and M. Tyler (2005), *An Introduction to Sociology: Feminist Perspectives*, 3rd edn, Abingdon: Routledge.

Abbott, S. (2007), *Celluloid Vampires: Life after Death in the Modern World*, Austin, TX: University of Texas Press.

Abbott, S. (2013), 'Vampires on My Mind', *CST Online*, 31 May. Available online: http://cstonline.tv/vampires-on-my-mind (accessed 18 March 2016).

Abbott, S. (2014), 'TV Vampires: From Barnabas Collins to Bill Compton', *OffScreen*, 18 (4). Available online: http://offscreen.com/view/tv-vampires (accessed 10 April 2021).

Abbott, S. (2016a), 'How to Navigate the Undead Apocalypse', Interview by R. Tranter, *RhysTranter.com – A Journal of Literature, Philosophy, and the Arts*, 3 October. Available online: https://rhystranter.com/2016/10/03/stacey-abbott-undead-apocalypse-interview-vampires-zombies-21st-century/ (accessed 10 April 2021).

Abbott, S. (2016b), *Undead Apocalypse: Vampires and Zombies in the Twenty-First Century*, Edinburgh: Edinburgh University Press.

Abele, E. (2016), 'Introduction: Liberating American Masculinity', in E. Abele and J. A. Gronbeck-Tedesco (eds), *Screening Images of American Masculinity in the Age of Postfeminism*, xiii–xxiv, Lanham, MD: Lexington Books.

Abele, E. and J. A. Gronbeck-Tedesco, eds (2016), *Screening Images of American Masculinity in the Age of Postfeminism*, Lanham, MD: Lexington Books.

'About', *SlutWalk Toronto*. Available online: www.slutwalktoronto.com/ (accessed 25 June 2017).

Aldana Reyes, X. (2014), 'Gothic Horror Film, 1960–Present', in G. Byron and D. Townshend (eds), *The Gothic World*, 388–98, Abingdon: Routledge.

Allen, R. C., ed. (1992), *Channels of Discourse, Reassembled: Television and Contemporary Criticism*, 2nd edn, London: Routledge.

Altman, R. ([1999] 2000), *Film/Genre*, London: BFI Publishing.

Amador, V. (2012), 'Blacks and Whites, Trash and Good Country People in *True Blood*', in B. Cherry (ed), *True Blood: Investigating Vampires and Southern Gothic*, 122–38, London: I. B. Tauris.

Ames, M. (2010), 'Twilight Follows Tradition: Analyzing "Biting" Critiques of Vampire Narratives for Their Portrayals of Gender and Sexuality', in M. A. Click, J. Stevens Aubrey and E. Behm-Morawitz (eds), *Bitten by Twilight: Youth Culture, Media, & the Vampire Franchise*, 37–53, New York, NY: Peter Lang.

Anatol, G. L., ed. (2011), *Bringing Light to Twilight: Perspectives on a Pop Culture Phenomenon*, New York, NY: Palgrave Macmillan.

Ang, I. ([1982] 1993), *Watching Dallas: Soap Opera and the Melodramatic Imagination*, trans. D. Couling, London: Routledge.

Ang, I. (1996), *Living Room Wars: Rethinking Media Audiences for a Postmodern World*, London: Routledge.

Antoni, R. (2008), 'A Vampiric Relation to Feminism: The Monstrous-Feminine in Whitley Strieber's and Anne Rice's Gothic Fiction', *Americana*, 4 (1). Available online: http://americanaejournal.hu/vol4no1/antoni (accessed 10 April 2021).

Anyiwo, U. M. (2012), 'It's Not Television, It's Transmedia Storytelling: Marketing the "Real" World of *True Blood*', in B. Cherry (ed), *True Blood: Investigating Vampires and Southern Gothic*, 157–71, London: I. B. Tauris.

Aquilina, C. (2013), 'The Deformed Transformed; or, from Bloodsucker to Byronic Hero: Polidori and the Literary Vampire', in S. George and B. Hughes (eds), *Open Graves, Open Minds: Representations of Vampires and the Undead from the Enlightenment to the Present Day*, 24–38, Manchester: Manchester University Press.

Auerbach, N. (1995), *Our Vampires, Ourselves*, Chicago: The University of Chicago Press.

Austen, J. (1813), *Pride and Prejudice*, London: T. Egerton.

Babuscio, J. ([1977] 1999), 'The Cinema of Camp (*aka* Camp and the Gay Sensibility)', in F. Cleto (ed), *Camp: Queer Aesthetics and the Performing Subject; a Reader*, 117–35, Edinburgh: Edinburgh University Press.

Backstein, K. (2009), '(Un)safe Sex: Romancing the Vampire', *Cineaste*, 35 (1): 38–41.

Bacon, S. (2011), 'Lost Boys: The Infernal Youth of the Cinematic Teenage Vampire', *Thymos: Journal of Boyhood Studies*, 5 (2): 152–62. doi:10.3149/thy.0502.152.

Badley, L. (1996), *Writing Horror and the Body: The Fiction of Stephen King, Clive Barker, and Anne Rice*, Westport, CT: Greenwood Press.

Baker, B. (2015), *Contemporary Masculinities in Fiction, Film and Television*, New York, NY: Bloomsbury.

Banet-Weiser, S. (2018), *Empowered: Popular Feminism and Popular Misogyny*, Durham, NC: Duke University Press.

Banks, M. J. (2004), 'A Boy For All Planets: *Roswell, Smallville* and the Teen Male Melodrama', in G. Davis and K. Dickinson (eds), *Teen TV: Genre, Consumption, Identity*, 17–28, London: BFI Publishing.

Bealer, T. L. (2011), 'Of Monsters and Men: Toxic Masculinity and the Twenty-First Century Vampire in the *Twilight Saga*', in G. L. Anatol (ed), *Bringing Light to Twilight: Perspectives on a Pop Culture Phenomenon*, 139–52, New York, NY: Palgrave Macmillan.

Beaver, F. E. (1994), *Dictionary of Film Terms: The Aesthetic Companion to Film Analysis*, New York, NY: Twayne Publishers.

Benshoff, H. M. and S. Griffin (2009), *America on Film: Representing Race, Class, Gender, and Sexuality at the Movies*, 2nd edn, Chichester: Wiley-Blackwell.

Blau DuPlessis, R. (1985), *Writing Beyond the Ending: Narrative Strategies of Twentieth-Century Women Writers*, Bloomington, IN: Indiana University Press.

Blayde, A. and G. A. Dunn (2010), 'Pets, Cattle and Higher Life Forms on *True Blood*', in W. Irwin, G. A. Dunn and R. Housel (eds), *True Blood and Philosophy: We Wanna Think Bad Things with You*, 33–48, Hoboken, NJ: Wiley.

Bloom, C., ed. (2020), *The Palgrave Handbook of Contemporary Gothic*, Cham: Palgrave Macmillan.

Bordo, S. (2003), *Unbearable Weight: Feminism, Western Culture, and the Body*, 10th edn, Berkeley, CA: University of California Press.

Botting, F. (1995), *The New Critical Idiom*: Gothic, London: Routledge.

Botting, F. (2008), *Gothic Romanced: Consumption, Gender and Technology in Contemporary Fictions*, Abingdon: Routledge.

Brabon, B. A. (2007), 'The Spectral Phallus: Re-Membering the Postfeminist Man', in B. A. Brabon and S. Genz (eds), *Postfeminist Gothic: Critical Interventions in Contemporary Culture*, 56–67, Basingstoke: Palgrave Macmillan.

Brabon, B. A. (2013), '"Chuck Flick": A Genealogy of the Postfeminist Male Singleton', in J. Gwynne and N. Muller (eds), *Postfeminism and Contemporary Hollywood Cinema*, 116–30, Basingstoke: Palgrave Macmillan.

Brabon, B. A. and S. Genz (2007a), 'Introduction: Postfeminist Gothic', in B. A. Brabon and S. Genz (eds), *Postfeminist Gothic: Critical Interventions in Contemporary Culture*, 1–15, Basingstoke: Palgrave Macmillan.

Brabon, B. A. and S. Genz, eds (2007b), *Postfeminist Gothic: Critical Interventions in Contemporary Culture*, Basingstoke: Palgrave Macmillan.

Braithwaite, A. (2002), 'The Personal, the Political, Third-Wave and Postfeminisms', *Feminist Theory*, 3 (3): 335–44. doi:10.1177/146470002762492033.

Braithwaite, A. (2004), 'Politics of/and Backlash', *Journal of International Women's Studies*, 5 (5): 18–33.

Branigan, E. (1984), *Point of View in the Cinema: A Theory of Narration and Subjectivity in Classical Film*, Berlin: Mouton.

Branston, G. and R. Stafford (2010), *The Media Student's Book*, 5th edn, Abingdon: Routledge.

Bridgeman, M. (2013), 'Forged in Love and Death: Problematic Subjects in *The Vampire Diaries*', *The Journal of Popular Culture*, 46 (1): 3–19. doi:10.1111/jpcu.12013.

Broders, S. (2011), '"Bitten Is the New Black": Images of Women in Canadian and US-American Vampire Chick Lit', in W. Bunn (ed), *The Centennial Reader: Current Readings – Reading Currents*, Calgary, AB: Mount Royal University. Available online: http://centennialreader.ca/bitten-is-the-new-black (accessed 1 February 2012).

Brontë, C. (1847), *Jane Eyre*, London: Smith, Elder & Co.

Brontë, E. (1847), *Wuthering Heights*, London: Thomas Cautley Newby.

Brooks, A. ([1997] 1998), *Postfeminisms: Feminism, Cultural Theory and Cultural Forms*, London: Routledge.

Broyles, K. (2010), 'Vampirism, and the Visual Medium: The Role of Gender within Pop Culture's Latest Slew of Vampires', *Journal of Dracula Studies*, 12. Available online: https://kutztownenglish.files.wordpress.com/2015/09/jds_v12_2010_broyles.pdf (accessed 10 April 2021).

Bucciferro, C. (2014a), 'Introduction', in C. Bucciferro (ed), *The Twilight Saga: Exploring the Global Phenomenon*, 1–13, Lanham, MD: The Scarecrow Press.

Bucciferro, C., ed. (2014b), *The Twilight Saga: Exploring the Global Phenomenon*, Lanham, MD: The Scarecrow Press.

Budgeon, S. (2001), 'Emergent Feminist (?) Identities: Young Women and the Practice of Micropolitics', *The European Journal of Women's Studies*, 8 (1): 7–28. doi:10.1177/135050680100800102.

Budgeon, S. (2011), 'The Contradictions of Successful Femininity: Third-Wave Feminism, Postfeminism and "New" Femininities', in R. Gill and C. Scharff (eds), *New Femininities: Postfeminism, Neoliberalism and Subjectivity*, 279–92, Basingstoke: Palgrave Macmillan.

Bunn, W., ed, (2011), *The Centennial Reader: Current Readings – Reading Currents*, Calgary, AB: Mount Royal University. Available online: http://centennialreader.ca/bitten-is-the-new-black (accessed 1 February 2012).

Burke, B. (2011), 'The Great American Love Affair: Indians in the *Twilight* Saga', in G. L. Anatol (ed), *Bringing Light to Twilight: Perspectives on a Pop Culture Phenomenon*, 207–19, New York, NY: Palgrave Macmillan.

Burns, A. (2013), 'The Chick's "New Hero": (Re)Constructing Masculinity in the Postfeminist "Chick Flick"', in J. Gwynne and N. Muller (eds), *Postfeminism and Contemporary Hollywood Cinema*, 131–48, Basingstoke: Palgrave Macmillan.

Busse, K. (2010), 'Vampire Shows and Gendered Quality Television', *Antenna*, 26 August. Available online: http://www.courses.commarts.wisc.edu/2010/08/26/vampire-shows-and-gendered-quality-television/ (accessed 10 April 2021).

Butler, J. (1990), *Gender Trouble: Feminism and the Subversion of Identity*, New York, NY: Routledge.

Butler, J. (1997), *The Psychic Life of Power: Theories in Subjection*, Stanford, CA: Stanford University Press.

Butler, J. (2005), *Giving an Account of Oneself*, New York, NY: Fordham University Press.

Butler, J. (2013), 'For White Girls Only? Postfeminism and the Politics of Inclusion', *Feminist Formations*, 25 (1): 35–58. doi:10.1353/ff.2013.0009.

Byron, G. (2008), '"As One Dead": Romeo and Juliet in the "Twilight" Zone', in J. Drakakis and D. Townshend (eds), *Gothic Shakespeares*, 167–85, Abingdon: Routledge.

Byron, G. and D. Townshend, eds (2014), *The Gothic World*, Abingdon, Oxon: Routledge.

Caine, R. (2006–14), *The Morganville Vampires series*, 15 vols., New York, NY: Berkley.

Campbell, R. and C. Campbell (2001), 'Demons, Aliens, Teens and Television', *Slayage*, 1.2 (2): pars. 1–21. Available online: www.whedonstudies.tv/uploads/2/6/2/8/26288593/campbell_campbell_slayage_1.2.pdf (accessed 10 April 2021).

Carroll, N. (1990), *The Philosophy of Horror Or, Paradoxes of the Heart*, New York, NY: Routledge.

Carter, M. L. (1997), 'The Vampire as Alien in Contemporary Fiction', in J. Gordon and V. Hollinger (eds), *Blood Read: The Vampire as Metaphor in Contemporary Culture*, 27–44, Philadelphia, PA: University of Pennsylvania Press.

Cast, P. C. and K. Cast (2007–14), *House of Night series*, 12 vols., New York, NY: St. Martin's Press.

Cast, P. C. and K. Cast (2017–), *House of Night: Other World series*, 4 vols., New York, NY: St. Martin's Press.

Chaplin, S. (2014), 'Gothic Romance, 1760–1830', in G. Byron and D. Townshend (eds), *The Gothic World*, 199–209, Abingdon: Routledge.

Cherry, B. (2012a), 'Before the Night Is Through: *True Blood* as Cult TV', in B. Cherry (ed), *True Blood: Investigating Vampires and Southern Gothic*, 3–21, London: I. B. Tauris.

Cherry, B., ed. (2012b), *True Blood: Investigating Vampires and Southern Gothic*, London: I. B. Tauris.

Christian-Smith, L. K. (1991), *Becoming a Woman through Romance*, New York, NY: Routledge.

Clare, C. (2007–14), *The Mortal Instruments Series*, 6 vols., New York, NY: Margaret K. McElderry.

Clarke, A. M. (2010), 'Introduction: Approaching Twilight', in A. M. Clarke and M. Osborn (eds), *The Twilight Mystique: Critical Essays on the Novels and Films*, 3–13, Jefferson, NC: McFarland & Company.

Clarke, A. M. and M. Osborn, eds (2010), *The Twilight Mystique: Critical Essays on the Novels and Films*, Jefferson, NC: McFarland & Company.

Clayton, W. and S. Harman (2014a), 'Introduction', in W. Clayton and S. Harman (eds), *Screening Twilight: Critical Approaches to a Cinematic Phenomenon*, 1–7, London: I. B. Tauris.

Clayton, W. and S. Harman, eds (2014b), *Screening Twilight: Critical Approaches to a Cinematic Phenomenon*, London: I. B. Tauris.

Clements, S. (2011), *The Vampire Defanged: How the Embodiment of Evil Became a Romantic Hero*, Grand Rapids, MI: Brazos Press.

Cleto, F., ed. (1999), *Camp: Queer Aesthetics and the Performing Subject; a Reader*, Edinburgh: Edinburgh University Press.

Click, M. A., J. Stevens Aubrey and E. Behm-Morawitz, eds (2010a), *Bitten by Twilight: Youth Culture, Media, & the Vampire Franchise*, New York, NY: Peter Lang.

Click, M. A., J. Stevens Aubrey and E. Behm-Morawitz (2010b), 'Introduction', in M. A. Click, J. Stevens Aubrey and E. Behm-Morawitz (eds), *Bitten by Twilight: Youth Culture, Media, & the Vampire Franchise*, 1–17, New York, NY: Peter Lang.

Clover, C. J. (1992), *Men, Women and Chain Saws: Gender in the Modern Horror Film*, Princeton, NJ: Princeton University Press.

Coffey, J., S. Budgeon and H. Cahill, eds (2016), *Learning Bodies: The Body in Youth and Childhood Studies*, Singapore: Springer.

Connell, R. W. (2005), *Masculinities*, 2nd edn, Cambridge: Polity.

Connell, R. W. and J. W. Messerschmidt (2005), 'Hegemonic Masculinity: Rethinking the Concept', *Gender & Society*, 19 (6): 829–59. doi:10.1177/0891243205278639.

Cook, P., ed. (2007), *The Cinema Book*, 3rd edn, London: British Film Institute.

Crawford, J. (2014), *The Twilight of the Gothic? Vampire Fiction and the Rise of the Paranormal Romance*, Cardiff: University of Wales Press.

Creeber, G. (2004), *Serial Television: Big Drama on the Small Screen*, London: BFI Publishing.

Creeber, G. (2006a), 'Analysing Television: Issues and Methods in Textual Analysis', in G. Creeber (ed), *Tele-Visions: An Introduction to Studying Television*, 26–38, London: BFI Publishing.

Creeber, G. (2006b), 'Decoding Television: Issues of Ideology and Discourse', in G. Creeber (ed), *Tele-Visions: An Introduction to Studying Television*, 44–55, London: BFI Publishing.

Creeber, G., ed. (2006c), *Tele-Visions: An Introduction to Studying Television*, London: BFI Publishing.

Creeber, G., T. Miller and J. Tulloch, eds (2008), *The Television Genre Book*, 2nd edn, London: Palgrave Macmillan.

Creed, B. ([1993] 2007), *The Monstrous-Feminine: Film, Feminism, Psychoanalysis*, Abingdon: Routledge.

Dana, R. (2008), 'It's No Gossip, Ratings Slip Threatens CW Network', *The Wall Street Journal*, 16 May. Available online: www.wsj.com/public/article/SB121089546043097065.html (accessed 10 April 2021).

Davis, G. and K. Dickinson (2004a), 'Introduction', in G. Davis and K. Dickinson (eds), *Teen TV: Genre, Consumption, Identity*, 1–13, London: BFI Publishing.

Davis, G. and K. Dickinson, eds (2004b), *Teen TV: Genre, Consumption, Identity*, London: BFI Publishing.

Davis, K. (2003), *Dubious Equalities and Embodied Differences: Cultural Studies on Cosmetic Surgery*, Lanham, MD: Rowman & Littlefield.
de la Cruz, M. (2006–13), *Blue Bloods Series*, 7 vols., New York, NY: Hyperion.
de Lauretis, T. (1984), *Alice Doesn't: Feminism, Semiotics, Cinema*, Bloomington, IN: Indiana University Press.
de Toro, F. (1999a), 'Explorations on Post-Theory: New Times', in F. de Toro (ed), *Explorations on Post-Theory: Toward a Third Space*, 9–23, Frankfurt am Main: Iberoamericana Vervuert.
de Toro, F., ed. (1999b), *Explorations on Post-Theory: Toward a Third Space*, Frankfurt am Main: Iberoamericana Vervuert.
Deffenbacher, K. and M. Zagoria-Moffet (2011), 'Textual Vampirism in The *Twilight* Saga: Drawing Feminist Life from *Jane Eyre* and Teen Fantasy Fiction', in G. L. Anatol (ed), *Bringing Light to Twilight: Perspectives on a Pop Culture Phenomenon*, 31–42, New York, NY: Palgrave Macmillan.
Dejmanee, T. (2016), 'Consumption in the City: The Turn to Interiority in Contemporary Postfeminist Television', *European Journal of Cultural Studies*, 19 (2): 119–33. doi:10.1177/1367549415585555.
Demory, P. H. (2010), 'The Pleasures of Adapting: Reading, Viewing, Logging On', in A. M. Clarke and M. Osborn (eds), *The Twilight Mystique: Critical Essays on the Novels and Films*, 202–16, Jefferson, NC: McFarland & Company.
Dietz, T. (2011), 'Wake Up, Bella! A Personal Essay on *Twilight*, Mormonism, Feminism, and Happiness', in G. L. Anatol (ed), *Bringing Light to Twilight: Perspectives on a Pop Culture Phenomenon*, 99–112, New York, NY: Palgrave Macmillan.
Dines, G. and J. M. Humez, eds (1995a), *Gender, Race and Class in Media: A Text-Reader*, Thousand Oaks, CA: SAGE.
Dines, G. and J. M. Humez (1995b), 'Modes of Sexual Representation 1: Romance Novels and Slasher Films', in G. Dines and J. M. Humez (eds), *Gender, Race and Class in Media: A Text-Reader*, 161–7, Thousand Oaks, CA: SAGE.
Doane, M. A. (1987), *The Desire to Desire: The Woman's Film of the 1940s*, Bloomington, IN: Indiana University Press.
Donnelly, A. (2011), 'Denial and Salvation: The *Twilight* Saga and Heteronormative Patriarchy', in M. Parke and N. Wilson (eds), *Theorizing Twilight: Critical Essays on What's at Stake in a Post-Vampire World*, 178–93, Jefferson, NC: McFarland & Company.

Douglas, S. J. (2010), *The Rise of Enlightened Sexism: How Pop Culture Took Us from Girl Power to Girls Gone Wild*, New York, NY: St. Martin's Griffin.

Drakakis, J. and D. Townshend, eds (2008), *Gothic Shakespeares*, Abingdon: Routledge.

Dugan, L. (2012), 'Twilight Becomes First Movie To Reach 1 Million Followers On Twitter', *Adweek*, 20 August. Available online: https://www.adweek.com/digital/twilight-million-followers/ (accessed 10 April 2021).

Dyhouse, C. (2017), *Heartthrobs: A History of Women and Desire*, Oxford: Oxford University Press.

Edwards, J. D. and A. Soltysik Monnet, eds (2012), *The Gothic in Contemporary Literature and Popular Culture: Pop Goth*, New York, NY: Routledge.

Edwards, K. (2009), 'Good Looks and Sex Symbols: The Power of the Gaze and the Displacement of the Erotic in Twilight', *Screen Education*, 53: 26–32.

Edwards-Behi, N. (2014), '"Flicks For Chicks (And Chicks With Dicks) Who Can't Take Serious Horror": The Generic Misrecognition of *The Twilight Saga*', in W. Clayton and S. Harman (eds), *Screening Twilight: Critical Approaches to a Cinematic Phenomenon*, 40–8, London: I. B. Tauris.

Elias, A. S., R. Gill and C. Scharff (2017a), 'Aesthetic Labour: Beauty Politics in Neoliberalism', in A. S. Elias, R. Gill and C. Scharff (eds), *Aesthetic Labour: Rethinking Beauty Politics in Neoliberalism*, 3–49, London: Palgrave Macmillan.

Elias, A. S., R. Gill and C. Scharff, eds (2017b), *Aesthetic Labour: Rethinking Beauty Politics in Neoliberalism*, London: Palgrave Macmillan. doi:10.1057/978-1-137-47765-1.

Em & Lo (2009), '"Twilight," Take Me Away! Teenage Vampires and the Others Who Love Them', *New York Magazine*, 11 November. Available online: http://nymag.com/movies/features/62027/ (accessed 10 April 2021).

Ermida, I., ed. (2016), *Dracula and the Gothic in Literature, Pop Culture and the Arts*, Leiden: Brill Rodopi.

Evans, J. and S. Hall, eds (1999), *Visual Culture: The Reader*, London: SAGE.

Faludi, S. ([1991] 1992), *Backlash: The Undeclared War against American Women*, New York, NY: Anchor Books.

Featherstone, M. (1991), 'The Body in Consumer Culture', in M. Featherstone, M. Hepworth and B. S. Turner (eds), *The Body: Social Process and Cultural Theory*, 170–96, London: SAGE.

Featherstone, M., M. Hepworth and B. S. Turner, eds (1991), *The Body: Social Process and Cultural Theory*, London: SAGE.

Fellner, A. M., M. Fernández Morales and M. Martausová, eds (2017), *Rethinking Gender in Popular Culture in the 21st Century: Marlboro Men and California Gurls*, Newcastle upon Tyne: Cambridge Scholars Publishing.

Ferguson Ellis, K. (1989), *The Contested Castle: Gothic Novels and the Subversion of Domestic Ideology*, Urbana, IL: University of Illinois Press.

Ferriss, S. (2008), 'Fashioning Femininity in the Makeover Flick', in S. Ferriss and M. Young (eds), *Chick Flicks: Contemporary Women at the Movies*, 41–57, New York, NY: Routledge.

Ferriss, S. and M. Young, eds (2008a), *Chick Flicks: Contemporary Women at the Movies*, New York, NY: Routledge.

Ferriss, S. and M. Young (2008b), 'Introduction: Chick Flicks and Chick Culture', in S. Ferriss and M. Young (eds), *Chick Flicks: Contemporary Women at the Movies*, 1–25, New York, NY: Routledge.

Fiske, J. (1989), *Reading the Popular*, London: Routledge.

Fiske, J. (1992), 'British Cultural Studies and Television', in R. C. Allen (ed), *Channels of Discourse, Reassembled: Television and Contemporary Criticism*, 284–326, 2nd edn, London: Routledge.

Flood, M., J. K. Gardiner, B. Pease and K. Pringle, eds (2007), *International Encyclopedia of Men and Masculinities*, Abingdon: Routledge.

Forrest-White, L. (2009), 'The *Twilight* of Feminism', *Caterwaul Quarterly*, 3: 28–31. Available online: http://caterwaulquarterly.com/node/82 (accessed 6 July 2010).

Four Gothic Novels (1994), Oxford: Oxford University Press.

Frantz, Sarah S. G. and E. M. Selinger, eds (2012), *New Approaches to Popular Romance Fiction: Critical Essays*, Jefferson, NC: McFarland & Company.

Fraser, M. and M. Greco (2005a), 'Introduction', in M. Fraser and M. Greco (eds), *The Body: A Reader*, 1–42, Abingdon: Routledge.

Fraser, M. and M. Greco, eds (2005b), *The Body: A Reader*, Abingdon: Routledge.

Freeman, H. (2017), 'Transparent's Jill Soloway: "The Words Male and Female Describe Who We Used to Be"', *The Guardian*, 21 May. Available online: www.theguardian.com/tv-and-radio/2017/may/21/transparents-jill-soloway-the-words-male-and-female-describe-who-we-used-to-be (accessed 10 April 2021).

Frohreich, K. A. (2013), 'Sullied Blood, Semen and Skin: Vampires and the Spectre of Miscegenation', *Gothic Studies*, 15 (1): 33–43. doi:10.7227/gs.15.1.4.

Gaines, J. (1999), 'White Privilege and Looking Relations: Race and Gender in Feminist Film Theory', in J. Evans and S. Hall (eds), *Visual Culture: The Reader*, 402–10, London: SAGE.

Gamble, S. ([1998] 2009a), 'Postfeminism', in S. Gamble (ed), *The Routledge Companion to Feminism and Postfeminism*, 43–54, Abingdon: Routledge.

Gamble, S., ed. ([1998] 2009b), *The Routledge Companion to Feminism and Postfeminism*, Abingdon: Routledge.

Gamman, L. and M. Marshment ([1988] 1994a), 'Introduction', in L. Gamman and M. Marshment (eds), *The Female Gaze: Women as Viewers of Popular Culture*, 1–7, London: Women's Press.

Gamman, L. and M. Marshment, eds ([1988] 1994b), *The Female Gaze: Women as Viewers of Popular Culture*, London: Women's Press.

Garofalo, A. (2014), 'How Successful Was "True Blood" for HBO? A Look Back at Ratings Before Series Finale', *International Business Times*, 19 August. Available online: https://www.ibtimes.com/how-successful-was-true-blood-hbo-look-back-ratings-series-finale-1663206 (accessed 28 August 2021).

Gelder, K. (1994), *Reading the Vampire*, London: Routledge.

Gelder, K. (2004), *Popular Fiction: The Logics and Practices of a Literary Field*, Abingdon: Routledge.

Genz, S. (2007), '(Re)Making the Body Beautiful: Postfeminist Cinderellas and Gothic Tales of Transformation', in B. A. Brabon and S. Genz (eds), *Postfeminist Gothic: Critical Interventions in Contemporary Culture*, 68–84, Basingstoke: Palgrave Macmillan.

Genz, S. (2017), '"I Have Work … I Am Busy … Trying to Become Who I Am": Neoliberal *Girls* and Recessionary Postfeminism', in M. Nash and I. Whelehan (eds), *Reading Lena Dunham's Girls: Feminism, Postfeminism, Authenticity and Gendered Performance in Contemporary Television*, 17–30, Cham: Palgrave Macmillan.

Genz, S. and B. A. Brabon (2009), *Postfeminism: Cultural Texts and Theories*, Edinburgh: Edinburgh University Press.

George, S. and B. Hughes (2013a), 'Introduction', in S. George and B. Hughes (eds), *Open Graves, Open Minds: Representations of Vampires and the Undead from the Enlightenment to the Present Day*, 1–23, Manchester: Manchester University Press.

George, S. and B. Hughes (2013b), *Open Graves, Open Minds: Representations of Vampires and the Undead from the Enlightenment to the Present Day*, Manchester: Manchester University Press.

George, S. and B. Hughes, eds (2020a), *In the Company of Wolves: Werewolves, Wolves and Wild Children*, Manchester: Manchester University Press.

George, S. and B. Hughes (2020b), 'Introduction: From Preternatural Pastoral to Paranormal Romance', in S. George and B. Hughes (eds), *In the Company of Wolves: Werewolves, Wolves and Wild Children*, 1–17, Manchester: Manchester University Press.

Gerhards, L. (2016), 'Vampires "on a Special Diet": Identity and the Body in Contemporary Media Texts', in I. Ermida (ed), *Dracula and the Gothic in Literature, Pop Culture and the Arts*, 235–56, Leiden: Brill Rodopi.

Gerhards, L. (2017), 'The Legacy of Lucy Westenra: Female Postfeminist Subjects in *The Vampire Diaries*, *True Blood* and *The Twilight Saga*', in A. M. Fellner, M. Fernández Morales and M. Martausová (eds), *Rethinking Gender in Popular Culture in the 21st Century: Marlboro Men and California Gurls*, 89–109, Newcastle upon Tyne: Cambridge Scholars Publishing.

Giddens, A. (1991), *Modernity and Self-Identity: Self and Society in the Late Modern Age*, Stanford, CA: Stanford University Press.

Gilbert, A. (2012), 'Between Twi-Hards and Twi-Haters: The Complicated Terrain of Online 'Twilight' Audience Communities', in A. Morey (ed), *Genre, Reception, and Adaptation in the "Twilight" Series*, 163–79, Farnham: Ashgate.

Gill, R. (2007), *Gender and the Media*, Cambridge: Polity.

Gill, R. (2016), 'Post-postfeminism? New Feminist Visibilities in Postfeminist Times', *Feminist Media Studies*, 16 (4): 610–30. doi:10.1080/14680777.2016.1193293.

Gill, R. (2017), 'The Affective, Cultural and Psychic Life of Postfeminism: A Postfeminist Sensibility 10 Years on', *European Journal of Cultural Studies*, 20 (6): 606–26. doi:10.1177/1367549417733003.

Gill, R. and E. Herdieckerhoff (2006), 'Rewriting The Romance: New Femininities in Chick Lit?', *Feminist Media Studies*, 6 (4): 487–504. doi:10.1080/14680770600989947.

Gill, R. and C. Scharff (2011a), 'Introduction', in R. Gill and C. Scharff (eds), *New Femininities: Postfeminism, Neoliberalism and Subjectivity*, 1–17, Basingstoke: Palgrave Macmillan.

Gill, R. and C. Scharff, eds (2011b), *New Femininities: Postfeminism, Neoliberalism and Subjectivity*, Basingstoke: Palgrave Macmillan.

Gillespie, R. (1997), 'Women, the Body and Brand Extension in Medicine', *Women & Health*, 24 (4): 69–85. doi:10.1300/J013v24n04_04.

Gleiberman, O. (2009), '"New Moon": Why Its Girl-Driven Success Is Good for the Future of Movies', *Entertainment Weekly*, 26 November. Available online: http://ew.com/article/2009/11/26/new-moon-why-its-good-for-the-future-of-movies/ (accessed 13 March 2017).

Goade, S., ed. (2007), *Empowerment versus Oppression: Twenty First Century Views of Popular Romance Novels*, Newcastle upon Tyne: Cambridge Scholars Publishing.

Godfrey, S. and H. Hamad ([2011] 2014), 'Save the Cheerleader, Save the Males: Resurgent Protective Paternalism in Popular Film and Television after 9/11', in K. Ross (ed), *The Handbook of Gender, Sex, and Media*, 157–73, Chichester: Wiley-Blackwell.

Godwin, V. (2014), '*Twilight* Anti-Fans: 'Real' Fans and 'Real' Vampires', in C. Bucciferro (ed), *The Twilight Saga: Exploring the Global Phenomenon*, 93–106, Lanham, MD: The Scarecrow Press.

Goodfriend, W. (2011), 'Relationship Violence in "Twilight": How "Twilight" Teaches Teens to Love Abusive Relationships', *Psychology Today*, 9 November. Available online: www.psychologytoday.com/us/blog/psychologist-the-movies/201111/relationship-violence-in-twilight (accessed 10 April 2021).

Gordon, J. and V. Hollinger (1997a), *Blood Read: The Vampire as Metaphor in Contemporary Culture*, Philadelphia, PA: University of Pennsylvania Press.

Gordon, J. and V. Hollinger (1997b), 'Introduction: The Shape of Vampires', in J. Gordon and V. Hollinger (eds), *Blood Read: The Vampire as Metaphor in Contemporary Culture*, 1–7, Philadelphia, PA: University of Pennsylvania Press.

Grant, B. K., ed. (1996), *The Dread of Difference: Gender and the Horror Film*, Austin, TX: University of Texas Press.

Gray, C. (2008–12), *Evernight Series*, 5 vols., New York, NY: HarperTeen.

Gross, E. (2010), 'True Blood: Executive Producer Alan Ball Discusses Vampires and Sex', *ComicBookMovie*, 6 December. Available online: http://www.comicbookmovie.com/fansites/vampiresandslayers/news/?a=26102 (accessed 12 May 2015).

Gwynne, J. and N. Muller (2013a), 'Introduction: Postfeminism and Contemporary Hollywood Cinema', in J. Gwynne and N. Muller (eds),

Postfeminism and Contemporary Hollywood Cinema, 1–10, Basingstoke: Palgrave Macmillan.

Gwynne, J. and N. Muller, eds (2013b), *Postfeminism and Contemporary Hollywood Cinema*, Basingstoke: Palgrave Macmillan.

Hall, S. (1997a), 'Introduction', in S. Hall (ed), *Representation: Cultural Representations and Signifying Practices*, 1–11, London: SAGE.

Hall, S., ed. (1997b), *Representation: Cultural Representations and Signifying Practices*, London: SAGE.

Hall, S. (1997c), 'The Work of Representation', in S. Hall (ed), *Representation: Cultural Representations and Signifying Practices*, 13–74, London: SAGE.

Hamad, H. (2013), 'Hollywood Fatherhood: Paternal Postfeminism in Contemporary Popular Cinema', in J. Gwynne and N. Muller (eds), *Postfeminism and Contemporary Hollywood Cinema*, 99–115, Basingstoke: Palgrave Macmillan.

Hamilton, L. K. (1993–), *Anita Blake: Vampire Hunter series*, 28 vols., New York, NY: Berkley.

Harkness, D. (2011–14), *All Souls Series*, 4 vols., London: Penguin Books.

Harman, S. (2014), 'The Pageant of Her Bleeding Twi-Hard Heart: *Twilight*, Femininity, Sexuality and Female Consumption', in W. Clayton and S. Harman (eds), *Screening Twilight: Critical Approaches to a Cinematic Phenomenon*, 49–56, London: I. B. Tauris.

Harris, C. (2001), *Dead until Dark*, New York, NY: Ace Books.

Harris, C. (2001–13), *The Southern Vampire Mysteries*, 13 vols., New York, NY: Ace Books.

Hawes, J. (2010), 'Sleeping Beauty and the Idealized Undead: Avoiding Adolescence', in A. M. Clarke and M. Osborn (eds), *The Twilight Mystique: Critical Essays on the Novels and Films*, 163–78, Jefferson, NC: McFarland & Company.

Hemmings, C. (2011), *Why Stories Matter: The Political Grammar of Feminist Theory*, Durham, NC: Duke University Press.

Herman, D., M. Jahn and M.-L. Ryan, eds (2005), *Routledge Encyclopedia of Narrative Theory*, Abingdon: Routledge.

Heywood, L. and J. Drake, eds (1997), *Third Wave Agenda: Being Feminist, Doing Feminism*, Minneapolis, MN: University of Minnesota Press.

Hills, M. (2012), '"Twilight" Fans Represented in Commercial Paratexts and Inter-Fandoms: Resisting and Repurposing Negative Fan Stereotypes', in A. Morey (ed), *Genre, Reception, and Adaptation in the "Twilight" Series*, 113–29, Farnham: Ashgate.

Hilton, M. and M. Nikolajeva, eds (2012a), *Contemporary Adolescent Literature and Culture: The Emergent Adult*, Farnham: Ashgate.

Hilton, M. and M. Nikolajeva (2012b), 'Introduction: Time of Turmoil', in M. Hilton and M. Nikolajeva (eds), *Contemporary Adolescent Literature and Culture: The Emergent Adult*, 1–16, Farnham: Ashgate.

Hollows, J. (2000), *Feminism, Femininity and Popular Culture*, Manchester: Manchester University Press.

Honneth, A. and M. Saar, eds (2003), *Michel Foucault: Zwischenbilanz einer Rezeption*, Frankfurt am Main: Suhrkamp.

hooks, b. (1984), *Feminist Theory: From Margin to Center*, Boston, MA: South End Press.

Hudson, D. (2013), '"Of Course There Are Werewolves and Vampires": True Blood and the Right to Rights for Other Species', *American Quarterly*, 65 (3): 661–87. doi:10.1353/aq.2013.0048.

Hughes, S. (2010), 'The Vampire Diaries – Fresh Blood for Teenage Vampire Lovers', *Independent*, 5 February. Available online: https://www.independent.co.uk/arts-entertainment/tv/features/the-vampire-diaries-fresh-blood-for-teenage-vampire-lovers-1889840.html (accessed 10 April 2021).

Hunt, L., S. Lockyer and M. Williamson, eds (2014), *Screening the Undead: Vampires and Zombies in Film and Television*, London: I. B. Tauris.

Hurrelmann, K. (2003), 'Der entstrukturierte Lebenslauf: Die Auswirkungen der Expansion der Jugendphase', *Zeitschrift für Soziologie der Erziehung und Sozialisation*, 23 (2): 115–26.

Irwin, W., G. A. Dunn and R. Housel, eds (2010), *True Blood and Philosophy: We Wanna Think Bad Things with You*, Hoboken, NJ: Wiley.

Jäckel, J. (2012), '"How Fucking Lame"? Zur Konstruktion von Weiblichkeit und Agency in True Blood', in P.-I. Villa (ed), *Banale Kämpfe? Perspektiven auf Populärkultur und Geschlecht*, 57–73, Wiesbaden: Springer VS.

James, E. L. (2011–17), *Fifty Shades Series*, 5 vols., New York, NY: Vintage Books.

Jancovich, M. (2014), '"Cue the Shrieking Virgins"? The Critical Reception of The Twilight Saga', in W. Clayton and S. Harman (eds), *Screening Twilight: Critical Approaches to a Cinematic Phenomenon*, 26–39, London: I. B. Tauris.

Jenkins, H. (2007), 'Transmedia Storytelling 101', *Confessions of an Aca-Fan. The Official Weblog of Henry Jenkins*, 22 March. Available online: http://henryjenkins.org/2007/03/transmedia_storytelling_101.html (accessed 10 April 2021).

Jensen, K. (2010), 'Noble Werewolves or Native Shape-Shifters?', in A. M. Clarke and M. Osborn (eds), *The Twilight Mystique: Critical Essays on the Novels and Films*, 92–106, Jefferson, NC: McFarland & Company.

Jenson, J. and A. Sarkeesian (2011), 'Buffy vs. Bella: The Re-Emergence of the Archetypal Feminine in Vampire Stories', in G. Schott and K. Moffat (eds), *Fanpires: Audience Consumption of the Modern Vampire*, 55–72, Washington, DC: New Academia Publishing.

Johnson, M. L. (2007a), 'Introduction: Ladies Love Your Box: The Rhetoric of Pleasure and Danger in Feminist Television Studies', in M. L. Johnson (ed), *Third Wave Feminism and Television: Jane Puts It in a Box*, 1–27, London: I. B. Tauris.

Johnson, M. L., ed. (2007b), *Third Wave Feminism and Television: Jane Puts It in a Box*, London: I. B. Tauris.

Jones, A. R. (1986), 'Mills & Boon Meets Feminism', in J. Radford (ed), *The Progress of Romance: The Politics of Popular Fiction*, 195–218, London: Routledge & Kegan Paul.

Jones, D. (2018), *Sleeping With the Lights On: The Unsettling Story of Horror*, Oxford: Oxford University Press.

Jowett, L. (2005), *Sex and the Slayer: A Gender Studies Primer for the Buffy Fan*, Middletown, CT: Wesleyan University Press.

Jowett, L. and S. Abbott (2013), *TV Horror: Investigating the Dark Side of the Small Screen*, London: I. B. Tauris.

Kandiyoti, D. (1988), 'Bargaining with Patriarchy', *Gender & Society*, 2 (3): 274–90. doi:10.1177/089124388002003004.

Kane, K. (2010), 'A Very Queer Refusal: The Chilling Effect of the Cullens' Heteronormative Embrace', in M. A. Click, J. Stevens Aubrey and E. Behm-Morawitz (eds), *Bitten by Twilight: Youth Culture, Media, & the Vampire Franchise*, 103–18, New York, NY: Peter Lang.

Kane, T. (2006), *The Changing Vampire of Film and Television: A Critical Study of the Growth of a Genre*, Jefferson, NC: McFarland & Company.

Kaplan, E. A. (1983), *Women and Film: Both Sides of the Camera*, New York, NY: Methuen.

Kapurch, K. (2012a), '"I'd Never Given Much Thought to How I Would Die": Uses (and the Decline) of Voiceover on the "Twilight" Films', in A. Morey (ed), *Genre, Reception, and Adaptation in the "Twilight" Series*, 181–97, Farnham: Ashgate.

Kapurch, K. (2012b), '"Unconditionally and Irrevocably": Theorizing the Melodramatic Impulse in Young Adult Literature through the *Twilight*

Saga and *Jane Eyre*', *Children's Literature Association Quarterly*, 37 (2): 164–87.

Kavka, M. (2002), 'Feminism, Ethics, and History, or What Is the "Post" in Postfeminism?', *Tulsa Studies in Women's Literature*, 21 (1): 29–44. doi:10.2307/4149214.

Keller, J. and M. Ryan (2015), 'Call for Papers: Emergent Feminisms and the Challenge to Postfeminist Media Culture', circulated 12 May.

Kheraj, A. (2018), 'How "Twilight" Changed Fan Culture Forever', *i-D Vice*, 26 October. Available online: https://i-d.vice.com/en_us/article/8xjydz/how-twilight-changed-fan-culture-forever (accessed 10 April 2021).

Knowles, C. (2007), 'Sensibility Gone Mad: Or, Drusilla, Buffy and the (D) evolution of the Heroine of Sensibility', in B. A. Brabon and S. Genz (eds), *Postfeminist Gothic: Critical Interventions in Contemporary Culture*, 140–53, Basingstoke: Palgrave Macmillan.

Kostihova, M. (2012), *How to Analyze the Works of Stephenie Meyer*, Edina, MN: ABDO Publishing Company.

Kristeva, J. ([1980] 1982), *Powers of Horror: An Essay on Abjection*, trans. L. S. Roudiez, New York, NY: Columbia University Press.

Kungl, C. T., ed. (2003), *Vampires: Myths & Metaphors of Enduring Evil*, Oxford: Inter-Disciplinary Press.

Kupers, T. A. (2005), 'Toxic Masculinity as a Barrier to Mental Health Treatment in Prison', *Journal of Clinical Psychology*, 61 (6): 713–24. doi:10.1002/jclp.20105.

Larsson, M. and A. Steiner, eds (2011a), *Interdisciplinary Approaches to Twilight: Studies in Fiction, Media, and a Contemporary Cultural Experience*, Lund: Nordic Academic Press.

Larsson, M. and A. Steiner (2011b), 'Introduction', in M. Larsson and A. Steiner (eds), *Interdisciplinary Approaches to Twilight: Studies in Fiction, Media, and a Contemporary Cultural Experience*, 9–28, Lund: Nordic Academic Press.

Levine, E. (2009), 'Feminist Media Studies in a Postfeminist Age', *Cinema Journal*, 48 (4): 137–43. doi:10.1353/cj.0.0129.

Levine, E. and L. Parks, eds (2007), *Undead TV: Essays on Buffy the Vampire Slayer*, London: Duke University Press.

Levy, A. ([2005] 2006), *Female Chauvinist Pigs: Women and the Rise of Raunch Culture*, New York, NY: Free Press.

Levy, D. P. (2007), 'Hegemonic Masculinity', in M. Flood, J. K. Gardiner, B. Pease and K. Pringle (eds), *International Encyclopedia of Men and Masculinities*, 253–255, Abingdon: Routledge.

Lindgren Leavenworth, M. (2011), 'Variations, Subversions, and Endless Love: Fan Fiction and the *Twilight* Saga', in G. L. Anatol (ed), *Bringing Light to Twilight: Perspectives on a Pop Culture Phenomenon*, 69–81, New York, NY: Palgrave Macmillan.

Lindgren Leavenworth, M. (2014), 'Transmedial Narration and Fan Fiction: The Storyworld of *The Vampire Diaries*', in M.-L. Ryan and J.-N. Thon (eds), *Storyworlds Across Media: Toward a Media-Conscious Narratology*, 315–31, Lincoln, NE: University of Nebraska Press.

Lorde, A., ed. (1984a), *Sister Outsider: Essays and Speeches*, Trumansburg, NY: The Crossing Press.

Lorde, A. (1984b), 'The Master's Tools Will Never Dismantle the Master's House', in A. Lorde (ed), *Sister Outsider: Essays and Speeches*, 110–113, Trumansburg, NY: The Crossing Press.

Lutz, D. (2007), 'The Haunted Space of the Mind: The Revival of the Gothic Romance in the Twenty-First Century', in S. Goade (ed), *Empowerment versus Oppression: Twenty First Century Views of Popular Romance Novels*, 81–92, Newcastle upon Tyne: Cambridge Scholars Publishing.

MacKenzie, C. (2010), '"Vampire Diaries" Star Nina Dobrev on Elena's Look-Alike Dilemma and More', *Los Angeles Times*, 21 January. Available online: http://latimesblogs.latimes.com/showtracker/2010/01/vampire-diaries-star-nina-dobrev.html (accessed 10 April 2021).

MacKinnon, K. (2003), *Representing Men: Maleness and Masculinity in the Media*, London: Arnold.

Mancusi, M. (2006–17), *Blood Coven Series*, 10 vols., New York, NY: Berkley.

Mann, P. S. (1994), *Micro-Politics: Agency in a Postfeminist Era*, Minneapolis, MN: University of Minnesota Press.

Margolis, R. (2005), 'Love at First Bite: Stephenie Meyer Interview, Undercover', *School Library Journal*, 1 October. Available online: www.slj.com/2005/10/interviews/under-cover/love-at-first-bite-stephenie-meyer-interview/ (accessed 10 March 2016).

Marion, I. (2010), *Warm Bodies*, New York, NY: Atria Books.

Masson, C. and M. Stanley (2006), 'Queer Eye of that Vampire Guy: Spike and the Aesthetics of Camp', *Slayage*, 6.2 (22): pars. 1–23. Available online: http://www.whedonstudies.tv/uploads/2/6/2/8/26288593/masson_stanley_slayage_6.2.pdf (accessed 10 April 2021).

McCracken, A. (2007), 'At Stake: Angel's Body, Fantasy Masculinity, and Queer Desire in Teen Television', in E. Levine and L. Parks (eds), *Undead*

TV: Essays on Buffy the Vampire Slayer, 116–44, London: Duke University Press.

McGeough, D. D. (2010), 'Twilight and Transformations of Flesh: Reading the Body in Contemporary Youth Culture', in M. A. Click, J. Stevens Aubrey and E. Behm-Morawitz (eds), *Bitten by Twilight: Youth Culture, Media, & the Vampire Franchise*, 87–102, New York, NY: Peter Lang.

McIntosh, J. (2009), 'Buffy vs Edward: Twilight Remixed – [original version]', *YouTube*, 20 June. Available online: https://www.youtube.com/watch?v=RZwM3GvaTRM (accessed 10 April 2021).

McLennan, R. (2012), 'Bella's Promises: Adolescence and (Re)capitulation in Stephenie Meyer's *Twilight* Series', in J. D. Edwards and A. Soltysik Monnet (eds), *The Gothic in Contemporary Literature and Popular Culture: Pop Goth*, 84–95, New York, NY: Routledge.

McLennon, L. M. (2014), 'Defining Urban Fantasy and Paranormal Romance: Crossing Boundaries of Genre, Media, Self and Other in New Supernatural Worlds', *Refractory: A Journal of Entertainment Media*, 23. Available online: http://refractory.unimelb.edu.au/2014/06/26/uf-mclennon/ (accessed 6 January 2016).

McRobbie, A. (1991), *Feminism and Youth Culture: From Jackie to Just Seventeen*, Basingstoke: Macmillan.

McRobbie, A. (2007), 'Postfeminism and Popular Culture: Bridget Jones and the New Gender Regime', in Y. Tasker and D. Negra (eds), *Interrogating Postfeminism: Gender and the Politics of Popular Culture*, 27–39, Durham, NC: Duke University Press.

McRobbie, A. (2015), 'Notes on the Perfect: Competitive Femininity in Neoliberal Times', *Australian Feminist Studies*, 30 (83): 3–20. doi:10.1080/08164649.2015.1011485.

Mead, R. (2007–10), *Vampire Academy Series*, 6 vols., London: Razorbill.

Mellins, M. (2013), *Vampire Culture*, London: Bloomsbury.

Menke, C. (2003), 'Zweierlei Übung: Zum Verhältnis von sozialer Disziplinierung und ästhetischer Existenz', in A. Honneth and M. Saar (eds), *Michel Foucault: Zwischenbilanz einer Rezeption*, 283–99, Frankfurt am Main: Suhrkamp.

Merskin, D. (2011), 'A Boyfriend to Die for: Edward Cullen as Compensated Psychopath in Stephanie [sic] Meyer's *Twilight*', *Journal of Communication Inquiry*, 35 (2): 157–78. doi:10.1177/0196859911402992.

Meyer, S. (2005), *Twilight*, London: Atom.

Meyer, S. (2007), *Eclipse*, London: Atom.
Meyer, S. (2015), *Life and Death: Twilight Reimagined*, London: Atom.
Meyer, S. (2020), *Midnight Sun*, London: Atom.
Meyer, S. (2005–08), *Twilight Series*, 4 vols., London: Atom.
Milestone, K. and A. Meyer (2012), *Gender and Popular Culture*, Cambridge: Polity.
Miller, K. (2010), 'A Little Extra Bite: Dis/Ability and Romance in Tanya Huff and Charlaine Harris's Vampire Fiction', *Journal of Popular Romance Studies*, 1 (1).
Miller, M. (2011), 'Maybe Edward Is the Most Dangerous Thing Out There: The Role of Patriarchy', in M. Parke and N. Wilson (eds), *Theorizing Twilight: Critical Essays on What's at Stake in a Post-Vampire World*, 165–77, Jefferson, NC: McFarland & Company.
Miller, S. (2003), '"Nursery Fears Made Flesh and Sinew": Vampires, the Body and Eating Disorders: A Psychoanalytic Approach', in C. T. Kungl (ed), *Vampires: Myths & Metaphors of Enduring Evil*, 53–8, Oxford: Inter-Disciplinary Press.
Modleski, T. (1982), *Loving with a Vengeance: Mass-Produced Fantasies for Women*, Hamden, CT: Archon Books.
Moers, E. ([1976] 1977), *Literary Women*, London: W.H. Allen.
Morey, A. (2012a), '"Famine for Food, Expectation for Content": Jane Eyre as Intertext for the "Twilight" Saga', in A. Morey (ed), *Genre, Reception, and Adaptation in the "Twilight" Series*, 15–27, Farnham: Ashgate.
Morey, A., ed. (2012b), *Genre, Reception, and Adaptation in the "Twilight" Series*, Farnham: Ashgate.
Morey, A. (2012c), 'Introduction', in A. Morey (ed), *Genre, Reception, and Adaptation in the "Twilight" Series*, 1–14, Farnham: Ashgate.
Moseley, R. (2008), 'The Teen Series', in G. Creeber, T. Miller and J. Tulloch (eds), *The Television Genre Book*, 52–54, 2nd edn, London: Palgrave Macmillan.
Mukherjea, A. (2011a), 'My Vampire Boyfriend: Postfeminism, "Perfect" Masculinity, and the Contemporary Appeal of Paranormal Romance', *Studies in Popular Culture*, 33 (2): 1–20. doi:10.2307/23416381.
Mukherjea, A. (2011b), 'Team Bella: Fans Navigating Desire, Security, and Feminism', in M. Parke and N. Wilson (eds), *Theorizing Twilight: Critical Essays on What's at Stake in a Post-Vampire World*, 70–83, Jefferson, NC: McFarland & Company.
Mukherjea, A. (2012), 'Mad, Bad and Delectable to Know: *True Blood*'s Paranormal Men and Gothic Romance', in B. Cherry (ed), *True Blood: Investigating Vampires and Southern Gothic*, 109–21, London: I. B. Tauris.

Mulvey, L. ([1975] 1989), 'Visual Pleasure and Narrative Cinema', in L. Mulvey (ed), *Visual and Other Pleasures*, 14–26, London: Macmillan.

Mulvey, L., ed. (1989), *Visual and Other Pleasures*, London: Macmillan.

Munford, R. and M. Waters (2014), *Feminism & Popular Culture: Investigating the Postfeminist Mystique*, London: I. B. Tauris.

Mussell, K. (1984), *Fantasy and Reconciliation: Contemporary Formulas of Women's Romance Fiction*, Westport, CT: Greenwood Press.

Nakagawa, C. (2011), 'Safe Sex with Defanged Vampires: New Vampire Heroes in *Twilight* and the *Southern Vampire Mysteries*', *Journal of Popular Romance Studies*, 2 (1).

Nash, M. and I. Whelehan, eds (2017), *Reading Lena Dunham's Girls: Feminism, Postfeminism, Authenticity and Gendered Performance in Contemporary Television*, Cham: Palgrave Macmillan.

Ndalianis, A. (2012), *The Horror Sensorium: Media and the Senses*, Jefferson, NC: McFarland & Company.

Neale, S. (2008a), 'Genre and Television', in G. Creeber, T. Miller and J. Tulloch (eds), *The Television Genre Book*, 5–6, 2nd edn, London: Palgrave Macmillan.

Neale, S. (2008b), 'Studying Genre', in G. Creeber, T. Miller and J. Tulloch (eds), *The Television Genre Book*, 3–5, 2nd edn, London: Palgrave Macmillan.

Negra, D. (2009), *What a Girl Wants? Fantasizing the Reclamation of Self in Postfeminism*, Abingdon: Routledge.

Ní Fhlainn, S. (2019), *Postmodern Vampires: Film, Fiction, and Popular Culture*, London: Palgrave Macmillan.

Nicol, R. (2011), '"When You Kiss Me, I Want to Die": Arrested Feminism in Buffy the Vampire Slayer and The Twilight Series', in G. L. Anatol (ed), *Bringing Light to Twilight: Perspectives on a Pop Culture Phenomenon*, 113–23, New York, NY: Palgrave Macmillan.

O'Brien, J., ed. (2009), *Encyclopedia of Gender and Society: Volume 1*, Thousand Oaks, CA: SAGE.

O'Reilly, J. D. (2013), *Bewitched Again: Supernaturally Powerful Women on Television, 1996–2011*, Jefferson, NC: McFarland & Company.

Parke, M. and N. Wilson, eds (2011), *Theorizing Twilight: Critical Essays on What's at Stake in a Post-Vampire World*, Jefferson, NC: McFarland & Company.

Pattman, R. (2007), 'Laddism', in M. Flood, J. K. Gardiner, B. Pease and K. Pringle (eds), *International Encyclopedia of Men and Masculinities*, 358–359, Abingdon: Routledge.

Paul, N. (2014), 'Other Ways of Looking: The Female Gaze in Jean Rhys' Wide Sargasso Sea', *eSharp*, 22: pars. 1–23. Available online: http://www.gla.ac.uk/research/az/esharp/issues/2/paul/ (accessed 10 April 2021).

Pearce, L. and G. Wisker, eds (1998), *Fatal Attractions and Cultural Subversions: Rescripting Romance in Contemporary Literature and Film*, London: Pluto Press.

Pender, P. (2016), *I'm Buffy and You're History: Buffy the Vampire Slayer and Contemporary Feminism*, London: I. B. Tauris.

Penley, C., C. Parreñas Shimizu, M. Miller-Young and T. Taormino (2013), 'Introduction: The Politics of Producing Pleasure', in T. Taormino, C. Parreñas Shimizu, C. Penley and M. Miller-Young (eds), *The Feminist Porn Book: The Politics of Producing Pleasure*, 9–20, New York, NY: The Feminist Press.

Percec, D., ed. (2012), *Romance: The History of a Genre*, Newcastle upon Tyne: Cambridge Scholars Publishing.

Perfetti-Oates, N. (2015), 'Chick Flicks and the Straight Female Gaze: Sexual Objectification and Sex Negativity in *New Moon*, *Forgetting Sarah Marshall*, *Magic Mike*, and *Fool's Gold*', *Gender Forum – An Internet Journal for Gender Studies*, 51, pars. 1–17. Available online: www.genderforum.org/issues/absolute-erotic/chick-flicks-and-the-straight-female-gaze-sexual-objectification-and-sex-negativity-in-new-moon-forgetting-sarah-marshall-magic-mike-and-fools-gold/ (accessed 31 May 2016).

Petersen, A. H. (2012), 'That Teenage Feeling: *Twilight*, Fantasy, and Feminist Readers', *Feminist Media Studies*, 12 (1): 51–67.

Pilcher, J. and I. Whelehan ([2004] 2011), *Fifty Key Concepts in Gender Studies*, London: SAGE.

Polidori, J. W., G. G. B. Byron and J. Mitford (1819), *The Vampyre: A Tale*, London: Sherwood, Neely and Jones.

Priest, H. (2011), 'What's Wrong with Sparkly Vampires?', *The Gothic Imagination Blog*, 20 July. Available online: www.gothic.stir.ac.uk/guestblog/whats-wrong-with-sparkly-vampires/ (accessed 8 April 2016).

Priest, H. (2014), 'Young Adults and the Contemporary Gothic', in G. Byron and D. Townshend (eds), *The Gothic World*, 274–83, Abingdon: Routledge.

Probyn, E. (1990), 'New Traditionalism and Post-Feminism: TV Does the Home', *Screen*, 31 (2): 147–59. doi:10.1093/screen/31.2.147.

Projansky, S. (2007), 'Mass Magazine Cover Girls: Some Reflections on Postfeminist Girls and Postfeminism's Daughters', in Y. Tasker and D.

Negra (eds), *Interrogating Postfeminism: Gender and the Politics of Popular Culture*, 40–72, Durham, NC: Duke University Press.

Purvis, T. and G. Longstaff (2009), 'Camp', in J. O'Brien (ed), *Encyclopedia of Gender and Society: Volume 1*, 104–6, Thousand Oaks, CA: SAGE.

Radford, J., ed. (1986), *The Progress of Romance: The Politics of Popular Fiction*, London: Routledge & Kegan Paul.

Radway, J. A. ([1984] 1991), *Reading the Romance: Women, Patriarchy, and Popular Literature*, Chapel Hill, NC: The University of North Carolina Press.

Recht, M. (2011), *Der Sympathische Vampir: Visualisierungen von Männlichkeiten in der TV-Serie Buffy*, Frankfurt am Main: Campus Verlag.

Regis, P. (2003), *A Natural History of the Romance Novel*, Philadelphia, PA: University of Pennsylvania Press.

Retallack, H., J. Ringrose and E. Lawrence (2016), '"Fuck Your Body Image": Teen Girls' Twitter and Instagram Feminism in and around School', in J. Coffey, S. Budgeon and H. Cahill (eds), *Learning Bodies: The Body in Youth and Childhood Studies*, 85–103, Singapore: Springer.

Rice, A. (1976–2018), *The Vampire Chronicles Series*, 13 vols., New York, NY: Knopf.

Rivers, N. (2017), *Postfeminism(s) and the Arrival of the Fourth Wave: Turning Tides*, Cham: Palgrave Macmillan. doi:10.1007/978-3-319-59812-3.

Roach, C. (2010), 'Getting a Good Man to Love: Popular Romance Fiction and the Problem of Patriarchy', *Journal of Popular Romance Studies*, 1 (1).

Roach, C. M. (2016), *Happily Ever After: The Romance Story in Popular Culture*, Bloomington, IN: Indiana University Press.

Roback, D. (2010), 'Facts and Figures 2009: Meyer's Reign Continues', *Publishers Weekly*, 22 March. Available online: https://www.publishersweekly.com/pw/by-topic/childrens/childrens-industry-news/article/42533-children-s-bestsellers-2009-the-reign-continues.html (accessed 28 August 2021).

Roberts, M. (2007), 'The Fashion Police: Governing the Self in *What Not to Wear*', in Y. Tasker and D. Negra (eds), *Interrogating Postfeminism: Gender and the Politics of Popular Culture*, 227–48, Durham, NC: Duke University Press.

Robinson, S. (2007), 'Crisis in Masculinity', in M. Flood, J. K. Gardiner, B. Pease and K. Pringle (eds), *International Encyclopedia of Men and Masculinities*, 90–91, Abingdon: Routledge.

Rogobete, D. (2012), 'The *Twilight* Saga: Teen Gothic Romance between the Dissolution of the Gothic and the Revival of Romance', in D. Percec (ed), *Romance: The History of a Genre*, 111–32, Newcastle upon Tyne: Cambridge Scholars Publishing.

Ross, K., ed. ([2011] 2014), *The Handbook of Gender, Sex, and Media*, Chichester: Wiley-Blackwell.

Roth, C. (2011), 'Twilight: 5 Lessons Your Business Can Learn from the Movie', *The Huffington Post – The Blog*, 28 November. Available online: www.huffingtonpost.com/carol-roth/business-lessons-twilight_b_1110342 .html (accessed 10 April 2021).

Rowling, J. K. (1997–2007), *Harry Potter series*, 7 vols., London: Bloomsbury.

Rowling, J. K. (2007), *Harry Potter and The Deathly Hallows*, London: Bloomsbury.

Ruddell, C. and B. Cherry (2012), 'More Than Cold and Heartless: The Southern Gothic Milieu of *True Blood*', in B. Cherry (ed), *True Blood: Investigating Vampires and Southern Gothic*, 39–55, London: I. B. Tauris.

Rutland, B. (1999), 'The Other of Theory', in F. de Toro (ed), *Explorations on Post-Theory: Toward a Third Space*, 71–83, Frankfurt am Main: Iberoamericana Vervuert.

Ryan, M.-L. and J.-N. Thon (2014a), 'Storyworlds Across Media: Introduction', in M.-L. Ryan and J.-N. Thon (eds), *Storyworlds Across Media: Toward a Media-Conscious Narratology*, 1–21, Lincoln, NE: University of Nebraska Press.

Ryan, M.-L. and J.-N. Thon, eds (2014b), *Storyworlds Across Media: Toward a Media-Conscious Narratology*, Lincoln, NE: University of Nebraska Press.

Ryder, M. E. (2005), 'Romance Novel', in D. Herman, M. Jahn and M.-L. Ryan (eds), *Routledge Encyclopedia of Narrative Theory*, 508–509, Abingdon: Routledge.

Saunders, C., ed. (2004), *A Companion to Romance: From Classical to Contemporary*, Malden, MA: Blackwell.

Schott, G. and K. Moffat, eds (2011), *Fanpires: Audience Consumption of the Modern Vampire*, Washington, DC: New Academia Publishing.

Schubart, R. (2018), *Mastering Fear: Women, Emotions, and Contemporary Horror*, New York, NY: Bloomsbury.

Selinger, E. M. (2013), 'Exploring Difference', *The Popular Romance Project*. Available online: http://popularromanceproject.org/wp-content/uploads/ ExploringDifference.pdf (accessed 16 May 2013).

Selinger, E. M. and S. S. G. Frantz (2012), 'Introduction: New Approaches to Popular Romance Fiction', in S. S. G. Frantz and E. M. Selinger (eds), *New Approaches to Popular Romance Fiction: Critical Essays*, 1–19, Jefferson, NC: McFarland & Company.

Senf, C. A. (1988), *The Vampire in Nineteenth-Century English Literature*, Madison, WI: The University of Wisconsin Press.

Șerban, A. (2012), 'Romancing the Paranormal: A Case Study on J.R. Ward's *The Black Dagger Brotherhood*', in D. Percec (ed), *Romance: The History of a Genre*, 89–110, Newcastle upon Tyne: Cambridge Scholars Publishing.

'Sexophone', *TV Tropes*. Available online: http://tvtropes.org/pmwiki/pmwiki.php/Main/Sexophone (accessed 19 May 2017).

Shary, T. (1997), 'The Teen Film and Its Methods of Study: A Book Review Essay', *Journal of Popular Film and Television*, 25 (1): 38–45. doi:10.1080/01956059709602748.

Sheffield, J. and E. Merlo (2010), 'Biting Back: Twilight Anti-Fandom and the Rhetoric of Superiority', in M. A. Click, J. Stevens Aubrey and E. Behm-Morawitz (eds), *Bitten by Twilight: Youth Culture, Media, & the Vampire Franchise*, 207–22, New York, NY: Peter Lang.

Siebert, M. V. (2011), 'Kidult Readers: The Cross-Generational Appeal of Harry Potter and Twilight', in M. Larsson and A. Steiner (eds), *Interdisciplinary Approaches to Twilight: Studies in Fiction, Media, and a Contemporary Cultural Experience*, 213–28, Lund: Nordic Academic Press.

Siegel, D. L. (1997), 'Reading between the Waves: Feminist Historiography in a "Postfeminist" Moment', in L. Heywood and J. Drake (eds), *Third Wave Agenda: Being Feminist, Doing Feminism*, 55–82, Minneapolis, MN: University of Minnesota Press.

Siegel, D. L. (2007), *Sisterhood, Interrupted: From Radical Women to Grrls Gone Wild*, New York, NY: Palgrave Macmillan.

Silver, A. (2010), '*Twilight* Is not Good for Maidens: Gender, Sexuality, and the Family in Stephenie Meyer's *Twilight* Series', *Studies in the Novel*, 42 (1&2): 121–38. doi:10.1353/sdn.2010.0009.

Smelik, A. (2007), 'Feminist Film Theory', in P. Cook (ed), *The Cinema Book*, 491–504, 3rd edn, London: British Film Institute.

Smith, A. and D. Wallace (2004), 'The Female Gothic: Then and Now', *Gothic Studies*, 6 (1): 1–7. doi:10.7227/GS.6.1.1.

Smith, L. J. (1991–2), *The Vampire Diaries Series*, 4 vols., New York, NY: Harper.

Smith, M. J. and K. Moruzi (2020), 'Gender and Sexuality in Young Adult Fiction', in C. Bloom (ed), *The Palgrave Handbook of Contemporary Gothic*, 609–22, Cham: Palgrave Macmillan.

Soloway, J. (2016), 'The Female Gaze: Tiff: Master Class', *Topple Productions*, 11 September. Available online: www.toppleproductions.com/the-female-gaze (accessed 10 April 2021).

Spieler, S. (2012), 'Stephenie Meyer's *Twilight* Series and the "Post(-)ing" of Feminism', *Aspeers. Emerging Voices in American Studies*, 5: 119–44. Available online: http://www.aspeers.com/sites/default/files/pdf/spieler.pdf (accessed 10 April 2021).

Spooner, C. (2006), *Contemporary Gothic*, London: Reaktion.

Spooner, C. (2017), *Post-Millennial Gothic: Comedy, Romance and the Rise of Happy Gothic*, London: Bloomsbury.

Steinhoff, H. and M. V. Siebert (2011), 'The Female Body Revamped: Beauty, Monstrosity and Body Transformation in the *Twilight* Saga', *Onlinejournal Kultur & Geschlecht*, 8: 1–19. Available online: https://kulturundgeschlecht.blogs.ruhr-uni-bochum.de/wp-content/uploads/2015/08/Steinhoff-Siebert_Female_Body_Revamped.pdf (accessed 10 April 2021).

Stoker, B. (1897), *Dracula*, London: Archibald Constable and Company.

Storey, J. (2011), *Cultural Theory and Popular Culture: An Introduction*, 5th edn, Harlow: Pearson Longman.

Strick, S. (2008), 'Vorher Nachher – Anmerkungen zur Erzählbarkeit des kosmetischen Selbst', in P.-I. Villa (ed), *Schön Normal: Manipulationen am Körper als Technologien des Selbst*, 199–217, Bielefeld: Transcript.

Taormino, T., C. Parreñas Shimizu, C. Penley and M. Miller-Young, eds (2013), *The Feminist Porn Book: The Politics of Producing Pleasure*, New York, NY: The Feminist Press.

Tasker, Y. ([1993] 2004), *Spectacular Bodies: Gender, Genre and the Action Cinema*, London: Routledge.

Tasker, Y. and D. Negra, eds (2007a), *Interrogating Postfeminism: Gender and the Politics of Popular Culture*, Durham, NC: Duke University Press.

Tasker, Y. and D. Negra (2007b), 'Introduction: Feminist Politics and Postfeminist Culture', in Y. Tasker and D. Negra (eds), *Interrogating Postfeminism: Gender and the Politics of Popular Culture*, 1–25, Durham, NC: Duke University Press.

Therrien, K. (2012), 'Straight to the Edges: Gay and Lesbian Characters and Cultural Conflict in Popular Romance Fiction', in S. S. G. Frantz and E. M.

Selinger (eds), *New Approaches to Popular Romance Fiction: Critical Essays*, 164–77, Jefferson, NC: McFarland & Company.

Thierauf, D. (2016), 'Forever After: Desire in the 21st-Century Romance Blockbuster', *The Journal of Popular Culture*, 49 (3): 604–26. doi:10.1111/jpcu.12423.

Thomas, G. (2012), 'Happy Readers or Sad Ones? Romance Fiction and the Problems of the Media Effects Model', in S. S. G. Frantz and E. M. Selinger (eds), *New Approaches to Popular Romance Fiction: Critical Essays*, 206–17, Jefferson, NC: McFarland & Company.

Thompson, L. J. (2013), 'Mancaves and Cushions: Marking Masculine and Feminine Domestic Space in Postfeminist Romantic Comedy', in J. Gwynne and N. Muller (eds), *Postfeminism and Contemporary Hollywood Cinema*, 149–65, Basingstoke: Palgrave Macmillan.

Thurber, A. (2011), 'Bite Me: Desire and the Female Spectator in *Twilight*, *The Vampire Diaries*, and *True Blood*', Dissertation, Emory University, Atlanta, GA.

Turner, G. (2002), *British Cultural Studies: An Introduction*, 3rd edn, Abingdon: Routledge.

Turner, G. (2008a), 'Genre, Hybridity and Mutation', in G. Creeber, T. Miller and J. Tulloch (eds), *The Television Genre Book*, 8, 2nd edn, London: Palgrave Macmillan.

Turner, G. (2008b), 'The Uses and Limitations of Genre', in G. Creeber, T. Miller and J. Tulloch (eds), *The Television Genre Book*, 6–7, 2nd edn, London: Palgrave Macmillan.

'Twilight', Box Office Mojo. Available online: http://www.boxofficemojo.com/franchises/chart/?id=twilight.htm (accessed 10 March 2017).

Utsch, C. (2014), 'True Blood: Scheiternde Rationalität', *POP-Zeitschrift*, 16 June. Available online: http://www.pop-zeitschrift.de/2014/06/16/true-bloodscheiternde-rationalitatvon-carolin-utsch16-6-2014/ (accessed 10 April 2021).

Valby, K. (2012), 'The "Twilight" effect', *Entertainment Weekly*, 16 November. Available online: https://ew.com/article/2012/11/16/twilight-effect/ (accessed 10 April 2021).

Vargo, L. (2004), 'Women's Gothic Romance: Writers, Readers, and the Pleasures of the Form', in C. Saunders (ed), *A Companion to Romance: From Classical to Contemporary*, 233–50, Malden, MA: Blackwell.

Veldman-Genz, C. (2011), 'Serial Experiments in Popular Culture: The Resignification of Gothic Symbology in *Anita Blake Vampire Hunter* and the *Twilight* Series', in G. L. Anatol (ed), *Bringing Light to Twilight: Perspectives on a Pop Culture Phenomenon*, 43–58, New York, NY: Palgrave Macmillan.

Veldman-Genz, C. (2012), 'The More the Merrier? Transformations of the Love Triangle Across the Romance', in S. S. G. Frantz and E. M. Selinger (eds), *New Approaches to Popular Romance Fiction: Critical Essays*, 108–20, Jefferson, NC: McFarland & Company.

Vera-Gray, F. (2017), *Men's Intrusion, Women's Embodiment: A Critical Analysis of Street Harassment*, Abingdon: Routledge.

Villa, P.-I. (2008a), 'Habe den Mut, Dich Deines Körpers zu bedienen! Thesen zur Körperarbeit in der Gegenwart zwischen Selbstermächtigung und Selbstunterwerfung', in P.-I. Villa (ed), *schön normal: Manipulationen am Körper als Technologien des Selbst*, 245–72, Bielefeld: Transcript.

Villa, P.-I., ed. (2008b), *Schön Normal: Manipulationen am Körper als Technologien des Selbst*, Bielefeld: Transcript.

Villa, P.-I., ed. (2012), *Banale Kämpfe? Perspektiven auf Populärkultur und Geschlecht*, Wiesbaden: Springer VS.

Vitellone, N. (2007), 'Male Sex Drive', in M. Flood, J. K. Gardiner, B. Pease and K. Pringle (eds), *International Encyclopedia of Men and Masculinities*, 377–378, Abingdon: Routledge.

Wagenseller Goletz, S. (2012), 'The Giddyshame Paradox: Why "Twilight"'s Anti-Fans Cannot Stop Reading a Series They (Love to) Hate', in A. Morey (ed), *Genre, Reception, and Adaptation in the "Twilight" Series*, 147–79, Farnham: Ashgate.

Wakefield, S. (2011), 'Torn between Two Lovers: Twilight *Tames* Wuthering Heights', in M. Parke and N. Wilson (eds), *Theorizing Twilight: Critical Essays on What's at Stake in a Post-Vampire World*, 117–31, Jefferson, NC: McFarland & Company.

Waller, A. (2009), *Constructing Adolescence in Fantastic Realism*, New York, NY: Routledge.

Walpole, H. ([1764] 1994), 'The Castle of Otranto, a Story', in *Four Gothic Novels*, 5–80, Oxford: Oxford University Press, https://global.oup.com/academic/product/four-gothic-novels-9780192823311?cc=de&lang=en&#.

Wester, M. and X. Aldana Reyes, eds (2019), *Twenty-First-Century Gothic: An Edinburgh Companion*, Edinburgh: Edinburgh University Press.

Wheatley, H. (2006), *Gothic Television*, Manchester: Manchester University Press.

Wheatley, H. (2015), 'Visual Pleasure and Narrative Television', *Feminist Media Studies*, 15 (5): 896–9. doi:10.1080/14680777.2015.1075276.

'WHY', *SlutWalk Toronto*. Available online: www.slutwalktoronto.com/about/why/ (accessed 25 May 2017).

Williams, L. (1996), 'When the Woman Looks', in B. K. Grant (ed), *The Dread of Difference: Gender and the Horror Film*, 15–34, Austin, TX: University of Texas Press.

Williams, R. (2013), 'Unlocking *The Vampire Diaries*: Genre, Authorship, and Quality in Teen TV Horror', *Gothic Studies*, 15 (1): 88–99. doi:10.7227/GS.15.1.9.

Williamson, M. (2003), 'Vampire Transformations: From Gothic Demon to Domestication?', in C. T. Kungl (ed), *Vampires: Myths & Metaphors of Enduring Evil*, 101–7, Oxford: Inter-Disciplinary Press.

Williamson, M. (2005), *The Lure of the Vampire: Gender, Fiction and Fandom from Bram Stoker to Buffy*, London: Wallflower Press.

Williamson, M. (2007), 'Television, Vampires and the Body: Somatic Pathos', *Intensities: The Journal of Cult Media*, 4: pars. 1–31. Available online: http://intensitiescultmedia.files.wordpress.com/2012/12/williamson-television-vampires-and-the-body.pdf (accessed 10 April 2021).

Williamson, M. (2014), 'Let Them All in: The Evolution of the "Sympathetic" Vampire', in L. Hunt, S. Lockyer and M. Williamson (eds), *Screening the Undead: Vampires and Zombies in Film and Television*, 71–92, London: I. B. Tauris.

Willms, N. (2014), '"Doesn't He Own a Shirt?" Rivalry and Masculine Embodiment in *Twilight*', in C. Bucciferro (ed), *The Twilight Saga: Exploring the Global Phenomenon*, 139–52, Lanham, MD: The Scarecrow Press.

Wilson, N. (2010), 'Civilized Vampires versus Savage Werewolves: Race and Ethnicity in the Twilight Series', in M. A. Click, J. Stevens Aubrey and E. Behm-Morawitz (eds), *Bitten by Twilight: Youth Culture, Media, & the Vampire Franchise*, 55–70, New York, NY: Peter Lang.

Wilson, N. (2011), *Seduced by Twilight: The Allure and Contradictory Messages of the Popular Saga*, Jefferson, NC: McFarland & Company.

Wilson Overstreet, D. (2006), *Not Your Mother's Vampire: Vampires in Young Adult Fiction*, Lanham, MD: The Scarecrow Press.

Wisker, G. (1998), 'If Looks Could Kill: Contemporary Women's Vampire Fictions', in L. Pearce and G. Wisker (eds), *Fatal Attractions and Cultural*

Subversions: Rescripting Romance in Contemporary Literature and Film, 51–68, London: Pluto Press.

Wisker, G. (2019), 'Postfeminist Gothic', in M. Wester and X. Aldana Reyes (eds), *Twenty-First-Century Gothic: An Edinburgh Companion*, 47–59, Edinburgh: Edinburgh University Press.

Wolf, N. ([1993] 1994), *Fire with Fire: The New Female Power and How It Will Change the 21st Century*, London: Vintage.

Zanger, J. (1997), 'Metaphor into Metonymy: The Vampire Next Door', in J. Gordon and V. Hollinger (eds), *Blood Read: The Vampire as Metaphor in Contemporary Culture*, 17–26, Philadelphia, PA: University of Pennsylvania Press.

Zeisler, A. (2016), *We Were Feminists Once: From Riot Grrrl to CoverGirl®, the Buying and Selling of a Political Movement*, New York, NY: Public Affairs.

Films

Alien (1979), [Film] Dir. Ridley Scott, UK/USA: 20th Century Fox.
Allegiant (2016), [Film] Dir. Robert Schwentke, USA: Lionsgate.
Black Widow (2021), [Film] Dir. Cate Shortland, USA: Walt Disney Studios Motion Pictures.
Bram Stoker's Dracula (1992), [Film] Dir. Francis Ford Coppola, USA: Columbia Pictures.
Breaking Dawn – Part 1 (2011), [Film] Dir. Bill Condon, USA: Summit Entertainment.
Breaking Dawn – Part 2 (2012), [Film] Dir. Bill Condon, USA: Lionsgate.
Breaking Wind (2012), [Film] Dir. Craig Moss, USA: Lionsgate Home Entertainment.
Byzantium (2014), [Film] Dir. Neil Jordan, Ireland/UK/USA: StudioCanal.
Crossroads (2002), [Film] Dir. Tamra Davis, USA: Paramount Pictures.
Demon Seed (1977), [Film] Dir. Donald Cammell, USA: United Artists.
Divergent (2014), [Film] Dir. Neil Burger, USA: Lionsgate.
Eclipse (2010), [Film] Dir. David Slade, USA: Summit Entertainment.
Fifty Shades Darker (2017), [Film] Dir. James Foley, USA: Universal Pictures.
Fifty Shades Freed (2018), [Film] Dir. James Foley, USA: Universal Pictures.

Fifty Shades of Grey (2015), [Film] Dir. Sam Taylor-Johnson, USA: Universal Pictures.

Ghost World (2001), [Film] Dir. Terry Zwigoff, USA/UK/Germany: Advanced Medien.

Insurgent (2015), [Film] Dir. Robert Schwentke, USA: Lionsgate.

Mean Girls (2004), [Film] Dir. Mark Waters, USA: Paramount Pictures.

New Moon (2009), [Film] Dir. Chris Weitz, USA: Summit Entertainment.

Rosemary's Baby (1968), [Film] Dir. Roman Polanski, USA: Paramount Pictures.

She's All That (1999), [Film] Dir. Robert Iscove, USA: Miramax Films.

Star Wars: Episode VIII – The Last Jedi (2017), [Film] Dir. Rian Johnson, USA: Walt Disney Studios Motion Pictures.

Taken (2008), [Film] Dir. Pierre Morel, France/USA: 20th Century Fox.

The Brood (1979), [Film] Dir. David Cronenberg, Canada: New World Pictures.

The Hunger Games (2012), [Film] Dir. Gary Ross, USA: Lionsgate.

The Hunger Games: Catching Fire (2013), [Film], Dir. Francis Lawrence, USA: Lionsgate.

The Hunger Games: Mockingjay – Part 1 (2014), [Film], Dir. Francis Lawrence, USA: Lionsgate.

The Hunger Games: Mockingjay – Part 2 (2015), [Film], Dir. Francis Lawrence, USA: Lionsgate.

The Princess Diaries (2001), [Film] Dir. Garry Marshall, USA: Walt Disney Pictures.

The Sisterhood of the Traveling Pants (2005), [Film] Dir. Ken Kwapis, USA: Warner Bros. Pictures.

The Unborn (1991), [Film] Dir. Rodman Flender, USA: Califilm.

Twilight (2008), [Film] Dir. Catherine Hardwicke, USA: Summit Entertainment.

Vampires Suck (2010), [Film] Dir. Jason Friedberg and Aaron Seltzer, USA: 20th Century Fox.

What We Do in the Shadows (2014), [Film] Dir. Jemaine Clement and Taika Waititi, New Zealand/USA: Madman Entertainment.

Wonder Woman (2017), [Film] Dir. Patty Jenkins, USA: Warner Bros. Pictures.

Wonder Woman 1984 (2020), [Film] Dir. Patty Jenkins, USA: Warner Bros. Pictures.

Television

Programmes

24 (2001–10), [TV programme] Fox.
Buffy the Vampire Slayer (1997–2003), [TV programme] The WB/UPN.
Dark Shadows (1966–71), [TV programme] ABC.
Dawson's Creek (1998–2003), [TV programme] The WB.
Degrassi: The Next Generation (2001–15), [TV programme] CTV/MuchMusic/MTV Canada.
I Love Dick (2016–17), [TV programme] Amazon Video.
Legacies (2018–), [TV programme] The CW.
Riverdale (2017–), [TV programme] The CW.
Roswell (1999–2002), [TV programme] The WB/UPN.
Six Feet Under (2001–05), [TV programme] HBO.
Stargirl (2020–), [TV programme] DC Universe/The CW.
The O.C. (2003–07), [TV programme] Fox.
The Swan (2004), [TV programme] Fox.
The Vampire Diaries (2009–17), [TV programme] The CW.
Transparent (2014–19), [TV programme] Prime Video.
True Blood (2008–14), [TV programme] HBO.
Veronica Mars (2004–19), [TV programme] UPN/The CW/Hulu.

Selected episodes

Dates given are original US airdates.

The Vampire Diaries (2009–17), The CW

'Pilot' (1.1). Writ. Kevin Williamson and Julie Plec. Dir. Marcos Siega. 10 September 2009.
'The Night of the Comet' (1.2). Writ. Kevin Williamson and Julie Plec. Dir. Marcos Siega. 17 September 2009.
'Friday Night Bites' (1.3). Writ. Barbie Kligman and Bryan M. Holdman. Dir. John Dahl. 24 September 2009.
'Family Ties' (1.4). Writ. Andrew Kreisberg and Brian Young. Dir. Guy Ferland. 1 October 2009.

'You're Undead to Me' (1.5). Writ. Sean Reycraft and Gabrielle Stanton. Dir. Kevin Bray. 8 October 2009.

'Haunted' (1.7). Writ. Andrew Kreisberg, Kevin Williamson and Julie Plec. Dir. Ernest Dickerson. 29 October 2009.

'162 Candles' (1.8). Writ. Barbie Kligman and Gabrielle Stanton. Dir. Rick Bota. 5 November 2009.

'The Turning Point' (1.10). Writ. Barbie Kligman, Kevin Williamson and Julie Plec. Dir. J. Miller Tobin. 19 November 2009.

'A Few Good Men' (1.15). Writ. Brian Young. Dir. Joshua Butler. 25 March 2010.

'Under Control' (1.18). Writ. Barbie Kligman and Andrew Chambliss. Dir. David Von Ancken. 15 April 2010.

'Miss Mystic Falls' (1.19). Writ. Bryan Oh and Caroline Dries. Dir. Marcos Siega. 22 April 2010.

'Blood Brothers' (1.20). Writ. Kevin Williamson and Julie Plec. Dir. Liz Friedlander. 29 April 2010.

'Isobel' (1.21). Writ. Caroline Dries and Brian Young. Dir. J. Miller Tobin. 6 May 2010.

'Founder's Day' (1.22). Writ. Bryan Oh and Andrew Chambliss. Dir. Marcos Siega. 13 May 2010.

'Brave New World' (2.2). Writ. Brian Young. Dir. John Dahl. 16 September 2010.

'Bad Moon Rising' (2.3). Writ. Andrew Chambliss. Dir. Patrick Norris. 23 September 2010.

'Plan B' (2.6). Writ. Elizabeth Craft and Sarah Fain. Dir. John Behring. 21 October 2010.

'Katerina' (2.9). Writ. Andrew Chambliss. Dir. J. Miller Tobin. 11 November 2010.

'The Sacrifice' (2.10). Writ. Caroline Dries. Dir. Ralph Hemecker. 2 December 2010.

'By the Light of the Moon' (2.11). Writ. Mike Daniels. Dir. Elizabeth Allen. 9 December 2010.

'Daddy Issues' (2.13). Writ. Kevin Williamson and Julie Plec. Dir. Joshua Butler. 3 February 2011.

'The Dinner Party' (2.15). Writ. Andrew Chambliss. Dir. Marcos Siega. 17 February 2011.

'Klaus' (2.19). Writ. Kevin Williamson and Julie Plec. Dir. Joshua Butler. 21 April 2011.

'The Last Day' (2.20). Writ. Andrew Chambliss and Brian Young. Dir. J. Miller Tobin. 28 April 2011.

'The Birthday' (3.1). Writ. Kevin Williamson and Julie Plec. Dir. John Behring. 15 September 2011.

'Our Town' (3.11). Writ. Rebecca Sonnenshine. Dir. Wendey Stanzler. 12 January 2012.

'Bringing Out the Dead' (3.13). Writ. Turi Meyer and Al Septien. Dir. Jeffrey Hunt. 2 February 2012.

'Dangerous Liaisons' (3.14). Writ. Caroline Dries. Dir. Chris Grismer. 9 February 2012.

'All My Children' (3.15). Writ. Evan Bleiweiss and Michael Narducci. Dir. Pascal Verschooris. 16 February 2012.

'1912' (3.16). Writ. Julie Plec and Elisabeth R. Finch. Dir. John Behring. 15 March 2012.

'The Departed' (3.22). Writ. Brett Matthews, Elisabeth R. Finch and Julie Plec. Dir. John Behring. 10 May 2012.

'Growing Pains' (4.1). Writ. Caroline Dries. Dir. Chris Grismer. 11 October 2012.

'The Rager' (4.3). Writ. Brian Young. Dir. Lance Anderson. 25 October 2012.

'The Killer' (4.5). Writ. Michael Narducci. Dir. Chris Grismer. 8 November 2012.

'My Brother's Keeper' (4.7). Writ. Caroline Dries and Elisabeth R. Finch. Dir. Jeffrey Hunt. 29 November 2012.

'Down the Rabbit Hole' (4.14). Writ. Jose Molina. Dir. Chris Grismer. 14 February 2013.

'She's Come Undone' (4.21). Writ. Michael Narducci and Rebecca Sonnenshine. Dir. Darnell Martin. 2 May 2013.

'For Whom the Bell Tolls' (5.4). Writ. Brett Matthews and Elisabeth R. Finch. Dir. Michael Allowitz. 24 October 2013.

'Monster's Ball' (5.5). Writ. Sonny Postiglione. Dir. Kellie Cyrus. 31 October 2013.

'Handle with Care' (5.6). Writ. Caroline Dries and Holly Brix. Dir. Jeffrey Hunt. 7 November 2013.

'The Cell' (5.9). Writ. Melinda Hsu Taylor. Dir. Chris Grismer. 5 December 2013.

'Gone Girl' (5.15 Supplement 1). Writ. Melinda Hsu Taylor. Dir. Lance Anderson. 6 March 2014.

'Promised Land' (5.21). Writ. Rebecca Sonnenshine. Dir. Michael Allowitz. 8 May 2014.
'Let Her Go' (6.15). Writ. Julie Plec. Dir. Julie Plec. 19 February 2015.
'The Downward Spiral' (6.16). Writ. Brian Young and Caroline Dries. Dir. Ian Somerhalder. 12 March 2015.
'A Bird in a Gilded Cage' (6.17). Writ. Neil Reynolds. Dir. Joshua Butler. 19 March 2015.
'Because' (6.19). Writ. Melinda Hsu Taylor. Dir. Geoffrey Wing Shotz. 23 April 2015.

True Blood (2008–14), HBO

'Strange Love' (1.1). Writ. Alan Ball. Dir. Alan Ball. 7 September 2008.
'The First Taste' (1.2). Writ. Alan Ball. Dir. Scott Winant. 14 September 2008.
'Mine' (1.3). Writ. Alan Ball. Dir. John Dahl. 21 September 2008.
'Escape from Dragon House' (1.4). Writ. Brian Buckner. Dir. Michael Lehmann. 28 September 2008.
'Sparks Fly Out' (1.5). Writ. Alexander Woo. Dir. Daniel Minahan. 5 October 2008.
'Cold Ground' (1.6). Writ. Raelle Tucker. Dir. Nick Gomez. 12 October 2008.
'Burning House of Love' (1.7). Writ. Chris Offutt. Dir. Marcos Siega. 19 October 2008.
'The Fourth Man in the Fire' (1.8). Writ. Alexander Woo. Dir. Michael Lehmann. 26 October 2008.
'I Don't Wanna Know' (1.10). Writ. Chris Offutt. Dir. Scott Winant. 9 November 2008.
'To Love Is to Bury' (1.11). Writ. Nancy Oliver. Dir. NancyOliver. 16 November 2008.
'Nothing but the Blood' (2.1). Writ. Alexander Woo. Dir, Daniel Minahan. 14 June 2009.
'Keep This Party Going' (2.2). Writ. Brian Buckner. Dir. Michael Lehmann. 21 June 2009.
'Scratches' (2.3). Writ. Raelle Tucker. Dir. Scott Winant. 28 June 2009.
'Never Let Me Go' (2.5). Writ. Nancy Oliver. Dir. John Dahl. 19 July 2009.
'Release Me' (2.7). Writ. Raelle Tucker. Dir. Michael Ruscio. 2 August 2009.
'New World in My View' (2.10). Writ. Kate Barnow and Elisabeth R. Finch. Dir. Adam Davidson. 23 August 2009.

'Beautifully Broken' (3.2). Writ. Raelle Tucker. Dir. Scott Winant. 20 June 2010.
'I Got a Right to Sing the Blues' (3.6). Writ Alan Ball. Dir. Michael Lehmann. 25 July 2010.
'Night on the Sun' (3.8). Writ. Raelle Tucker. Dir. Lesli LinkaGlatter. 8 August 2010.
'I Wish I Was the Moon' (4.6). Writ. Raelle Tucker. Dir. Jeremy Podeswa. 31 July 2011.
'Spellbound' (4.8). Writ. Alan Ball. Dir. Daniel Minahan. 14 August 2011.
'Let's Get Out of Here' (4.9). Writ. Brian Buckner. Dir. Romeo Tirone. 21 August 2011.
'And When I Die' (4.12). Writ. Raelle Tucker. Dir. Scott Winant. 11 September 2011.
'We'll Meet Again' (5.4). Writ. Alexander Woo. Dir. Romeo Tirone. 1 July 2012.
'Let's Boot and Rally' (5.5). Writ. Angela Robinson. Dir. Michael Lehmann. 8 July 2012.
'Save Yourself' (5.12). Writ. Alan Ball. Dir. Michael Lehmann. 26 August 2012.
'You're No Good' (6.3). Writ. Mark Hudis. Dir. Howard Deutch. 30 June 2013.
'At Last' (6.4). Writ. Alexander Woo. Dir. Anthony Hemnigway. 7 July 2013.
'Fuck the Pain Away' (6.5). Writ. Angela Robinson. Dir. Michael Ruscio. 14 July 2013.
'Don't You Feel Me' (6.6). Writ. Daniel Kenneth. Dir. Howard Deutch. 21 July 2013.
'In the Evening' (6.7). Writ. Kate Barnow. Dir. Scott Winant. 28 July 2013.
'Thank You' (7.10). Writ. Brian Buckner. Dir. Scott Winant. 24 August 2014.

Index

24 193

agency   65, 112–15, 117–18, 120, 122–4, 132–3, 139–40, 146–9, 152–3, 179–81, 184, 210–12, 214, 216, *see also* subjectivity
   lack of   112, 124, 126, 136–8, 141–6, 148–9, 153, 180, 185, 197, 211
Alien   224 n.2
All Souls series   217 n.1
Anita Blake: Vampire Hunter series   4
audience
   active   8, 10, 18–19, 36–8, 41, 48, 52–8, 62, 101, 181, 206–7
   cross-generational   11, 12, 37, 51–2, 57, 59–60, 62, 67
   female   10, 11, 12, 44, 48, 51, 57–61, 69, 72–3, 116, 157, 158, 163, 165, 167–8, 178–9, 187, 192, 197, 198–9, 202, 207, 209, 211–13, 225 n.3 (*see also* gaze, female)
   male   96, 219 n.3, 223 n.3, 225 n.1, 225 n.3
   teen   5, 6, 8–9, 10, 11, 20, 38, 49–51, 60, 69, 73, 202, 207, 221 n.9, 225 n.3 (*see also* teenager)

Ball, Alan   7, 8
Black Widow   10
Blood Coven series   217 n.1
Blue Bloods series   217 n.1
body   13–14, 119, 201, 205

body work   21, 120–6, 130–1, 133–5, 137–8, 140–1, 142–9, 150–5, 168–9, 175–80, 184–7, 190–1, 196–7, 210–13 (*see also* postfeminism, and neoliberalism; self-surveillance)
   female   21, 34, 67, 75–81, 83–4, 92–7, 110, 113–18, 121–49, 150, 153–5, 177–8, 209–12
   male   21–2, 86–93, 97–108, 112, 134, 153, 161–2, 165, 169, 174–80, 182, 184–7, 190–2
   vampiric   14, 20–2, 69, 86–93, 97–108, 109, 127, 131–5, 137–8, 141, 142–9, 150–5, 164–6, 167–9, 174, 175–80, 182, 184–7, 190–2, 210–13 (*see also* vampire)
both/and moment, *see* contradiction
Bram Stoker's Dracula (film)   4
Breaking Dawn – Part 1   127–31, 173
Breaking Dawn – Part 2   75, 131–5, 144, 150
Breaking Wind   217 n.1
Brood, The   224 n.2
Buffy the Vampire Slayer   4–5, 48–51, 59, 89–90, 103–5, 202–3
Byronic hero   43–5, 48
Byzantium   8

camp   101–8, 203, 208
Castle of Otranto, a Story, The   42
Collins, Barnabas, *see Dark Shadows*
Compton, Bill   5, 14, 21–2, 46, 79–81, 92–5, 115, 142–6, 157–9, 187–99, 208,

212–14, 219 n.3, 224 n.1, 227 n.9
Connell, R. W.   197, 198, 213, 225–6 n.4
contradiction   12–13, 15, 18, 20–2, 30–2, 35–8, 62, 64, 66–7, 92–7, 110–11, 114, 117–18, 119–20, 125, 151–2, 153–5, 159, 161, 163, 164, 165, 167, 179–80, 181, 188, 193, 195, 197–9, 203, 204–6, 209–12, 215–16
Crossroads   5
Cullen, Edward   14, 21–2, 40, 46, 56, 71, 84–92, 126, 127, 129–34, 144, 157–9, 166, 169–80, 192–9, 208, 212–14

Dark Shadows   47–8, 59, 167–8, 225 n.3
Dawson's Creek   5, 221 n.10
Dead until Dark   7
Degrassi: The Next Generation   5
Demon Seed   224 n.2
desire   14–15, 170–1, 201–2, *see also* gaze; sexuality
　　and bloodthirst   141, 144–5, 147–8, 175–80, 186–7, 226 n.7
　　female   11, 20–1, 45, 57, 69–73, 85–9, 92–101, 108–9, 111–12, 116–18, 123, 127, 134, 144–5, 147–8, 149, 154, 164, 171, 173, 176–81, 208, 210, 213–14, 223 n.3, 224 n.7
　　male   69–70, 72–3, 166, 168, 176–80, 186–7, 198–9
Divergent series   10
Dracula (novel)   4, 102, 136, 151, 176, 208

Eclipse (film)   126, 132, 133, 154, 170–4, 219–20 n.4, 221 n.13
Eclipse (novel)   43

empowerment   20–1, 28–9, 33, 69, 92–7, 111–20, 122–5, 130–5, 137–55, 205, 208–12, 214, 215, 220–1 n.8
Evernight series   217 n.1

femininity   20–1, 30, 33, 34, 57–61, 69–118, 119–55, 176–80, 193, 202, 208–12, 216
Fifty Shades of Grey series   10, 56, 217 n.4
Forbes, Caroline   21, 119–20, 126, 130, 132, 133, 135–42, 144, 147, 149–55, 208, 210–12, 225 n.3

gaze, *see also* desire; pleasure, visual; sexuality
　　classist   71, 87, 91–2
　　desiring   20–1, 84–93, 98–9, 101, 108–9, 111–12, 115, 116, 118, 209–10, 223 n.3
　　female   3, 16, 20–1, 69–118, 165, 174, 202–3, 209–10, 222–3 n.1, 223 n.3, 224 n.7 (*see also* audience, female)
　　'gazed'   21, 69, 72–84, 108–9, 117–18, 209–10
　　investigative   84–6, 89, 98–101
　　male   16, 20–1, 69–84, 85, 93–7, 108–9, 113–15, 117–18, 168, 208–10, 223 n.2
　　white   16, 71, 90–2, 112–13, 215, 224 n.7
Gelder, Ken   9, 37
Ghost World   5
Gilbert, Elena   56, 97–101, 106, 108–18, 135, 137–8, 144, 180–8, 224 n.1, 226 n.7
Gothic   2, 6, 8, 15, 20, 38, 39, 119, 188, 205, 225 n.3, *see also* horror
　　Female   48, 60, 63–4, 168, 222 n.15

Index

Gothic hero   42–9, 63
Gothic heroine   43–4, 49, 63–4, 167–9, 185, 191–2
happy   202–4
history of   42–50, 60, 61, 67
postfeminist   62–4, 66, 155, 168–9, 202–4
Southern   39, 78

Hall, Stuart   18–19, 33, 206
Hamby, Jessica   21, 51, 55–6, 119–20, 126, 130, 132, 133, 141–55, 208, 210–12
Harris, Charlaine, *see Southern Vampire Mysteries, The*
Harry Potter and the Deathly Hallows   5
Harry Potter series   5
hooks, bell   214
horror   38, 50, 51, 55, 59, 93, 102–3, 119, 128, 136, 168, 188, 191, 222 n.15, *see also* Gothic
House of Night: Other World series   217 n.1
House of Night series   217 n.1
Hunger Games, The   10

identity   13, 16, 35, 50, 112, 119, 121, 127, 205
  female   30, 122, 153–5, 206, 207
  male   159–60, 168–9, 173–4, 213
  multi-faceted   15, 65, 114, 123
I Love Dick   222–3 n.1
irony   52, 101, 102, 104, 106, 107, 162, 181

Jane Eyre   43–4, 219–20 n.4

Kristeva, Julia   127

Legacies   2

Life and Death: Twilight Reimagined   2
Lorde, Audre   29

makeover   21, 33, 34, 120, 125–50, 152–5, 210–12
masculinity   45, 57–60, 69–118, 157–99, 202, 208, 212–14, 216, 227 n.8
Mean Girls   5
Meyer, Stephenie, *see Twilight* series (novels)
Midnight Sun   2
Modleski, Tania   64–6, 157, 163, 196, 205
Moers, Ellen   60, 63, 205, 222 n.15
Morganville Vampires series, *The*   217 n.1
Mortal Instruments series, *The*   217 n.1
Mulvey, Laura   16, 20, 69–73, 78, 81, 85, 215

New Moon   3, 91, 126, 132, 166, 170–2, 175–6
Northman, Eric   5, 46–7, 93–5, 106–8, 115, 219 n.3
nostalgia   51, 158–9, 169, 212, *see also* postfeminism, and new traditionalism

O.C., The   5

paranormal romance   180, 188, 198–9, 217 n.1, 219 n.1, 219 n.2
  definition of   38–41, 61–2
  development of   1, 4–10, 20, 42–9, 203
  and postfeminism   2–3, 20–2, 37–8, 61–7, 157–9, 201–5
  reception of   1–13, 57–61
pleasure

and popular culture 40, 54–6, 64–5, 206–9
postfeminist 16, 28, 69, 109, 117, 124–5, 199, 201–2, 205, 206, 208–13, 215
visual 69–73, 76, 86–99, 105–8, 209–10, 215 (*see also* gaze)
Plec, Julie 6, 9, 221 n.10
postfeminism
and aging 66–7, 110, 112, 113, 122, 152–4, 164, 165, 214
as backlash 15, 19, 25, 29–33, 35–6, 66–7, 161, 162, 204
and choice 19, 31–3, 114, 117, 121–5, 130, 153–5, 162, 166, 209, 211–12
and class 16, 26, 79, 123, 135, 162, 214
and consumer culture 13, 15, 19, 21, 28, 33–6, 38, 52–4, 56, 59, 62, 64, 110, 116–17, 120, 122, 124, 148, 150, 152–3, 161–2, 165, 181, 193, 204, 206–7, 209, 214–16
definition of 13–15, 19, 23–36, 204–5
and homosexuality 29, 101–2, 112–13, 162, 223 n.6, 225 n.1
and hybridity 13, 15, 19, 23–4, 35–6, 66, 159–63, 194, 204
and individualism 13, 15, 19, 21, 28, 31–4, 52, 65, 79, 113–14, 116–18, 119–25, 126, 130, 140, 142, 149–52, 161–2, 204, 205, 208–12, 216
and mainstream media 13, 15, 19, 28, 30, 32–6, 112–13, 115–17, 123, 149, 158, 193, 204, 205–6, 214–15
and neoliberalism 13, 15, 19, 21, 24, 31–5, 64, 115–17, 120–5, 150–2, 159, 203, 204, 210–12, 216 (*see also* body, body work; self-surveillance)
and new traditionalism 11–12, 29, 31–2, 126, 130, 132–4, 154–5, 158–9, 164, 169–72, 179–80, 180–1, 185–6, 187–9, 193, 206, 212, 215, 224 n.1 (*see also* nostalgia)
as politicized 18, 27, 35, 57, 59, 61–3, 65–7, 72, 117–18, 122–3, 201, 204–5, 214–16, 227–8 n.2
and race 16, 26–9, 32, 71, 79, 87, 91–2, 109, 112–13, 123, 135, 153, 165–6, 192, 214–15
and second wave feminism 13, 24–36, 204–5, 208–9, 212, 216 (*see also* postfeminism, as backlash)
power 10, 11, 16, 17, 36, 91, 119, 123, 124, 151–2, 192, 206
and gender 13–14, 42–5, 69, 70, 77, 82, 84–7, 92–101, 109, 113–15, 117–18, 122, 125, 126–7, 132–3, 134, 136, 141–49, 153–5, 159, 165, 166, 168, 171, 176, 184–7, 195–8, 202, 204, 205, 210–15
subversion of 13, 17, 44, 69, 70, 84–7, 92–101, 109, 113–15, 132–3, 146–9, 153–5, 196–8, 204, 210–12
Pride and Prejudice 43, 219–20 n.4
Princess Diaries, The 120

Radway, Janice A. 64–6, 157, 163, 175, 176, 205, 213
Rice, Anne, *see Vampire Chronicles* series, *The*
Riverdale 51

romance (genre)   11, 20, 39, 42–5, 48–9, 57–61, 64–7, 157, 187–8, 205, 208, *see also* paranormal romance
  hero   44–9, 157, 163, 166, 172–3, 175–7, 185–6, 194, 196, 205, 208
  heroine   101, 108, 163, 166–7, 173, 175–7, 179, 180, 187, 189, 194–6, 205, 208
Rosemary's Baby   224 n.2
Roswell   5

Salvatore, Damon   5, 9, 46–7, 56, 101–8, 136, 139, 180, 183–4, 186, 188
Salvatore, Stefan   5, 14, 21–2, 46–7, 56, 98–101, 104–5, 144, 157–9, 180–8, 192–9, 208, 212–14, 219–20 n.4, 226 n.7
self-surveillance   14, 21, 33, 34, 119–25, 126–7, 133–8, 141–53, 175–80, 184–7, 191, 205, 210–13, 225 n.3, 226 n.7, *see also* body, body work; postfeminism, and neoliberalism
sexism   21, 35, 78–84, 94–7, 114, 116, 123, 162, 164, 181, 192, 205, 208, 210, 223 n.3
sexuality   11, 12, 15, 31, 51, 57, 60, 61, 64, 85, 109–10, 125, 153, 170, 203, 205, 220–1 n.8, 226 n.7, *see also* desire; gaze, desiring
  female   59, 67, 74–5, 92–7, 110–17, 132, 145, 147–8, 168, 176–80, 208, 224 n.8
  male   176–80, 208
She's All That   120
Sisterhood of the Traveling Pants, The (film)   5
Six Feet Under   7

Smith, L. J., *see Vampire Diaries series, The* (novels)
Soloway, Joey   16, 20, 71–2, 74, 78, 84, 108, 118, 209, 222–3 n.1
Southern Vampire Mysteries, The   6, 7, 9
Stackhouse, Sookie   21, 78–84, 92–7, 108–18, 130, 187–9, 191–2, 209–10, 219 n.3, 224 n.1, 227 n.9, 228 n.4
Stargirl   51
Star Wars: Episode VIII – The Last Jedi   10
subjectivity   17, 20–1, 32, 50, 66–7, 70–101, 108–9, 111–18, 120–3, 126, 127, 138, 150–1, 153, 155, 176, 208–11, 222–3 n.1, 223 n.3, *see also* agency
  postmodern   12, 32, 205, 209–10
subjectivation   14, 21, 33, 120, 130–55, 210–12, 214
Swan, Bella   16, 21–2, 71, 73–8, 84–92, 108–20, 125–35, 137, 144, 149–55, 170–80, 194, 208, 210–12, 219–20 n.4, 223 n.3
Swan, The   120, 131, 141

Taken   193
teenager   4, 49–52, 59, 66–7, 119, 216, 220–1 n.8, 226 n.7, *see also* audience, teen
Transparent   222–3 n.1
True Blood   5–9, 20–2, 38–40, 46, 49, 51–2, 54–6, 59–60, 67, 69, 71, 78–84, 92–7, 106–7, 108–20, 130, 141–59, 163, 165, 169, 187–99, 201–16, 219 n.3, 224 n.1, 227 n.9
  success of   3, 6–7, 11–12
Twilight (film)   3, 6, 7, 73–8, 84–91, 126, 172, 175, 178

Twilight (novel)   5–8, 43, 75
Twilight franchise   3, 7–12, 51, 56–61, 202, 205–6
Twilight Saga (films)   7–9, 11–12, 20–2, 38–40, 46, 49, 51, 56, 57–9, 60–1, 67, 69, 71, 73–8, 84–92, 108–20, 125–35, 149–59, 163–6, 169–80, 192–9, 201–16, 223 n.3
   success of   3–4, 6, 10–12
Twilight series (novels)   1–3, 5–6, 8–9, 12, 43, 57–61, 91, 120, 125, 129, 154, 206, 207, 219–20 n.4

Unborn, The   224 n.2

vampire   14–15, 39, 50, 58, *see also* body, vampiric
   as defanged/domesticated   8, 11–12, 47, 58–9
   and gender   11–15, 20, 84–5, 89–90, 105–9, 132–5, 149–55, 157–9, 163–9, 169–99, 205, 208, 210–13
   humanized/reluctant/sympathetic   4, 14, 21–2, 45–9, 150–1, 163–9, 175–6, 184–5, 191–3, 196–7, 212–13
   as object of the gaze   20, 69, 84–90, 92–3, 97–101, 105–9, 165, 174, 182, 210
   as Other   14, 39, 45–7, 82, 87, 89–90, 109, 111, 164–5, 178, 191–220, 227 n.9
   in popular culture   1–2, 4–10, 14, 43, 45–9, 164–7

   and postfeminism   13–15, 20–2, 108–10, 150–5, 163–99, 205, 210–13
   and race   13–14, 45–6, 71, 82–3, 87, 91–2, 153, 165–6, 192
   as romantic hero   1, 4, 5, 14, 21–2, 39, 45–9, 56, 102, 109, 151, 157–99, 208, 212–14, 217 n.1
   and sexuality   4, 11, 13–15, 43, 82–3, 144–8, 171, 176–80
Vampire Academy series   217 n.1
Vampire Chronicles series, *The*   4, 48
Vampire Diaries, The (TV series)   4–6, 9, 20–2, 38–40, 46–7, 49–52, 56, 59–60, 67, 69, 71, 97–120, 135–41, 149–59, 163–5, 169, 180–7, 188, 192–9, 201–16, 220 n.6, 224 n.1, 225 n.3, 226 n.7
   success of   3, 6, 11–12
Vampire Diaries series, *The* (novels)   6
Vampires Suck   217 n.1
Vampyre: A Tale, The   43
Veronica Mars   5
violence against women   21, 35, 48–9, 63, 75–84, 142, 203, 205, 224 n.8, 227 n.9

Warm Bodies   9
werewolf   14, 40, 74, 90–1, 129, 132
What We Do in the Shadows   8
Williamson, Kevin   6, 9, 221 n.10
Wonder Woman   10
Wonder Woman 1984   10
Wuthering Heights   43, 44, 219–20 n.4

young adult, *see* teenager